Critical acclaim for *Bobby and Jackie*

"Pulitzer-nominated biographer Heymann delivers a gawk-worthy beach read with this fascinating look at Jackie and the Kennedy clan in the aftermath of John F. Kennedy's assassination. . . . Heymann's research is top notch, with plentiful attributions, making this trainwreck love story a substantial guilty pleasure and a sizzling reminder of how the rich are different."

—*Publishers Weekly*

"Full of gossipy tidbits—Bobby's wife, Ethel, knew about the affair; it was Jackie who told doctors to pull the plug after Bobby's shooting—this book is shocking, yearningly romantic and tons of fun."

—*People*

"A fast and fascinating read."

—*Winnipeg Free Press* (Canada)

Praise for *American Legacy*

"[A] page turner."

—*Daily Mail* (London)

"The first dual biography of JFK's children is a far cry from the glitzy, superficial star bios that litter bookstore shelves. . . . There's no denying that Heymann knows how to make a biography read like an epic novel. A must for committed Kennedy watchers."

—*Booklist*

"A fine, emotional summer read for anyone who daydreams of American royalty."

—*Publishers Weekly*

Praise for *The Georgetown Ladies' Social Club*

"A winning combination of sex, scandal and political escapade."
—*Publishers Weekly*

"One juicy story after another. Mr. Heymann doesn't hold back. I couldn't put this book down. . . . Extremely readable . . . Don't miss it!"
—Liz Smith, *New York Post*

"A massively researched study of five of Washington's leading grandes dames."
—*The Washington Times*

"This is a superb book which harkens back to the mid-twentieth century when life was lived differently. . . . A testament to prodigious research, and it is a fascinating look into a hierarchical world that ultimately governs our own small slices of life."
—*The Kingston Observer* (Kingston, Mass.)

"Delivers dishy tidbits about the patrician ladies who ruled Georgetown from the Truman administration until sometime in the 1980s. Think *Entertainment Tonight* does Georgetown."
—*The Washington Post*

"Heymann reveals Washington's most enduring power brokers—from the Cold War to the Gulf War—to be a circle of wealthy, connected, and ambitious women."
—*Elle*

"Gossip or not, just watch this book climb to the best seller list."
—*Daily Oklahoman* (Oklahoma City, Okla.)

"Heymann pulls out all the stops here, and the result is a well-researched, fast-paced, and fascinating look at dinner-party power-brokering."

—Booklist

"Heymann's book takes readers into a world where sex, politics, scandal, and power mix."

—The Hartford Courant

"A gossipy, informative and entertaining book—like the women it profiles."

—Toronto Sun

These titles are also available as eBooks.

BOBBY
AND
JACKIE

A Love Story

———◆———

C. DAVID HEYMANN

ATRIA PAPERBACK
New York   London   Toronto   Sydney

To RKH

1912–2008

◆

ATRIA PACERBACK

A Division of Simon & Schuster, Inc.
1230 Avenue of the Americas
New York, NY 10020

First Atria Paperback edition April 2010

ATRIA PACERBACK and colophon are trademarks of Simon & Schuster, Inc.

For information about special discounts for bulk purchases, please contact Simon & Schuster Special Sales at 1-866-506-1949 or business@simonandschuster.com.

The Simon & Schuster Speakers Bureau can bring authors to your live event. For more information or to book an event, contact the Simon & Schuster Speakers Bureau at 1-866-248-3049 or visit our website at www.simonspeakers.com.

Manufactured in the United States of America

10 9 8 7 6 5 4 3 2 1

The Library of Congress has cataloged the hardcover edition as follows:

Heymann, C. David (Clemens David).
Bobby and Jackie : a love story / C. David Heymann.
p. cm.
1. Kennedy, Robert F., 1925–1968—Relations with women.
2. Onassis, Jacqueline Kennedy, 1929–1994—Relations with men.
3. Legislators—United States—Biography. 4. Presidents' spouses—
United States—Biography. 5. United States. Congress. Senate—
Biography. 6. Celebrities—United States—Biography. 7. United
States—Biography. I. Title.
E840.8.K4H493   2009
973.922092—dc22   2009008257

ISBN 978-1-4165-5624-4
ISBN 978-1-4165-5629-9 (pbk)
ISBN 978-1-4391-6547-8 (ebook)

AUTHOR'S NOTE

◆

I FIRST HEARD hints and whispers of a romantic involvement between Robert and Jacqueline Kennedy while researching and conducting interviews for *A Woman Named Jackie,* my 1989 biography of the former First Lady. Because Jackie was still very much alive at the time, it is easy to understand why interviewees were reluctant to discuss the romance in great depth or detail. Following Jacqueline's death in 1994—and after I had begun work on *RFK,* my 1998 biography of Robert Kennedy—interview subjects, old and new, were suddenly much more eager to explore the topic. Thereafter nearly every biography of Bobby or Jackie, including volumes by Edward Klein, Christopher Andersen, Sarah Bradford, and Peter Evans, capitalized on my research and reported on the Bobby-Jackie affair, in certain instances adding new details to those already known.

After the publication of *RFK,* I continued to probe the subject, collecting further material and information. I was aided in part by the release in 2007 of a set of previously unavailable reports and briefs prepared by the Secret Service and the FBI, released to me under the Freedom of Information Act. Covering the years 1964 to 1968, when the liaison took place, these documents confirmed what I had already ascertained by way of personal interviews. I was thus able to piece together a complete picture of the complex relationship that existed between two of the most heralded figures of the twentieth century.

Too often in earlier biographies, Robert Kennedy was depicted as something of a choirboy when, in fact, he enjoyed the same proclivity for extramarital affairs as his brothers, Jack and Ted Kennedy. Insiders, among them Ted Kennedy as well as his sisters, were evidently well aware of the circumstances. Given Bobby's and Jackie's shared grief over the 1963 assassination of Jack Kennedy, it is not difficult to imagine how such an unlikely union could begin. The relationship grew and continued on its own, ending not because of lack or loss of affection but out of pure practical necessity when RFK decided to run for president in 1968. It is also clear, in the confusing days following Bobby's death, why Jackie turned to Aristotle Onassis for solace, agreeing to marry him and to leave the United States and raise her children abroad.

Despite the conclusive accounts of those insiders quoted in this volume, I don't doubt for a moment that some readers will remain skeptical that a romance actually took place. In the course of writing four books on the Kennedys, I have come across individuals who still deny the rampant womanizing of JFK, both before and after he became president. It took *The New York Times,* often cited as our most authoritative newspaper, some thirty years to admit in print that Jack Kennedy had numerous affairs outside his marriage. With all this purported womanizing, the doubters ask, how is it possible that JFK still had time to run the country? A somewhat related query might be posed regarding Bobby and Jackie. If such an affair took place, how is it conceivable that they managed to keep it out of the public eye? The answer to the first question is that President Kennedy compartmentalized his life to such an extent that he was able to preside over the nation while at the same time pursuing a hyperactive social schedule. The answer to the second question is that in the 1960s, the private lives of public figures were simply not covered by the media, certainly not to the extent that they are today when even the slightest impropriety, sexual or otherwise, gets reported, probed, and reported again.

Certain readers may also wonder or ask if it is even necessary to divulge the inner (or private) lives of biographical figures such as Robert and Jacqueline Kennedy. As a biographer, it has always been my con-

viction that sexual (or personal) behavior is integral to a fuller understanding of a person's life, particularly in the case of a public personality. Knowing that Robert and Jackie Kennedy became romantically
involved following JFK's death—and for reasons that this volume
attempts to reveal—sheds a whole new light on who they were and what
made them tick. It demonstrates, among other things, that they were
motivated by many of the same temptations and emotions that drive
the rest of us. It helps us gain a fuller comprehension not only of them
but also of ourselves.

Chapter 1

◆

A T 12:30 P.M. (CST) ON Friday, November 22, 1963, as President John Fitzgerald Kennedy's motorcade approached the Texas School Book Depository at Dealey Plaza in downtown Dallas, a series of gunshots rang out. Six minutes later the Lincoln Continental limousine carrying the president and his wife, as well as Texas governor John Connally and his wife, lurched to a halt in front of the emergency entrance to Parkland Memorial Hospital. Cradling her dying husband in her arms, Jacqueline Bouvier Kennedy refused to allow the waiting medics to lift the president out of the backseat until Secret Service agent Clint Hill wrapped JFK's gaping head wound in his own suit jacket.

Jackie's clothes were so heavily splattered with blood and gore that the first hospital security guard she encountered thought she'd been wounded along with the governor and the president. Lady Bird Johnson, the wife of Vice President Lyndon Johnson, arrived at Parkland shortly after the First Lady and saw her standing by herself in the narrow corridor outside the trauma room where they had taken the president. "Jackie looked more alone and vulnerable at that moment," Lady Bird later told White House chief of staff Ken O'Donnell, "than anyone I'd ever seen." Embracing the First Lady, Mrs. Johnson asked if she needed a change of clothing. Jackie shook her head from side to side. "I want people to see what they've done to Jack," she responded.

In the car, as bullets rained upon the open convertible from above,

1

Jackie had clambered onto the trunk of the vehicle in what appeared to be an attempted escape, only to be pushed back into her seat by Clint Hill. The Lincoln rapidly accelerated from eight to eighty miles per hour. Now, with her husband close to death, she wanted more than anything to be with him. After trying to push aside the head nurse, she turned to Dr. George Burkley, the president's personal physician, whose first impulse was to offer her a sedative. "I don't want a sedative—I want to be with my husband when he dies," she said. Although the doctors in the trauma room objected, Dr. Burkley insisted that she be permitted to enter.

Once in the room, which was filled with medical personnel, Jackie knelt on one knee to pray. Two priests suddenly appeared and administered the last sacraments of the Church. Jackie rose. A tall doctor stood before her. "Mrs. Kennedy, your husband has sustained a fatal wound," he said. "I know," she whispered. Dr. Burkley felt for the president's pulse: there was none.

A trauma room attendant pulled up a sheet to cover the president's body. It was too short, and his feet stuck out, whiter than the sheet. Jackie took his right foot and kissed it. Then she pulled back the sheet. She kissed him on the lips. His eyes were open, and she kissed them as well. She kissed his hands and fingers. She held on to his hand and for the longest time wouldn't let go.

At 2:31 p.m., Mac Kilduff, acting press secretary on the Texas trip, made the official announcement of the president's death.

"I went to Ken O'Donnell, who had joined Jackie in the trauma room," said Kilduff. "I told him I would have to make some sort of announcement. There were too many reporters running around who already knew—or at least had deep suspicions. It was only a matter of time. Ken said, 'Why are you asking me? Ask the president.'

"I knew exactly what he meant, so I went and found Lyndon Johnson. They had sequestered him in another trauma room with Lady Bird and Secret Service agent Rufus Youngblood. I didn't know what to call him. I wasn't going to call him Lyndon. I called him Mr. President, and Lady Bird let out an audible gasp. I said, 'We have to announce President Kennedy's death.' I could see his mind clicking. He said, 'I have no idea what kind of conspiracy this might be. They could be after me, the Speaker [of the House], the secretary of state. Who knows? We'd better get out of Dallas as soon as possible. I'll wait until you make your announcement, and then we'll leave.' "

Godfrey McHugh, the president's Air Force aide and a good friend of the Kennedy clan, ran into the First Lady and Ken O'Donnell outside the trauma room. "Jackie looked frightful," recalled McHugh. "Her pillbox hat, stockings, and pink wool suit were splattered with blood and brain matter. I handed her my handkerchief, and she handed it back without bothering to use it. After a moment or two, she removed her hat. It was the only attempt she made to tidy herself up."

Next Jackie asked McHugh if he would put through a call to Bobby Kennedy on the East Coast. She had always been close to Bobby, in certain respects closer than she'd been to Jack. McHugh asked a security guard for access to a private telephone. The guard led them to an empty administration office on the same floor.

"I think Bobby's at home," Jackie told McHugh. She recited the phone number for Hickory Hill, RFK's sprawling family residence in McLean, Virginia, and McHugh placed the call. Handing Jackie the receiver, McHugh exited the office. Three or four minutes later, the office door opened and Jackie emerged. "It's so sad," she said. "Bobby just celebrated his thirty-eighth birthday a few days ago. And now this."

Without knowing the full extent of the president's injuries, FBI director J. Edgar Hoover had already notified the attorney general of the shooting. Bobby had followed up Hoover's call (which he later termed "dispassionate") by telephoning Clint Hill in Dallas. "Is it serious?" Bobby inquired. "I'm afraid it is, sir," said Hill. Jackie's telephone call a few minutes later had confirmed Bobby's worst fears. The Kennedy administration had come to an unexpected and abrupt end.

As had Jack on August 1, 1944, with the wartime death of his older brother, Joseph Kennedy Jr., so Robert Francis Kennedy on November 22, 1963, stepped up to a new position in the family hierarchy: he was now patriarch Joseph P. Kennedy's eldest son. With barely enough time to compose himself, Bobby was soon on the phone again, taking command of the clan's response to the assassination. Rose Kennedy, the patriarch's wife, at the family compound in Hyannis Port, Massachusetts, had already seen and heard the news on television. Mother and son agreed that the old man, having suffered a severe stroke two years earlier, should not be told just yet. RFK called his younger brother, Ted Kennedy, in Washington, D.C., and assigned the junior senator from Massachusetts the unenviable task of flying to the Cape the following day to break the news to their ailing father in person. Bobby asked his sister Eunice Shriver to join Teddy at the compound. He couldn't reach his sister Jean, but asked her husband, Steve Smith, in charge of the Joseph P. Kennedy Foundation, to relay her assignment: since she was the Kennedy sister closest to Jackie, she would fly from New York to Washington to comfort the First Lady upon her return from Dallas. Their sister Patricia, the estranged wife of British actor Peter Lawford, would take the next plane to the nation's capital from California. Stanislas (Stas) and Lee Radziwill, Jackie's brother-in-law and younger sister, would fly in from London. And Sargent Shriver, perhaps the most reliable of the Kennedy in-laws, would help Bobby and Jackie organize the funeral.

As Hickory Hill began to fill with close friends and family members, Bobby remained the least anguished among them. Subdued and somber, he nevertheless tried to console those around him, including his wife, Ethel, and their children, by issuing words of confidence and comfort. CIA director John McCone, whom Bobby had asked to make the five-minute drive from Central Intelligence headquarters, later avowed that at the beginning of this ordeal, "as severe a trial as a man can go through, Bobby never faltered. He remained steady. It was remarkable. Obviously he was seriously affected, but at no point did he lose his composure." RFK did not have time for his own grief on this particular day. At a near future point in time, the attorney general would ask McCone whether certain CIA operatives had somehow been involved in his brother's assassination—and if not the CIA, then who?

At about 2:30 p.m., Bobby received a telephone call from Lyndon Johnson. The nation's new chief executive had returned to Love Field, where he had boarded Air Force One instead of Air Force Two, the vice presidential aircraft. The rest of the Kennedy party, including Jackie and Ken O'Donnell, had also returned to Air Force One, bringing with them a vital piece of cargo: the casket containing President Kennedy's body. Sounding harried, even frightened, LBJ told Bobby more or less what he had earlier revealed to Mac Kilduff—he suspected a worldwide plot of some sort, a plot so sinister it could result in the overthrow of the government. In no uncertain terms, Johnson felt that he should be sworn in as president at once, before leaving Texas.

"Who can swear me in?" Johnson asked RFK, whose position as attorney general marked him as the top lawman in the land.

Annoyed by Johnson's impatience, RFK nevertheless said he would find out and get back to him.

The attorney general promptly contacted his deputy, Nicholas Katzenbach, who in turn checked with Harold Reis of the Justice Department's Office of Legal Counsel. According to Reis, the oath of office was a mere formality. The truth of the matter was that by virtue of JFK's death, Johnson had automatically assumed the presidency. Anyone, added Reis, authorized to administer federal and state oaths could administer the presidential oath, the wording of which could be found in the Constitution. Johnson could safely wait until Air Force One reached Washington to be sworn in.

Katzenbach relayed this information to Bobby, but by the time the attorney general got back to Johnson, the new president had taken matters into his own hands. Having decided he wanted to be sworn in while still on the ground, Johnson—a diehard Texan—had summoned Sarah T. Hughes, whom John F. Kennedy had appointed to the federal bench. When no one aboard Air Force One could find a copy of the Constitution, Johnson suggested that a member of his staff contact Katzenbach. Katzenbach subsequently dictated the proper constitutional text to one of LBJ's secretaries. As soon as Judge Hughes arrived, accompanied by a police escort, Johnson asked Ken O'Donnell to find Jackie Kennedy. "I would like to have her come and stand next to me while I take the oath," he said.

"I knew how much Bobby had long detested Lyndon Johnson," recalled O'Donnell. "As JFK's campaign manager, he'd openly opposed his brother's choice of Johnson as a running mate. The last thing Bobby would have wanted now was to have Jackie stand up for him. So I said to Johnson, 'Please don't ask me to do that. The poor lady has been through enough for one day. You can't do that to her, Mr. President.' Johnson countered by saying that Jackie had requested she be part of the swearing-in process. He also stated that Bobby had advised him to take the oath before leaving Texas."

Joined by General Chester V. Clifton, a military advisor to JFK, in addition to Larry O'Brien and Dave Powers, two of JFK's most loyal aides, O'Donnell approached Jackie. "Johnson would like you to be with him when he gets sworn in," said O'Donnell. "Are you up for it?" The former First Lady agreed to stand by her husband's successor. "At least I owe that much to the country," she said.

Jackie followed the men into the gold-carpeted midsection of the jet. She stood to Johnson's left, Lady Bird to his right, as LBJ raised his right hand to take the oath as the thirty-sixth president of the United States.

White House photographer Cecil Stoughton recorded the impromptu ritual with his camera.

"Though dry-eyed, Jackie seemed completely out of it," said Stoughton. "She appeared to be in a state of shock. Only a few hours earlier she'd been First Lady. In little more than the blink of an eye, she had become a grieving thirty-four-year-old widow."

Following the hurried ceremony, Jackie returned to her seat at the rear of the aircraft next to her husband's casket. Ken O'Donnell, Larry O'Brien, and Dave Powers—affectionately known as "the Irish Mafia"—sat nearby. As quickly as she'd arrived, Judge Hughes departed the plane. Moments later Air Force One took off.

Twice during the flight, Lyndon Johnson sent Bill Moyers, soon to become a presidential assistant, to the back of the plane to ask O'Donnell and O'Brien to join him, and on both occasions JFK's lieutenants declined.

"We wanted to be with Jackie," said O'Brien. "We needed her and she needed us. Finally Dave Powers went up front to see Johnson. When he returned, he said Johnson had told him he wanted JFK's entire staff to stay on with him. Dave imitated Johnson with that Texas drawl of his. 'You fellas can't leave me now,' he quoted Johnson as saying. 'I don't know a single soul north of the Mason-Dixon Line. I want all of you to remain on board with me.' "

It was at this juncture that Ken O'Donnell asked one of the flight attendants for a bottle of scotch. "I don't know about you guys," he said, "but I sure as hell can use a stiff drink." The others joined him, including Jackie, who had never tried scotch before. She didn't care for it particularly, but she drained her drink in a single gulp.

"All in all," said Larry O'Brien, "I don't think I've ever experienced the kind of courage Jackie exhibited, first at the hospital in Dallas and on that plane to Washington, and then during the three days before the funeral. She undoubtedly endured her private moments of grief, but on the whole she acquitted herself magnificently and became a symbol for all of us, a symbol of great nobility and character in an age of general impoverishment of soul."

During the flight, the former First Lady placed two calls. She spoke to Angier Biddle Duke, the White House chief of protocol, and also to Bobby Kennedy. Ken O'Donnell overheard a portion of the latter conversation. "Bobby, how could this have happened?" she asked. Then she said, "Life has no meaning for me anymore."

Bobby Kennedy, meanwhile, had been picked up by the Secret Service and driven to the Pentagon, from which he would soon depart by helicopter for Andrews Air Force Base to await the arrival of the presidential jet. With him were Secretary of Defense Robert McNamara and Army General Maxwell Taylor, an intimate family friend. They arrived at Andrews at 5:30 p.m. and secluded themselves in a U.S. Army transport truck adjacent to the runway. Thirty minutes later, in the gathering dark, the aircraft bearing RFK's dead brother touched down.

As the jetliner taxied to a halt, a ground crew began wheeling a yellow ramp toward the plane's front entrance. With the ramp still in motion, Bobby raced up the steps and into the aircraft. Jack Valenti, a Texas Democratic Party advertising manager soon to become an LBJ White House aide, recalled the attorney general "elbowing his way, darting down the aisle, looking neither right nor left as he headed for the tail section of the jet. He passed Lyndon and Lady Bird Johnson without so much as a nod. He looked like a man possessed." RFK didn't stop until he reached his sister-in-law. "Hi, Jackie," he said softly, placing his arm around her shoulder. "I'm here."

"Oh, Bobby," she responded, and she might well have thought how like Bobby this was—he was always there when you needed him.

Despite the arrival aboard Air Force One of a half-dozen U.S. Army personnel, the late president's casket was ultimately removed from the plane by JFK's Secret Service detail. Lost in the commotion of crowds and cameras, the new president later complained that nobody had paid him the slightest heed. "Nobody said a word to me," LBJ told Jack Valenti the following day. "And here I am, the goddamn president of the United States."

Bobby and Jackie sat in the back of a military ambulance as they accompanied Jack's body to Bethesda Naval Hospital in Bethesda, Maryland, for the autopsy. While en route, Jackie asked Bobby about Lyndon Johnson's claim that the attorney general advised him to take the oath of office before leaving Dallas. When Bobby denied the story, Jackie said, "The last thing Jack told me about Lyndon is that he's incapable of telling the truth."

Jackie had asked Ken O'Donnell and Larry O'Brien to remain with her during the autopsy and then to stay at the White House as her personal guests. Dr. John Walsh, Jackie's gynecologist and obstetrician, also joined her at Bethesda. "He recommended that she rest for an hour or two while the autopsy proceeded," recalled O'Brien. "To help her relax, he injected her with one hundred milligrams of Vistaril, which under normal circumstances would have enabled her to sleep for a good twelve hours without interruption. As it happened, the shot seemed only to stimulate her."

Robert McNamara, having likewise joined the group at Bethesda, listened for hours as Jackie recounted every morbid detail of the assassination. "From the moment they reached Parkland Hospital," said McNamara, "she remembered everything. Talking it all out over and over again became a kind of purgation for her, a way of unburdening her soul. Bobby, on the other hand, didn't want to hear about it. If she felt more comfortable sharing her grief, he had to camp alone with his. Without comment or facial expression, he nevertheless listened to her describe the horror of Dallas, after which he turned and walked away."

At a certain point, Bobby left the room to make a telephone call. When he returned, he beckoned Jackie aside. "They think they've found the man who did it," he told her. "He's a small-time Communist sympathizer named Lee Harvey Oswald."

Jackie stared at her brother-in-law. "Oh my God," she whispered, "but that's too absurd." It sickened her that such a "silly little man," as she subsequently referred to him, could actually murder the leader of the Free World. It robbed her husband's death of all moral significance. It trivialized the act. "If it had at least been for his civil rights stand," she proclaimed at a later date.

As the night wore on, others began to drift in. Ethel Kennedy approached Jackie. "At least you have the comfort of knowing that Jack has found eternal happiness," she said.

"I would have hoped for more," responded the former First Lady. "You're lucky to have Bobby—he's here for you."

"He's here for you too, Jackie."

Jackie's stepfather and mother, Hugh and Janet Auchincloss, arrived. "As terrible as this was," Janet told her daughter, "think how much worse it would have been had Jack lived and been maimed." Jackie urged her mother and stepfather to stay at the White House and gave them Jack's bedroom for the night.

At 4:30 a.m., the autopsy completed, Bobby and Jackie brought the body, in a coffin of African mahogany, back to the executive mansion. Following a brief Catholic service in the East Room, RFK conferred with advisors and decided, in accord with Jackie's wishes, to keep the coffin closed throughout all the ceremonial rites. At 6:00 a.m., Jackie retired to her bedroom. Bobby retired to the Lincoln Bedroom for a few hours of rest. After swallowing a sleeping pill provided by Charles (Chuck) Spalding, one of JFK's most devoted friends, Bobby said, "Why now, God? Why now?"

As Spalding left the room and shut the door behind him, he heard the stricken younger brother of the slain president begin to weep. "As much as I wanted to go in there and console him," remarked Spalding, "I couldn't bring myself to intrude upon his private grief. As I retreated down the corridor, Bobby's sobbing rose in pitch until it became a wail."

It had been Maud Shaw, the stouthearted British nanny to Caroline and John Jr., who told Caroline on the night of November 22 of her father's death. Caroline, about to turn a precocious six, fully comprehended many of the tragic implications of the moment. "She cried so hard I thought she might choke," Shaw revealed in her 1965 tell-all book, *White House Nanny.*

It was left to Bobby Kennedy, the following day, to impart the sorrowful news to John-John, whose third birthday fell on November 25. "Your daddy has gone to heaven to be with Patrick," he told the boy, referring to the prematurely born baby Jack and Jackie had lost because of a respiratory ailment on August 9, 1963, just two days after the infant's birth.

The explanation, for all its simplicity, passed over John Jr.'s head. Nor did the handwritten letters that he and Caroline received that day from Lyndon Johnson make an impression on him. Writing the letters—which praised their father's valor and service to the country—had been Johnson's first order of business as Kennedy's successor.

Shortly before 10:00 a.m., November 23, Jackie arrived at the White House nursery. She hadn't seen her children since the assassination. Holding them in her arms, she soon led them downstairs to the East Room, where mother and daughter knelt and prayed before John F. Kennedy's coffin, which had been placed upon a simple funeral bier draped in black. A four-man honor guard stood watch over the president's coffin. Bobby Kennedy and other family members joined Jackie and her children for a private mass led by Father John Cavanaugh. That evening Bobby joined Jackie, Caroline, and John-John for dinner in the family dining room on the second floor of the White House. "Every time I look at Caroline and John, I want to cry," RFK told Dave Powers.

Later that evening, in tears and unable to sleep, Jackie wrote her husband a long letter in which she spoke of their life together, of Caroline and John, of Patrick, of their dreams and plans for the future now shattered forever. She then gathered together a few of JFK's favorite personal articles, including several samples of scrimshaw and a pair of engraved gold cuff links she'd given him as a birthday present. The next morning, November 24, she asked Caroline and John to write to their father, telling him how much they loved and missed him. Not yet able to write and uncertain as to the reason for the letter, John Jr. scribbled and colored with a crayon on a blank sheet of paper. His sister printed her message in blue ballpoint. "Dear Daddy," she wrote on a separate sheet. "We are all going to miss you, Daddy. I love you very much. Caroline."

The package of personal articles and letters—her own and those of her children—in hand, Jackie asked Bobby Kennedy to accompany her to the East Room. Waiting for them was Godfrey McHugh. Having been placed in charge of the honor guard, McHugh helped Bobby open the coffin. Jackie laid the letters and several other keepsakes inside the coffin. Bobby had brought along several items of his own to add to Jackie's offerings, including a silver rosary and a PT-109 tie clasp commemorating his brother's World War II naval service in the Pacific. RFK and McHugh watched in silence as Jackie arranged and then rearranged the articles the way she wanted them. She gazed at her husband's face and gently stroked his reddish-brown hair. The minutes ticked by as she continued to caress him. Sensing what she wanted to do next, McHugh excused himself and quickly returned with a pair of scissors, which he handed to Jackie. Leaning forward, she carefully cut a lock of the president's hair. Bobby lowered the coffin lid, and he and Jackie left the room.

At 1:21 p.m., word arrived from Dallas that Jack Ruby, a former nightclub owner with ominous underworld connections, had shot Lee Harvey Oswald at close range while the suspect was being transferred from local to federal authorities. Less than two hours later, at 2:07 p.m. CST, Oswald succumbed at Parkland, the same hospital in which JFK had perished. When asked why he'd shot Oswald, Ruby insisted that he'd wanted to spare the former First Lady the anguish of having to return to Dallas to testify at Oswald's trial. Jackie summarized her reaction to Ruby's intervention with a single poignant phrase: "one more awful thing," she said to RFK.

Later that day, following the arrival from London of Stas and Lee Radziwill, JFK's coffin was removed from the White House to the Capitol Rotunda, where Kennedy's body would lie in state. More than 250,000 mourners, forming a line three miles long, filed past the flag-draped coffin in less than a day. Meanwhile, Sarge Shriver worked out the administration's plans for JFK's formal funeral rites. Assisted by Angier Biddle Duke, Shriver requested that the Library of Congress provide him with the details of the state funerals that had been held for George Washington, Abraham Lincoln, Woodrow Wilson, and Ulysses S. Grant. At every stage of the planning process, Shriver and Duke kept Jacqueline Kennedy fully apprised.

Shortly after 9:00 p.m., Bobby and Jackie visited the Rotunda. Back at the White House, within the hour, Jackie was seen by Dr. Max Jacobson, her late husband's favorite physician, who had flown down from New York at the former First Lady's behest. Best known as "Dr. Feelgood," Jacobson had been treating Jack and Jackie since 1960, when they were still on the campaign trail seeking the presidency. Learning of Jacobson's use of methamphetamines in conjunction with other unconventional materials such as crushed monkey glands, RFK had attempted to convince his brother to stop using Jacobson. "I don't care if it's porcupine piss," JFK had supposedly responded, "it relieves my chronic back pain." That night Jacobson injected Jackie with one of his patented medicinal cocktails. "I have no idea what the shot contained," Jackie told her brother-in-law. "All I know is that my nerves have finally begun to settle."

Rising above her grief, Jacqueline Kennedy resolved to imprint on the American consciousness her husband's place in history, to remind Americans what had been taken from them. The funeral, on Monday morning, November 25, provided her a means of demonstrating John Fitzgerald Kennedy's importance as both a national and a global leader.

Lyndon and Lady Bird Johnson joined Jackie and her children as well as Robert Kennedy for the limousine ride from the White House to the Capitol Rotunda, the site of JFK's funeral. According to Lady Bird's published diaries, a restless John Jr. vaulted across seats and from one person's lap to another until Bobby managed to calm him with a few quiet words. When they reached the Capitol, the boy was led away by Maud Shaw, who had made the trip with Secret Service agents. Following the eulogies, including a moving presentation by Senator Mike Mansfield, television viewers around the world watched as Jackie and her young daughter approached the coffin, knelt and kissed it, then rose and walked slowly away.

At 11:00 a.m., following the funeral, JFK's coffin was lifted onto a caisson, the same one that had been used to carry President Franklin D. Roosevelt's body in 1945. As in Roosevelt's day, the caisson was drawn by six white horses. A riderless horse with boots reversed in the stirrups to signify a fallen hero fell into place behind the caisson as it made its way from Capitol Hill to St. Matthew's Cathedral for the formal funeral mass. With muffled drums sounding behind them, Jackie, Bobby, and Ted Kennedy led the procession on foot. Caroline and John Jr. were transported from the Capitol by car. Hundreds of thousands of spectators, the majority in tears, lined the funeral route.

Richard Cardinal Cushing, whose ring Jackie kissed upon entering St. Matthew's with her children, conducted the forty-five-minute mass. The most memorable and perhaps theatrical gesture of the day took place outside St. Matthew's following the mass. Dressed in a resplendent blue overcoat and squinting into the sun, little John-John suddenly raised his right hand in a military salute just as his father's coffin rolled by on the horse-drawn caisson. Like the eternal flame that would adorn her husband's grave site, her son's salute had been Jackie's idea.

After JFK's burial service at Arlington National Cemetery—Air Force One dipped its wings as it flew over the president's freshly dug grave—Jackie, Bobby, and Ted Kennedy returned to the White House, where they met privately with French president Charles de Gaulle, Prince Phillip of England, Ireland's President Eamon de Valera, and Emperor Haile Selassie of Ethiopia. The three Kennedys then formed a reception line to greet the hundreds of other foreign dignitaries and statesmen who had flocked to Washington from every corner of the globe to pay homage to the late president.

Another visitor, an unexpected houseguest at that, was spotted early that evening emerging from the former First Lady's bedroom. Aristotle Onassis, the self-made Greek shipping tycoon, had received a personal invitation to the White House from none other than Jacqueline Kennedy. Jackie had first met Onassis in 1960, when she and Jack, during a short stay in Greece, attended a banquet aboard the *Christina*, Ari's legendary yacht.

"Onassis's presence in the White House during the funeral period took everyone by surprise," noted Ken O'Donnell. "He wasn't exactly a Kennedy family favorite." In early 1963, Onassis and Lee Radziwill had become involved in a highly publicized affair. Then, in October of that year, Ari and Lee invited Jackie to join them on a leisurely cruise of the Aegean Sea, suggesting it would help her recuperate from the recent death of Patrick Bouvier Kennedy. Jackie accepted the invitation. Needless to say, the president objected. So did Bobby. Ari's reputation as a womanizing social climber and a kind of pirate of the high seas had been firmly established years before. The attorney general was once quoted as saying to Ken O'Donnell, "If it were up to me, I'd sink his fucking yacht—and the goddamn Greek with it."

At 7:00 p.m. that evening, not wanting to disappoint her son, Jackie celebrated his third birthday with a modest party attended predominantly by members of the Kennedy clan. Jackie also invited Aristotle Onassis. John Jr. seemed to enjoy the party—which featured horns, balloons, and ice cream cake—whereas Caroline appeared remote and withdrawn. She spent the evening by herself in a corner of the room, for the most part ignoring her rambunctious Kennedy cousins. She brightened only briefly when Uncle Bobby arrived bearing what turned out to be John-John's favorite gift: a scale model of Air Force One.

According to the actor Peter Lawford, at the time still married to Patricia Kennedy, a sister of the late president, the party "felt uncomfortable, full of forced frivolity." Aristotle Onassis became the target of some extremely unflattering remarks. Although he took it in good humor, the Kennedys began making snide comments about his yacht and his wealth. Teddy drew up an ersatz contract calling for the billionaire to give half his material assets to the poor in South America. Going along with the joke, Onassis signed the document, appending several codicils in Greek.

At evening's end, after the party had emptied and Caroline and John had been put to bed, the only mourners left in the room were Bobby and Jackie. The two who were most afflicted by the death of their loved one sat and chatted for a while. Close to midnight, his soul stirred by sudden memories of his brother, Bobby leaned toward his sister-in-law and said, "Shall we go visit our friend?"

While Clint Hill called ahead to Arlington, Jackie gathered a small bouquet of lilies of the valley from an eighteenth-century vase she kept on a second-floor hall table. Jack Metzler, superintendent of the cemetery, met the black Mercury at Arlington's main gate. The car drove in and parked along Hatfield Drive. Accompanied by Metzler, Clint Hill, a second Secret Service agent, and a pair of military policemen, Bobby and Jackie walked up between clumps of cedar and oak to a high white picket fence that had been newly installed to mark off the Kennedy plot. The vast throngs that had flocked to the cemetery that afternoon were now gone. The rolling grounds of Arlington were damp and dark and quiet. Robert E. Lee's mansion stood atop a steep slope overlooking Kennedy's grave. Concentric rows of uniform white gravestones, beneath which lay the bodies of American soldiers killed in battle, stretched as far as the eye could see.

One of the military policemen unlatched a metal gate that divided the fence in half. Jacqueline and Robert Kennedy entered the plot and approached the glowing torch of the eternal flame that Jackie had lit as part of the funeral service earlier in the day. The flame flickered blue in the cool wind. Bobby and Jackie spotted a cap—a green beret—which had been placed near the grave that afternoon by a sergeant major as a token of respect. An MP had left his black-and-white brassard; next to the brassard, a member of the Third Infantry had propped his buff strap and Old Guard cockade. Such symbols of military tradition were not lost on the two mourners. Together they dropped to their knees, bowed their heads, and offered their prayers. When they were done, Jackie rose and placed her spray of flowers upon the earth. Then, holding hands, the widow and younger brother of John Fitzgerald Kennedy rejoined the others and walked back to the waiting car.

Chapter 2

◆

FROM THE MOMENT Jacqueline Lee Bouvier married John F. Kennedy at Newport, Rhode Island, on September 12, 1953, the family member with whom she felt most comfortable was Bobby Kennedy.

The seventh child of Joseph P. and Rose Fitzgerald Kennedy, Robert Francis Kennedy was born at home in Brookline, Massachusetts, on November 20, 1925. Although he would later become known for his aggressive, driven, often ruthless demeanor, as a child he was considered the sweetest and gentlest of the Kennedy offspring. Bobby spent two years at Portsmouth Priory School, the only son of Joe Kennedy to stay in a Catholic school for more than a single term. He graduated from Milton Academy, a prestigious boarding school twelve miles from Boston, and began his studies at Harvard University, where he at first struggled to maintain passing grades. When America entered World War II, he interrupted his education to enlist in the navy. After the war, he returned to Harvard, graduating in 1948 as an American history major. Despite his relatively small frame—he stood five foot nine and weighed 140 pounds—he played on Harvard's football team and earned his varsity letter, a feat that had eluded his brother Jack. Following Harvard, he attended the University of Virginia Law School, from which he received his degree in 1951. On June 17, 1950, while still in law school, he married Ethel Skakel, a college roommate of his sister Jean. The Skakels, a large Catholic family from Greenwich, Connecticut, were as wealthy and outspoken as the Kennedys.

In 1952 Robert Kennedy accepted a job offer with the Justice Department in New York City, but he soon resigned to manage his brother Jack's senatorial campaign in Massachusetts. When JFK won, Bobby and Ethel moved to Washington, where RFK began working as consulting counsel for several select Senate subcommittees. Wisconsin Republican senator Joseph R. McCarthy, a Kennedy family friend, invited him to join the controversial, much reviled, and feared Senate Investigations Subcommittee, which in turn led to his involvement as minority counsel in the Army-McCarthy hearings. Later he worked tirelessly for the anti-Communist committee investigating labor racketeering, a position that brought him into direct conflict with Teamsters boss Jimmy Hoffa. Hoffa described his young adversary as "an arrogant little prick, born with a silver spoon in his mouth." RFK portrayed Hoffa as "a crime-bound mobster masquerading as a concerned union organizer." Their major detractors claimed they were both right.

In the end it was Bobby—not Joe Kennedy, as is commonly asserted—who convinced his brother to marry Jacqueline Bouvier. More than any of the other Kennedys, RFK saw Jackie as a potentially invaluable political weapon. Her background as a Miss Porter's School debutante and honors student at Vassar and the Sorbonne, her French Catholic heritage, her facility with foreign languages, her academic grounding in French art and literature—even her current employment as the personable and amusing "Inquiring Camera Girl" at the *Washington Times-Herald*—made Jackie an ideally suited mate for an ambitious, up-and-coming senator bent on one day attaining the presidency. Jacqueline gave the Kennedys the social respectability they otherwise lacked. The future First Lady's East Coast finishing-school polish complemented her husband's quick wit, intelligence, and youthful vitality. Individually and as a couple, they were also astonishingly photogenic, more Hollywood than Washington in appearance. Compared to the aging dowdiness of their immediate presidential predecessors—the Roosevelts, Trumans, and Eisenhowers—the Kennedys seemed the picture of health and vigor. They were the perfect specimens for a new age: the age of television. They had what legendary fashion doyenne Diana Vreeland termed "allure." "Allure," Vreeland observed, "isn't something you can buy; nor is it something you acquire. You either have it or you don't." Jack and Jackie had it.

RFK fully understood that while the Kennedys were one of the most successful and influential clans in America, they likewise harbored their fair share of closeted skeletons and shady characters. Chief among the latter was Joseph P. Kennedy. A rampant womanizer whose primary fortune had been made in the film business and by importing gin and whiskey during Prohibition, Kennedy methodically increased his financial holdings by implementing a number of complex real estate deals and questionable Wall Street stock and security manipulations. Appointed the first Irish Catholic ambassador from America to Great Britain, Kennedy became an ardent admirer of the leaders of the Third Reich. His shameful support of the Nazi regime resulted in his forced resignation as ambassador and return to the United States.

For better or worse, Kennedy's feats left an indelible mark upon all nine of his children. Joseph P. Kennedy Jr., his oldest child, founded an isolationist, pro-Hitler fan club while attending Harvard Law School in 1939 and 1940. Groomed for success, Joe Jr. redeemed himself by joining the Naval Aviation Reserve in 1942. He died in an explosion over the English Channel two years later while flying a dangerous bombing mission on behalf of the Allied command. Another familial airplane fatality was that of Kathleen (Kick) Kennedy, the fourth child of Joe and Rose Kennedy, who moved to England during World War II and married William Cavendish, the Marquess of Hartington. Cavendish died in action three months after marrying Kathleen. Two years later, in early 1946, Kick began an affair with Lord Peter Fitzwilliam, a titled Brit not yet divorced from his wife. The romance, which created a furor in the English press, ended in May 1948 when a private plane carrying Peter and Kathleen from Paris to the south of France crashed and burned.

Then there was Rosemary, the eldest Kennedy daughter, whose erratic mood swings as a teenager alarmed her parents to such an extent that they began sending her to a series of psychologists and psychiatrists, none of whom could help her. Finally, without consulting with his wife, Joe Kennedy authorized a specialist to perform a lobotomy on his daughter. The procedure left Rosemary profoundly retarded and partially paralyzed. Joe made immediate arrangements to have her placed in a Catholic nursing home in Wisconsin, where she languished for the remainder of her life.

"If truth be told, the Kennedys were a highly dysfunctional family," claimed Oleg Cassini, Jackie's chief fashion designer during her days as First Lady. "Jack Kennedy was a sex and amphetamine addict, and Teddy was an out-and-out alcoholic. Joan Kennedy, Teddy's wife, drank more than he did. Jack's sisters, particularly Pat Lawford and Jean Smith, also drank to excess. They had good reason. Their spouses, Peter Lawford and Steve Smith, thought nothing of stepping out on them. Lawford was a drug abuser, while Smith had sadomasochistic tendencies—he paid women for the express privilege of beating them up. Ethel Kennedy, on the other hand, has always been an emotional cripple. She's unstable. She gave birth to eleven children but knew nothing about raising a family. She's the world's worst mother."

Although such disclosures are by now largely familiar to most Kennedy watchers, they came as a complete surprise to Jackie when she first entered the family circle. Former society columnist Igor Cassini, Oleg's older brother, remembered visiting Jackie a year into her marriage. "With the exception of Jack and Bobby," he said, "the Kennedys had a confrontational relationship with Jackie. She wasn't a team player. She didn't care for all that rah-rah business, those interminable touch football and baseball games that took place at the beachfront estate in Florida and at the Kennedy compound in Hyannis. Jack's sisters simply didn't get along with Jackie. The Kennedys were political animals, and Jackie wasn't exactly a politico—at least not in the beginning."

Jack's sisters—as well as Rose and Ethel—more than once accused Jackie of being an elitist, an effete snob. When the future First Lady expressed her desire to be called Jacqueline rather than Jackie, Eunice Shriver let out a squeal. "That's *Jack-leen,* rhymes with *queen!*" she exclaimed. When Jackie confessed that as a child she'd wanted to become a ballerina, Ethel Kennedy pointed at her sister-in-law's size 9 shoes and quipped, "With those feet, kiddo, you'd have been better off taking up soccer."

Igor Cassini recalled an outing at Hyannis one afternoon when Jack's sisters packed several picnic baskets and a cooler with peanut butter and jelly sandwiches, hot dogs, potato chips, and beer. Jackie's picnic basket contained foie gras, caviar, and a chilled bottle of champagne. The sisters wore T-shirts and blue jeans, while Jackie had on a white sleeveless Christian Dior sheath. "Pat Lawford and Eunice Shriver never got over that little picnic," said Igor. "Years later they were still jabbering away about it."

A major obstacle for Jackie, one that she never completely overcame, involved JFK's overactive libido. Although her father, John Vernon "Black Jack" Bouvier III, had been a playboy in his own right, nothing in Jackie's background had quite prepared her for what she was about to experience firsthand.

Longtime *Washington Times-Herald* reporter John White, a pal of Jackie's during her stint at the paper, attempted to warn her about her future husband. White, a former suitor of Kick Kennedy, had frequently double-dated with Jack and whatever female companion he happened to be squiring on that particular day. "I knew what a womanizer he was," said White. "I told Jackie I didn't think he'd make a very good husband, that he was nice to play around with but nobody to bring home to Momma. I knew a lot of girls who had dealt with him. I used to hear their stories. Most of them would say that to deal with such raw power and with such open contempt—being checked off in a little black book—turned out to be one hell of a challenge. They probably thought they could break through to him. The fact that he was such a cold fish also played a role. He had warm blood but a cold heart. He was totally cold and ruthless toward women, which I imagine many of them found charming. It was almost the idea of being able to say the next morning that you were drunk and didn't know what you were doing."

J. Edgar Hoover's personal files literally bulged with the names of John Kennedy's myriad sex partners. They included secretaries, nurses, interns, housewives, striptease artists, prostitutes, showgirls, models, airplane hostesses, college coeds, socialites, Mafia molls, European aristocrats, the wives of good friends, and such well-known Hollywood sirens as Laraine Day, Jean Simmons, Gene Tierney, Angie Dickinson, Jayne Mansfield, and Marilyn Monroe. Marilyn, a cash contributor to Kennedy's presidential slush fund, defended her affair with Jack, remarking, "I'd rather have a president who does it to a woman than one who does it to the country." JFK White House special counsel and speechwriter Ted Sorensen, often credited with having ghostwritten Kennedy's Pulitzer Prize–winning *Profiles in Courage,* put it a bit differently. "The Kennedy administration," he said, "is going to do for sex what the Eisenhower administration did for golf." Joan Lundberg Hitchcock, the West Coast socialite who carried on with Kennedy while he was still a senator, acknowledged that she was "just one of Jack's many women. He wasn't exactly monogamous. He went through women like a Russian tank."

Not even on their 1953 Mexican honeymoon did JFK remain faithful to his bride. Michael Diaz, a lawyer from Mexico City, recalled a cocktail reception he attended for the newlyweds at a cliffside villa overlooking the sea in Acapulco. "It turned out to be a rather awkward occasion," said Diaz. "There were more women than men, and they all seemed to be hovering around JFK. Mrs. Kennedy spent most of the evening by herself on the verandah, while her husband busied himself collecting names and numbers. At one point he brazenly walked off with one of the better-looking women and headed for a bedroom. They emerged twenty minutes later, looking flushed and spent. You had to feel sorry for Mrs. Kennedy."

Over the ensuing years, JFK's sexual exploits with women other than his wife only increased in number. In the summer of 1956, after narrowly missing out on becoming Adlai Stevenson's vice presidential running mate at the Democratic National Convention in Chicago, Jack took off on a European vacation with his brother Teddy and Florida senator George Smathers. Jackie, seven months pregnant, remained behind with her mother and stepfather at Hammersmith Farm, their Newport estate. Arriving in France, the three men chartered a forty-foot sloop complete with a captain and a galley cook for a cruise of the Mediterranean. What Jackie didn't know was that the passenger list included three young Scandinavian ladies the trio had met on the Riviera and invited along. The truth emerged when the captain of the vessel, unaware that any of the men was currently married, gave a candid interview to a French journalist. The story quickly reached Jackie in the States.

On August 23, two days after learning of her husband's infidelity, Jackie experienced severe stomach cramps and soon began to hemorrhage. An ambulance rushed her to Newport Hospital, where doctors performed an emergency Caesarean. When she regained consciousness following surgery, the first person she saw was Robert Kennedy. Taking his brother's place, Bobby had raced to Jackie's side. Without flinching, he delivered the sad news: the infant, an unnamed baby girl, had died before drawing her first breath. It was Jackie's second failed pregnancy; the year before, she'd suffered a miscarriage. Then, too, Bobby had reached her bedside before Jack. "Thanks, Bobby," she'd said on that occasion. "Thanks for always being there for me."

Not until August 26, when the sloop docked at Genoa, Italy, did JFK hear about the stillbirth of his daughter. He called Newport Hospital and spoke to his wife; he'd tried to reach her earlier, he said, but the boat's ship-to-shore radio had broken down. Jackie made no mention of her husband's latest indiscretion, but made it clear that she expected him to return to the United States as soon as possible. Jack's reaction was one of mild annoyance. He would be home, he said, in a few days. He telephoned Bobby, and his brother set him straight. "If you ever want to run for president," he remarked, "you had better haul ass back to your wife." George Smathers seconded the motion. Jack flew home the next day.

Rumor had it that Jackie nearly left her husband that year. "It was the closest they ever came to a full-blown divorce," said George Smathers. Indeed, a story circulated in the press that Joe Kennedy had offered Jackie $1 million to stay with his son. The story wasn't true. What was true is that Jackie was depressed and demoralized. She thought that Jack should have been there for her and not off on a pleasure cruise with a trio of young, sexy bimbos.

Jacqueline's usual approach to her husband's frequent indiscretions involved a smattering of good humor and teasing in conjunction with a string of offhand remarks. Despite her growing skepticism over the conventional institution of marriage, she tended to make light of the situation. When Joan Kennedy complained to her that Teddy was seeing other women, Jackie immediately dismissed her sister-in-law's lament. "All Kennedy men are like that," she said. "It doesn't mean a thing."

Jack's latest infidelity toward the end of 1956, and his absence from his wife's bedside following the stillbirth of their daughter, evidently hurt Jackie more than she was willing (or able) to admit. In January 1957, Jackie accompanied her friend Bill Walton, a gay artist and former journalist from Washington (whom JFK later appointed director of the White House Fine Arts Commission), on a ten-day trip to California without JFK. While in Los Angeles, they attended a dinner party at the Coldwater Canyon home of Charlie Feldman, one of Hollywood's most powerful agents and producers. Feldman's other guests that evening included film star William Holden and Brenda Marshall, his dutiful actress wife. The couple had been married since 1941 and had two sons. Known as Hollywood's "Golden Boy" for his clean good looks and lead role in a 1939 boxing film by the same title, the thirty-nine-year-old, Oscar-winning actor owned residences in Switzerland and Kenya, where he had started the Mount Kenya Safari Club. Jacqueline later told Walton that the actor reminded her of her father. Although the two men looked not at all alike, they had other traits in common. Like Black Jack Bouvier, William Holden had a dark side. An unrepentant alcoholic, he loved adventure, wild animals, and women, though not necessarily in that order. Jackie took to him at once and evidently let her feelings be known.

After checking with Feldman the following day, Holden telephoned Jackie at the Beverly Hills Hotel, where she and Walton were staying in separate cottages. An accomplished equestrienne, Jackie invited the actor to go horseback riding. Afterward they returned to Charlie Feldman's house and began an affair that, according to Bill Walton, was "primarily driven by Jackie's desire to seek revenge on Jack." Flying back to Washington, the once irreproachable wife of John F. Kennedy told Walton that the actor had been "an unselfish lover." Her only complaint was that William Holden was a registered Republican, but then, so too was her father.

The affair did not end there. In a seemingly reckless bid to pay back her husband for his recent disloyalty, she told him of her fling with Holden. "By flaunting it," said Bill Walton, "Jackie probably hoped to reawaken Jack's romantic interest in her. I suppose she wanted to redefine herself as the kind of flirtatious woman Jack usually found irresistible."

Jackie's ploy appears to have had some effect on her husband, at least for the moment. By April 1957 she was again pregnant, this time with Caroline. Whatever the extent of JFK's feelings toward his wife, he soon resumed his extramarital lifestyle. Frank Sinatra introduced him to Judith Campbell, a leggy Las Vegas showgirl whose boyfriend at the time happened to be Sam Giancana, the notorious Mafia kingpin. For the next three years, Campbell shifted back and forth between the politician and the crime chieftain, sleeping with both and delivering messages from one to the other. Kennedy continued to see Campbell a year into his presidency, ending the relationship only after Bobby Kennedy warned him that J. Edgar Hoover had compiled a voluminous file charting the affair.

In general, JFK carried on with complete abandon, impervious to the perils of exposure. "He was the son of a man who thought nothing of bringing his mistresses home to the dinner table," said Langdon Marvin, a longtime congressional and senatorial aide to JFK. Marvin was given the dubious assignment of lining up women for Kennedy during the 1960 presidential campaign. "He'd dispatch me to a given town or city as a kind of advance man," said Marvin. "I'd set things up for him.

When he arrived, I'd pick him up at the airport. He'd clamber off the *Caroline,* the campaign plane his father had purchased for him, and he'd say to me, 'Where are the broads?' "

Another of Marvin's tasks involved hiring prostitutes for JFK before each of his four nationally televised debates with Republican Party presidential candidate Richard Nixon. Kennedy would spend time with the prepaid call girl just before going on the air. The results of the exercise were obvious to anyone who watched the debates. Kennedy looked refreshed and composed on camera, whereas Nixon seemed nervous and out of sorts.

The gossip surrounding Jack Kennedy's pressing need for other women inevitably reached Jackie at home in Washington and at Hyannis. Again pregnant, on this occasion with John Jr., the future First Lady walked around in a daze, doing her utmost to hide her embarrassment and shame, her anguish exacerbated by her knowledge that the rest of the clan knew of Jack's extracurricular activities. She told JFK's White House press secretary, Pierre Salinger, that she suspected certain family members of practically "pimping" for Jack, particularly Peter and Pat Lawford, at whose Santa Monica beach house JFK had met dozens of aspiring actresses. Ironically, Salinger too had from time to time played the role of procurer.

"Once Jack won the presidency," said Salinger, "he asked me to convince Jackie that as First Lady she would need her own press secretary. He had in mind Pamela Turnure, a young lady he'd been secretly dating since 1958. In her mid-twenties, Pamela knew almost nothing about secretarial work and even less about journalism and the press. Jack didn't care—he wanted her on the payroll. So I approached Jackie with the idea. 'Why do I need my own press secretary?' she inquired. 'Well, Jackie,' I responded, 'it's going to get pretty hectic around here. We're going to need all the help we can get.' I'm certain she knew all about Jack and Pamela, but she agreed to the arrangement. She was well acquainted with the theory that you should keep your friends close and your enemies closer. Or, as Jack used to put it, 'Forgive your enemies, but never forget their names.' "

Pamela Turnure was only one of countless women placed at JFK's disposal during his tenure in the White House. Kennedy's daily noontime swim-and-exercise sessions in the Executive Mansion's basement pool were nothing less than full-blown orgies, women of every description being snuck into the White House to party with the president and his cronies. The sole witnesses to this midday regimen, aside from those who participated, were the Secret Service agents assigned to President Kennedy's detail. While most of them simply could not believe what they were seeing, they soon learned to keep their thoughts and impressions to themselves. For his part, Kennedy enjoyed having the agents around. They were young, handsome, well-educated men who liked women and parties almost as much as did their boss.

"This was the James Bond era," said White House Secret Service operative Marty Venker, "and Kennedy was intrigued by the whole mystique of the Secret Service. He identified with us and knew we would never betray him. There was a tacit agreement within the agency that went something like, 'You protect my ass, and I'll protect yours.' We weren't going to talk to the press about his sexual proclivities, because we were doing more or less the same thing. That's not to say we didn't wonder about his behavior. After all, he was the president of the United States. We likewise wondered about the First Lady. Why would such a desirable and scintillating young wife put up with this nonsense? I could only surmise that either she didn't love her husband and therefore didn't care what he did, or if she did love him, she had to be the world's greatest masochist. The one thing you could say for JFK is that he successfully compartmentalized his life. He could be screwing a woman in the basement of the White House one minute, and the next minute he'd be playing family man with his wife and kids—or he'd be in the Oval Office discussing strategy with the prime minister of England."

Morton Downey Jr., the son of Irish crooner Mort Downey, Joe Kennedy's closest friend, suggested that Jack and Jackie's marriage had all the makings of an arranged (or brokered) union. "She wanted fame and fortune," maintained Downey, "and he needed a beautiful wife with lots of polish and panache. I don't think either of them had illusions about what they were getting into. Jackie may have gone into it with an open mind, but she soon recognized that Jack wasn't about to change. She often joked about it. When asked by a *New York Times* reporter what she thought Jack would do after his term or two in the White House, she remarked, 'He'll probably take a job as headmaster of an exclusive, all-girls prep school.' "

Jack and Jackie's Faustian pact had been more his idea than hers, though she gradually adjusted to it. While her husband explored pleasures of the flesh, Jacqueline Kennedy engaged in delights of a more material nature, traveling to New York or Paris on costly shopping binges for jewelry, clothing, artworks, and antiques. But her most profitable acquisition came when Jack gave her the funds to build Wexford, her expensively appointed weekend retreat in Atoka, Virginia. While she went horseback riding in the rolling foothills of Virginia's verdant countryside, Jack carried on with a consortium of mistresses; his latest batch featured deposed Princess Elizabeth of Yugoslavia (the wife of Howard Oxenberg, a wealthy New York businessman) and Mary Pinchot Meyer (the former wife of CIA bigwig Cord Meyer Jr.). Mary, who also happened to be the sister-in-law of *Washington Post* executive editor Ben Bradlee, later admitted that she and the president had done pot and LSD together. Lest it be forgotten, this was before the crazy sixties came into full bloom.

Because of his bad back, the result of injuries sustained during World War II, JFK added a physical therapist named Susan Sklover to his personal staff. Nicknamed "S. K. LOVER" by members of the president's Secret Service detail (in whose logbooks her name never appeared), Susan waited forty-five years to discuss the true nature of her employment by JFK. "I'd been recommended for the position by Peter Lawford, whom I'd known in Los Angeles, where I studied for my degree in physical therapy. I flew to Washington and was interviewed by Pierre Salinger, of all people. To my surprise, he asked me nothing about my professional training or experience as a physical therapist. Instead he told me how wonderful it was to work for the president.

When I asked him for a copy of JFK's medical history so I could arrange a treatment plan, Salinger hemmed and hawed—in the end, these documents never materialized. When I finally met the president, I realized why I'd been hired. The only kind of physical therapy he wanted was sexual in nature, and I was too young and dumb to refuse."

For all his sexual experience, Jack Kennedy struck Susan Sklover as "an ordinary lover." Mechanical and cold, Kennedy insisted Sklover perform fellatio but never offered to reciprocate. Afterward he lay on his back and asked her to "climb aboard." The entire act lasted no more than a minute or two. "He wanted to be serviced," she said, "but couldn't have cared less about his partner's satisfaction. I spent a weekend alone with him at Camp David while Jackie went to New York on what JFK called 'the ultimate shopping spree.' "

Sklover quit after six weeks on the job. Pierre Salinger wrote her a personal check for $5,000 and made her sign an invasion of privacy contract. "If you ever discuss the terms or details of your employment with the chief executive," he warned, "you'll never work again."

Before returning to Los Angeles, Sklover received a telephone call from Attorney General Robert Kennedy, inviting her to meet him at a hotel in Washington. "I never went," she said, "but it became clear that the Brothers Kennedy, Teddy included, enjoyed trading their women back and forth. I subsequently read that Bobby inherited both Marilyn Monroe and Jayne Mansfield from the president. I couldn't help but wonder how the Kennedy wives dealt with all that philandering."

The most egregious example of sexual impropriety on the part of the Kennedy boys involved the youngest brother. During the second year of JFK's presidency, Teddy took a trip to Europe without his wife. One day, finding himself in Antwerp, Belgium, he learned about a dinner party to be given that evening by a wealthy Belgian couple in honor of the country's king and queen. Teddy decided he wanted to attend. Even though the hostess had no desire to have a Kennedy as her guest, she could hardly refuse after the American ambassador called her to request an invitation for the visiting brother of the president.

Hearst newspaper society columnist Doris Lilly, a friend of the wealthy couple, noted that they lived in a grand eighteenth-century palazzo, with Aubusson carpeting on the floors and paintings by Flemish masters on the walls. The mansion abounded with valuable antiques, glittering jewels, polished silver.

Despite the invitation he'd gone to some trouble to get, Ted never showed up for dinner. But after everyone had eaten, he arrived, staggering, red-faced, obviously plastered. With him was a young trollop he'd picked up that afternoon in the red-light district. She had on a tiny skirt—hardly the sort of thing one wears to greet royalty. They both just stood there, bleary eyed, swaying to and fro.

After the hostess hustled the king and queen of Belgium into another room, Teddy and his companion plopped onto one of the many couches in this large, exquisite room. As the two of them sat there, holding hands, with the hostess trying to figure out what to do with them, everyone except Ted suddenly noticed that liquid was running down the woman's leg onto the priceless antique sofa. Ted noticed only when the urine, running in a rivulet, wet his own trousers.

The formally attired butler rushed off to find some large towels to try to clean up the mess, but by the time he returned, the damage had been done. The hostess resolved never again to allow a Kennedy into her house.

When he heard the Teddy-in-Belgium saga from Doris Lilly, author Truman Capote (a onetime close friend of Jackie's) used the anatomical reference to uric acid in a somewhat altered context. "Those Kennedy men are like dogs," he said. "They have to stop and piss at every fire hydrant."

In a less titillating vein, Capote observed that Jackie knew all about the Kennedy brothers and their sophomoric sexual antics. "I sometimes wondered," the author said, "what it must have been like for her to be married to a charming and handsome man, talented and accomplished, in many respects admirable, who had reached the apex of government, who even at times professed undying love for his wife and probably meant it, but who couldn't stop himself from repeatedly cheating on her. That she remained by his side probably had more to do with her allegiance to the nation than it did with her devotion to him. Except for the children—Caroline and John-John—their relationship had become an utter farce by the time he became president. My sense is she fell in love with him again only after the assassination. The shock and horror of the event ignited her romantic imagination. But as First Lady, she constantly turned to RFK for advice and support. He served as her Rock of Gibraltar."

As for RFK, he was always rather bedazzled by Jackie. If he never intervened to halt the endless humiliation inflicted upon her by her husband, he nevertheless willingly served as her sounding board, as somebody she could count on in her darker moments. In addition, RFK shared with his sister-in-law a distinct interest in the arts, a field of study that quite frankly bored JFK, whose recreational reading was limited to American history and mystery novels. When master cellist Pablo Casals performed at the White House, JFK nearly fell asleep. Despite his closeness to Jackie and his firsthand knowledge of her suffering at the hands of her lascivious husband, RFK (like his brothers) indulged in his share of extramarital sexual interludes.

"Bobby was more selective than either of his brothers," said the late Abe Hirschfeld, a New York real estate developer who regularly contributed to Kennedy campaigns. "He was also a bit more discreet. When he did go with other women, it was as if they were second or third wives. He remained loyal to them."

Although the attorney general participated in some of the notorious White House swimming pool parties with Jack (and Teddy), he managed to maintain a lower personal profile than either of his brothers. Yet for all his efforts, there were several notable exceptions. Peter Jay Sharp, owner of the Carlyle Hotel on Madison Avenue in Manhattan (where the Kennedys maintained a penthouse suite), remembered one such occasion.

"I didn't own the Carlyle when JFK was president," remarked Sharp. "I acquired the property in 1967, but I knew President Kennedy and his brothers and would visit them at the hotel whenever they came to town. Once, in early 1962, I went up to the suite and encountered a

Secret Service agent posted in front of the door. He ushered me inside, and there I found Jack in bed with a blonde and Bobby on the living room floor with a brunette. I was really looking for Teddy, but Bobby told me he was in the bathroom with another girl. I didn't want to bother Ted, so as I was leaving, I asked Bobby to have his younger brother call me that evening. Bobby carried on a conversation with me without missing a beat. Caught up in the moment, his companion barely noticed me."

The young lady writhing on the Carlyle penthouse living room floor with Bobby was Carol Bjorkman, a personalities columnist for *Women's Wear Daily,* whom RFK had met the year before at a Manhattan cocktail party. "Carol was not only chic but very bright," said Marianne Strong, then society editor of the now defunct *New York World-Telegram and Sun.* "She exercised a great deal of influence in the world of fashion. In this respect she reminded me of Jackie. Moreover, she was a Jackie look-alike."

During their nearly two years together, Bjorkman and Bobby saw each other predominantly at the Carlyle. But the attorney general and his mistress didn't shun all public outings. "They were quite an item in those days," said Marianne Strong. They were occasionally seen together at Broadway plays and in upscale New York restaurants, usually in company with other couples. Another witness, Peter Lawford, recalled that Bobby would sometimes pick Bjorkman up at her Madison Avenue hairdresser. "The day I accompanied him, he seemed extremely impatient," said Lawford. " 'When are you going to be ready?' he kept saying. 'When are you going to be done?' I heard a rumor—and only a rumor—that he asked Carol to marry him. He promised he would divorce Ethel. Carol purportedly turned him down. She had no intention of becoming a home wrecker."

Another of Bobby's affairs during his brother's presidency, according to Peter Lawford, involved Hollywood film star Lee Remick, to whom he was introduced in 1961 at a Justice Department dinner party in Washington. The next time he traveled to Los Angeles, the attorney general asked Lawford to set up a second meeting for him with Lee.

Lawford, who subsequently also became romantically involved with Remick, did more than schedule a meeting—he arranged for RFK and the then twenty-six-year-old actress to spend a weekend together at a friend's secluded home in Malibu. Remick evidently fell for Bobby, despite being married at the time to producer-director Bill Colleran, with whom she had two young children. Even after she and Peter Lawford became an item, Lee continued to pursue Bobby, whose high energy and boldness impressed her. She and Bobby spent several weekends together in 1962, once at the Palm Bay Club in Miami Beach, Florida.

"As far as I recall," said Bill Walton, "Bobby abandoned his friendship with Lee Remick when she became overly aggressive, calling him at all hours at home and in his office. Unlike Jack and Teddy, Bobby always exercised discretion and insisted his female partners comport themselves similarly. His attitude toward women stood in sharp contrast to his personality. Jack Kennedy tended to be subtle and slick; Bobby was forceful and direct. Jack would slip it to you behind your back; Bobby would tell you to your face to go fuck yourself. Jack had a wonderful sense of humor; Bobby had none. He was all business all the time. But by the same token, RFK seemed more sensitive than the president, more attuned to the women in his life."

"Why can't Jack be more like Bobby?" Jackie once asked Pierre Salinger. JFK's press secretary took the question as an indication of the First Lady's frustration over the president's seemingly incessant need to cheat on his wife in the most flagrant and demeaning ways, as opposed to Bobby's more acceptable "undercover operations." The one thing Jackie couldn't tolerate was to be embarrassed by Jack's very public flings, many of which took place directly under her nose.

Only once during his presidency—in the days immediately following Patrick's August 1963 death—did JFK make a sincere effort to contain his insatiable need for other women. His transformation was short-lived. By the time Jackie left on her cruise aboard the *Christina* with Lee Radziwill and Aristotle Onassis, Jack had resumed his errant lifestyle. A final schismatic confrontation between the president and his brokenhearted spouse would play itself out at a White House reception the night before the couple's ill-fated departure for Texas. The event— a reception for the Supreme Court justices, their wives, and other judicial officials, spouses, and guests—marked Jackie's first appearance at an Executive Mansion social function since August.

White House correspondent Jessie Stearns noted that as usual there was great interest among the press corps in how the First Lady looked, how she dressed, and how she had arranged the details of the evening. "I remember the reception very clearly," said Stearns, "because it took place just two or three days before the assassination and because we were given unprecedented access to the president and his wife. Jackie had never been a lover of the press. She had previously banished a White House photographer simply because he'd snapped a picture of her smoking a cigarette. She'd been nasty to us from the start. Suddenly we were being encouraged to cover the function, take photographs, and mingle with the guests. Such openness on the part of Jackie Kennedy was uncharacteristic and signaled a new policy on the part of the White House."

It was a period, Stearns further recalled, when JFK was supposedly "settling down" with Jackie but in reality was still "playing around" with other women. "He had evidently stopped for a while," said Stearns, "but he'd begun again. There was ample evidence to support this notion, including actual sightings by a number of very credible eyewitnesses. That nobody reported these activities in the press was due to the fact that the president's personal sex life was then considered off-limits."

At that particular reception, Stearns planted herself near the foot of the grand stairway, down which marched the honor guard carrying the presidential flag and the Stars and Stripes, followed by John F. Kennedy, Jackie, and guests of honor. They emerged to the Marine Band's playing of "Hail to the Chief."

All of a sudden, Stearns heard some scuffling on the staircase, a kind of pushing and pulling. Heads began to turn in the direction of the noise. A moment later, the procession came into view. President Kennedy's hair stood up on one side as though somebody had grabbed hold of a clump and given it a hard yank. JFK appeared momentarily ruffled and flustered. Jackie looked upset. As they continued to emerge, the president tried patting down his hair, smoothing it back into place. "As I recall," said Stearns, "the members of the press were quickly rounded up and moved out of the area. For obvious reasons, Kennedy's people didn't want us standing around and asking questions. Only later did I ascertain what had happened."

Returning an hour before the start of the reception from a day of horseback riding at Atoka, the First Lady learned (thanks to an East Wing maid) that her husband had spent an hour that afternoon in the Lincoln Bedroom with Mary Pinchot Meyer, frequently identified by biographers as JFK's last mistress. Seething with anger, Jacqueline flew at her husband with words and everything else in her arsenal, including her fists. They quarreled again later that evening after the reception. JFK's excessive self-indulgence had finally proved too much for Jackie. She must have understood once and for all that the man she had married—and campaigned for—could never be trusted. The man she'd married could never remain faithful to her. This final realization would forever tarnish Jacqueline Kennedy's conception of marriage. Yes, she would accompany her husband to Dallas, but only in body and not in soul or spirit.

Chapter 3

◆

F OR ALL HER post-assassination regrets and self-recriminations, Jacqueline Kennedy wanted more than anything to place her husband's administration in the best possible historic light. At the end of November 1963, while still residing in the White House, she telephoned journalist Theodore H. White in New York and invited him to visit her at Hyannis Port, Massachusetts, where she intended to go for a few days of rest and to see Joe Kennedy, whom she hadn't seen since September. "She knew I was writing a summation of the assassination for *Life*," said White, "and she wanted to discuss her husband's legacy—would I be willing to come up and talk with her?"

Life magazine provided White with a town car and a chauffeur, and in early December he drove up to the Cape. Jackie was staying in the house that she and Jack had owned at the Kennedy compound. On arriving, she had spent an hour alone with her father-in-law, whose stroke had rendered him speechless. In great detail, she told the old man how his son had lost his life. A day later, looking pale and drained, she met with Teddy White.

"She and I spoke for nearly four hours," said White. "She mentioned Patrick's death as a prelude to the assassination. The infant's passing had been a very emotional experience for both parents, and I think it made JFK reach out for her in a way he hadn't before. There weren't too many of these moments in their lives. I had the distinct sense that their marriage hadn't always been so good. The baby's death had provided a bond of intimacy between them. Without citing specifics, Jackie seemed to imply that the moment of closeness had gradually elapsed, and that their difficulties had prevailed to the bitter end."

Jackie provided the journalist with a minute-by-minute account of the assassination. She recalled the pink-rose rings on the inside of the president's skull after the top had been blown off. "The inside of his head was so beautiful," Jackie told White. "I tried to hold the top of his head down, so more of his brains wouldn't spill out. I knew he was dead. His blood and matted clumps of his hair were stuck to my clothes and my face. From the moment we arrived at Parkland Hospital, everyone kept trying to convince me to change my clothes. I wouldn't do it. I wanted the world to see what they'd done to Jack."

Jackie's only solace, she said, was that Jack hadn't suffered. He had made a point of telling her on any number of occasions that he never wanted to end up like his father—mute, half-paralyzed, and confined to a wheelchair. He preferred death to permanent impairment. He had told her this for the first time before undergoing radical back surgery early in their marriage.

White brought up the subject of the political climate as it existed in the country at the time of the assassination—the possibility of a conspiracy or even of governmental involvement in the murderous act. To the journalist's surprise, Jackie had no interest in the myriad theories as to who might have been behind her husband's murder. "What difference does it make," she asked, "whether he was killed by the CIA, the FBI, the Mafia, or simply some half-crazed misanthrope? It won't change anything. It won't bring him back. What matters now is that Jack's death be placed in some kind of lasting historical context."

As she continued to speak, it became obvious to White that the former First Lady had given the matter a great deal of thought, and in so doing had come up with the concept of Camelot, a term never before connected to the Kennedy administration. "It was an ingenious conceit," said White. The explicit association of the thirty-fifth president of the United States with King Arthur's court, its high ideals and progressive ideology, was Jacqueline Kennedy's invention, her contribution to the cause. If nothing else, she hoped to commemorate her husband's memory in such a way that his presidency would never be forgotten.

The *Camelot* symbol seemed an appropriate choice. Alan Jay Lerner, JFK's classmate at the Choate School and then Harvard, had written the lyrics for the musical and had been a frequent guest at the White House. By ironic coincidence, the Marine Band played excerpts from *My Fair Lady* and *Camelot* at the White House reception for the Supreme Court justices the night before the Kennedys departed for Texas, the same night Jackie learned of yet another of her husband's indiscretions. The selections that evening included the tune whose words Jackie now chose as a nostalgic summation of JFK's term as chief executive:

> *Don't let it be forgot*
> *That once there was a spot*
> *For one brief shining moment*
> *That was known as Camelot. . . .*

After reciting the lines for Teddy White, Jackie said, "When Jack quoted anything, it was usually classical, but I'm so ashamed of myself because all I keep thinking of are these lyrics from the musical. They were among his favorites. He identified with them, and he often played them on his phonograph at night before he went to sleep."

Continuing her presentation, the former First Lady told White, "Bitter old men write history. Jack's life had more to do with myth and magic than political theory or political science. History belongs to heroes, and heroes must not be forgotten. If only for my children, I want Jack to be remembered as a hero. There will be great presidents again, but there will never be another Camelot."

Jacqueline spoke so passionately that, seen in a certain light, it almost began to make sense to White. "I realized it was a misreading of history," he said, "but I was taken with Jackie's ability to frame the tragedy in such romantic and human terms. There was something extremely compelling about it, particularly since her marriage had been so problematic."

White understood that Jackie wanted him to hang his *Life* epilogue on the *Camelot* conceit. "Under the circumstances, it didn't seem like a hell of a lot to ask," said the journalist. "So I said to myself, why not? If that's all she wants, let her have it. As a result, the epitaph of the Kennedy administration became Camelot—a magic moment in American history when gallant men danced with beautiful women, when great deeds were done, and when the White House became the center of the universe."

When Art Buchwald, the Washington humorist and newspaper columnist, read Ted White's article in *Life*, he had to laugh. "I knew how compelling and earnest Jackie could be—and must have been—for Ted White to swallow all that *Camelot* business," said Buchwald. "I'd known Jack and Jackie for years and had never heard either of them so much as mention *Camelot*. To be honest, Jack couldn't stand Broadway musicals. He told me so himself in 1962, when I profiled him for the Paris edition of the *Herald Tribune*. The only connection between *Camelot* and JFK is that he 'came a lot.' Now, that made sense to me."

Chapter 4

◆

N OW THAT THE president was gone, Jacqueline Kennedy became preoccupied with where she and her two young children would live. In 1962 she and Jack had sold the three-story Georgetown townhouse they'd purchased six years earlier. Jackie's mother and stepfather offered to take them in temporarily, but the prospect of residing with family members didn't appeal to Jackie. She considered moving into Wexford, her weekend retreat at Atoka, Virginia, but ultimately decided against it. She wanted to remain within commuting distance of Washington so that Caroline could complete first grade at the White House school.

She eventually sought advice from John Kenneth Galbraith, the Harvard economist and American ambassador to India under JFK. Having returned to the States for the president's funeral, Galbraith discussed the situation with Averell and Marie Harriman, longtime Washingtonians and key players in the Democratic Party. The Harrimans offered Jackie their landmark eleven-room Georgetown residence at 3038 N Street, a mere three blocks from the house formerly owned by Jack and Jackie. To make room, the Harrimans acquired adjoining suites at the nearby Georgetown Inn. Ten days after the assassination, Jackie, Caroline, and John vacated the White House and moved into the Harriman house. With them came a contingent of retainers, including Maud Shaw, Nancy Tuckerman (Jackie's White House social secretary), and a team of Secret Service agents made available to the family by Lyndon Johnson. The presidential act (passed by Congress) called for the Secret Service to remain with the Kennedys until Caroline and John each in turn reached the age of sixteen; they would remain with Jackie until such time as she might remarry, and for the rest of her life if she didn't.

To welcome Jackie, the Harrimans gave her a dinner party at the Jockey Club. Kentucky senator John Sherman Cooper and his wife, Lorraine, close friends of the family, did the same. Ambassador Charles Whitehouse, a horseback riding partner of Jackie's, hosted a cocktail party for the former First Lady at Washington's F Street Club. White-house later described JFK's term in office as a "beautiful sunset before an endlessly bitter night."

In mid-December 1963, following the publication in *Life* of Theodore White's *Camelot* salute to JFK, Bobby and Ethel Kennedy organized a buffet luncheon for Jackie at the Harriman townhouse. Among the invitees were Randolph Churchill (Winston's son), Robert McNamara, Ted and Joan Kennedy, Steve and Jean Kennedy Smith, Pat Lawford, Pierre Salinger, Secretary of the Interior Stewart Udall, Ben and Tony Bradlee, Stas and Lee Radziwill, George Kennan (the states-man, back from an ambassadorship to Yugoslavia), and *Washington Post* owner Katharine Graham. Also included on the guest list was President Lyndon Johnson, who found himself shut out by the predominantly pro-Kennedy crowd. The common lament among most Kennedyites had it that LBJ was an interloper, with no real claim to the throne. What's more, he spoke with a pronounced Texas drawl and lacked JFK's polish and sophistication. Even Jackie got in on the act. Although she'd written him a letter on November 26 expressing her gratitude for all his help and understanding, she began referring to the president and First Lady as "Colonel Cornpone and his little Pork Chop."

"At this particular buffet," recalled Pierre Salinger, "nobody went near Johnson. You had to feel for him. After all, he'd done everything he could to ease Jackie's plight. At her request, because JFK had initi-ated the U.S. space program, he issued an executive order changing the name of the Cape Canaveral Air Force Station and the Launch Operation Center of the National Aeronautics and Space Administration [NASA] to the John F. Kennedy Space Center. He issued a second executive order granting Jackie a $50,000-per-year budget to pay for all staff and office expenses for a period of two years. He even offered her the position of ambassador to France. In return, the Kennedys treated him miserably. During his presidency, the only member of the clan who maintained decent relations with LBJ was Teddy Kennedy. The rest of them treated him like a leper."

Following the initial spree of parties, Jackie suffered a mental collapse. She rarely left her bedroom and almost never left the house. She became a compulsive nail-biter. She stopped taking telephone calls. With the exception of Bobby Kennedy, she refused to see anyone, ordering Nancy Tuckerman to clear her appointment calendar. Lyndon Johnson invited her to visit the White House, but she declined—it was far too soon. He then asked her to join Lady Bird's Washington beautification committee, Mrs. Johnson's version of Jackie's White House renovation project; Jackie refused. Over Christmas vacation 1963, she brought Caroline and John Jr. to Palm Beach, Florida, to visit with their Kennedy grandparents. Bobby Kennedy also flew down and gave Jackie the Christmas present Jack had intended to give her that year: a small sculpture of the Egyptian goddess Isis. For New Year's, Jacqueline and her children joined Ted Kennedy and his brood at a ski lodge in Aspen, Colorado. While her children went skiing, Jackie purportedly drank herself into a stupor.

Aware that she couldn't impose on the Harrimans indefinitely, Jackie returned to Washington and began searching for a home of her own. Accompanied by John Kenneth Galbraith, she looked at a dozen houses before settling on a three-story, fourteen-room, fawn-colored brick Colonial at 3017 N Street, on the same block as the Harriman townhouse. The asking price was $215,000. Lacking the necessary funds and unwilling to take out a mortgage, Jackie turned to Bobby Kennedy for assistance. The attorney general talked the seller into accepting $195,000 for the property; he then authorized Steve Smith to advance his sister-in-law $100,000 from the Joseph P. Kennedy Jr. Foundation. Jackie paid the remainder in cash.

One problem with 3017 N Street was that it stood on a rise high above the sidewalk, a steep set of wooden stairs leading to the front door. As a result, it was easy to peer into the house from the street below. Even with the draperies drawn, the interior of the house was clearly visible from certain angles, and it soon became the number one tourist attraction in Washington. Day after day, the narrow streets of Georgetown filled with tourists and strangers eager to catch a glimpse of the fabled trio. They stood on the sidewalk in front of the house or sat on the curb eating their lunch, leaving behind crumpled paper bags and empty bottles of Coke. The more brazen members of the crowd climbed the magnolia trees that stood in a clump before the house, or they perched atop the hoods and roofs of parked cars. They double-parked in their own vehicles, obstructing traffic, chanting Jackie's name over and over like a mantra. Some of them slept in their cars at night, buying their meals from street vendors hawking an array of fast-food products. Other street vendors sold Kennedy-related trinkets and souvenirs, including postcards, T-shirts, and key chains. In addition, dozens of reporters and news photographers maintained a round-the-clock vigil, as did a battery of radio technicians and television crews.

"Now that Jackie and her children have taken possession of their new home on N Street," read a *Washington Post* editorial, "the once quaint and quiet district of Georgetown has begun to resemble one of the many hurly-burly casbahs of Morocco." Indeed, whenever Jackie or her children emerged from their house, the Washington police and Secret Service cordoned off the block and cleared a path for them through the clamoring throngs. The same procedure was applied when any of them returned. Despite these efforts, onlookers were known to break through police barricades in an effort to touch or embrace the children. On one occasion, a crazed woman grabbed hold of Caroline's hair and refused to let go until the police stepped in and carted her off to jail. Professional as well as amateur photographers often popped their flashbulbs in the children's startled faces. The tour bus operators of

Washington made Jackie's house a mandatory stop as they cruised through Georgetown, stopping to disgorge hundreds of rowdy passengers in need of a closer look.

The freakish atmosphere that pervaded Georgetown, the constant din and clamor, gradually eroded all hope Jackie might have had of starting a new life in the Washington area. She became more depressed than ever. A prisoner in her own home, she spent her days in bed leafing through family photograph albums, often breaking down in tears. To prove to her that she could leave her house without being mobbed, Secretary of Defense Robert McNamara (one of the few members of JFK's cabinet to stay on with LBJ) convinced her to accompany him to lunch one afternoon. "It turned into a disaster," he said. As they walked down the street, they were trailed by dozens of tourists. One hysterical woman ran up and thrust a Bible at Jackie. Another woman accosted her verbally, accusing her in a loud voice of having been behind her husband's assassination. When they entered the restaurant, the place fell silent. Fellow diners gawked at Jackie. Waiters, waitresses, and busboys gathered around for a closer look. "I feel like the bearded lady in a circus side show," said Jackie. "Her presence brought out every crazy in town," said McNamara.

The secretary of defense had another unhappy experience with Jackie. Soon after she moved into her new Georgetown house, McNamara brought over an unfinished oil painting of JFK he had purchased from a Washington art gallery. Jackie placed the painting on the floor of her dining room, against the wall where she hoped to mount it. When Caroline first saw the portrait, she approached it and began kissing her father's face. She then began to cry. The following day, Jackie telephoned McNamara and reported what had happened. "Caroline went nuts when she saw the painting," she said. "I had to hide it in a closet. You have to come and take it back."

Others had similarly emotional stories to tell. Franklin D. Roosevelt Jr., who had chaperoned Jackie on her 1963 cruise aboard the *Christina*, recalled driving the former First Lady home from a small get-together at his house one evening. As he pulled up in front of 3017 N Street, he noticed a gaggle of strangers seated on the wooden steps leading to her front door. "I can't take it anymore," said Jackie. "They're like locusts— they follow me wherever I go. They're driving me crazy." Roosevelt stepped out of the car first and chased off the trespassers. He then accompanied Jackie into the house and spent a few minutes trying to calm her.

"She told me that even though she was taking antidepressants and sleeping pills, she couldn't sleep at night," said Roosevelt. "She'd become an insomniac. She kept reliving the assassination, replaying it in her mind, wondering if there had been anything she could've done to save Jack's life on that terrible day. She discussed Caroline and John Jr. She pledged to be both mother and father to them, to raise them in as normal a manner as possible. She also brought up Bobby Kennedy. If not for Bobby, she said, she might well have ended it, by which I think she meant she would've taken her life."

A number of Jackie's Washington friends and associates noticed a marked change in her personality. Susan Mary Alsop, the wife of journalist Joseph Alsop, joined her for tea one day. "I hadn't seen her since the funeral, and I wanted to offer a few consoling words to make her feel better," remarked Mrs. Alsop, "so I mumbled something like, 'At least Jack is resting peacefully with God.' She gave me a look and shot back, 'That's the silliest thing I've ever heard, Susan.' I apologized. She quickly finished her tea and practically threw me out of the house. I wrote to her several times and tried calling, but I never heard from her again."

Following the assassination, Evelyn Lincoln, JFK's senatorial and White House secretary, was placed in charge of organizing and cataloguing the president's personal and presidential papers. After some time on the job, she complained to Jackie that she hadn't had a day off in months. "Mrs. Lincoln, why are you whining?" said the unsympathetic former First Lady. "You still have your husband, and you're still gainfully employed. All I have to look forward to is the presidential library they're planning to build for Jack in Boston." The relationship between the two ladies continued to disintegrate. Jackie later accused the secretary of taking certain documents and other materials from the collection, a charge that Lincoln flatly denied. In the end, Evelyn Lincoln refused to give her own personal files to the Kennedy Library; instead, in 1972 she donated them to the Lyndon Baines Johnson Presidential Library and Museum in Austin, Texas.

Mary Gallagher, Jackie's personal secretary in the White House, received equally poor treatment. Hired to help Evelyn Lincoln process JFK's executive papers, Mary made the mistake of asking Jackie for a small raise. After upbraiding her secretary for nearly an hour, the former First Lady fired her without a penny of severance pay, giving her just two weeks' notice. Gallagher subsequently wrote her own account of working for the Kennedys, including in the book some less than complimentary statements about the former First Lady.

George Plimpton remembered seeking Jackie's permission to publish a perfectly harmless article he'd written for *Harper's* magazine on JFK and Caroline attending the America's Cup yacht race off Newport the year before. "She reacted to my request by throwing a fit," said Plimpton. "She absolutely opposed the idea and threatened to sue if the article appeared anywhere in print. 'But Jackie,' I said, 'you've known me for years. You know perfectly well I'd never write anything of a negative nature.' 'I don't care if you write about me,' she responded, 'but leave my daughter out of it.' So I canned the piece, and published it years later, after Jackie's death in 1994."

A second publishing fracas occurred when *Paris Match* ran an article suggesting that ever since her father's assassination, Caroline had been seeing a child psychiatrist. When Jackie read the article, she contacted Pierre Salinger and forced him to call the Paris-based magazine to demand a retraction. Philippe de Bausset, a senior editor at *Paris Match,* informed Salinger that it had based the story on information provided by a reliable source.

"And who might that be?" inquired Salinger.

"Like any respectable publication, we protect our sources," said the editor. "But in this case, I don't mind divulging his name. It was Steve Smith, the late president's brother-in-law."

"I find it difficult to believe that Steve Smith would comment on such a personal matter," remarked Salinger. "But in any case, Mrs. Kennedy demands a retraction. If you refuse, she is going to sue."

After an emergency meeting of the magazine's editorial board, de Bausset got back to Salinger and advised him that *Paris Match* stood behind its article and had no intention of running a retraction. Knowing full well that the story was true and unable to bully the periodical, Jackie withdrew her complaint, but not before serving notice on the press that they had better check their facts before publishing anything in the future about the Kennedy children.

LeMoyne (Lem) Billings, one of JFK's oldest and dearest friends, felt that Jackie was suffering from a form of manic depression. "You never knew what to expect of her, or what kind of mood she'd be in at any given moment," he said. "She phoned me late one night, practically in tears. She said she'd asked to have one of her children's Secret Service agents [Bob Foster] transferred to another detail because John-John had begun to call him 'Daddy.' 'That's not so bad, Jackie,' I said. 'It's almost to be expected.' She exploded. 'How would you know, Lem? You're gay—you never had children of your own.' "

Billings recalled a luncheon invitation he received from Jackie in early 1964. He arrived at her Georgetown home just as another visitor, Dr. Max Jacobson, was leaving. "I knew Jacobson, because Jack had sent me to see him on several occasions during 1961 and '62. He dispensed methamphetamine injections. It was dangerous stuff. Several of his patients had developed serious infections from the shots; others had become addicted. In no uncertain terms, I told Jackie what I thought of him. The next day I called Bobby Kennedy. I reported seeing Jacobson at Jackie's house, and Bobby went ballistic. He telephoned Jacobson's office in New York and warned the good doctor to stay away from his sister-in-law. 'If you show up again,' Bobby told him, 'I'll see to it that you never practice medicine again.' "

Several days after receiving one of Jacobson's shots, Jackie was spotted eating a late lunch with Secret Service agent Clint Hill at Washington's Jockey Club. "They were seated at a rear banquette," said real estate broker Carl Franks. "There weren't many people around. I happened to be there with my wife. It was obvious that Jackie had been drinking. She was carrying on, conversing in a loud voice, slurring her words, laughing hysterically. Then, without warning, she suddenly slid off the banquette and onto the floor. The Secret Service agent jumped up and helped her back into her seat. When they were done eating, he practically carried her out of the restaurant. If he hadn't held on to her, she would've toppled over again."

William Manchester, the historian chosen by Jackie (and Bobby Kennedy) to pen the official story of the assassination (*The Death of a President*), reported that whenever he interviewed the former First Lady for the book, she felt compelled to fortify herself with alcohol. "I conducted six or seven separate interviews with her, sometimes late at night," said Manchester. "It must have been terribly painful for her, because she drank heavily. Several times we had to stop so she could regain her composure. I noticed that her moods shifted drastically from session to session. The drinking may have had something to do with it."

Jackie's erratic mood swings did not go unnoticed by her children. Jacqueline Hirsh, a French instructor at Caroline's White House school, had begun tutoring the child privately. Every Monday she took Caroline on an afternoon outing during which they spoke only in French. According to her oral history at the JFK Library, Hirsh soon observed how "wan and unhappy" Caroline looked. "My mommy lies in bed all day and can't stop crying," the little girl told her tutor. Whenever a reporter or press photographer came around, she'd hide behind Hirsh or cower on the floor of Hirsh's car. She disrupted a weekly religious training class she'd been taking by announcing that her mother cried all day long. "I tell her everything's going to be all right," Caroline noted, "but she never stops."

Mother and daughter quickly became the talk of Caroline's White House school. Washington attorney William Joyce, whose daughter attended the same school, saw the former First Lady at a birthday party for one of the children in the class. "Jackie had on a pair of lavender sandals," said Joyce, "and an old, rumpled pants suit. Her hair looked dirty, and her makeup wasn't well applied. She looked terrible. Caroline looked worse. She was one of the most miserable-looking little creatures I've ever seen. I went over to her and said, 'Hi, Caroline, how're you doing?' 'I'm okay,' she said. But she wasn't okay. She appeared to be extremely tense and despondent."

While Jacqueline Kennedy grieved the loss of a husband with whom she'd had a dizzying, roller-coaster relationship, Bobby Kennedy grieved the death of a brother for whom he had nothing but unconditional love. Believing that his life had been destroyed, RFK found insufficient solace in the nostrums he'd learned as a boy in church. Ethel Kennedy's religious faith was more basic than his, with fewer questions. As such, her ability to comfort her husband had been compromised. Her friend Coates Redmon recalled several of the conversations that took place at Hickory Hill following JFK's demise: "Someone would say, 'Well, what are we going to do about such-and-such?' You know, government talk. And Ethel would say, 'Well, Jack will take care of that. He's up in heaven, and he's looking down on us, and he'll show us what to do.' She often said things like that. And one time Bobby sat back and said, audibly, to everyone, 'The voice you just heard belongs to the wife of the attorney general of the United States. Let's hear no more out of her.' "

Bobby's despair was in no small measure a result of survivor's guilt. Given the climate of hatred that existed in Dallas at the time of his brother's assassination, he felt he should have done something to prevent the trip. Senator William J. Fulbright and UN ambassador Adlai Stevenson had both been the victims of editorial attacks by *The Dallas Morning News* and had been greeted by egg-pelting mobs during their respective visits to the city. Byron Skelton, the Democratic National Committeeman from Texas, had written to RFK on November 4, 1963, "Frankly, I'm worried about President Kennedy's proposed trip to Texas." The city wasn't safe, Bobby agreed, but political commitments took precedence over concern for the president's personal security.

The attorney general's failure to intervene in JFK's visit to Dallas, however, weighed less heavily on his conscience than did his conduct over the whole of his brother's term in office, for he had been the driving force in the Kennedy administration's most dangerous and aggressive operations. He had pushed the government to eliminate Fidel Castro, to probe and prosecute Jimmy Hoffa, and to destroy the Mafia and all other facets of organized crime in America. He personally had dealt with Marilyn Monroe after the actress threatened to go public with details of her failed affair with JFK. He deported another of his brother's love interests, an East German showgirl named Ellen Rometsch, because he suspected her of being a Russian spy. There was little question that these and other actions perpetrated by RFK in the name of justice may well have played a role in his brother's murder. Less than a day after the assassination, Bobby told Larry O'Brien, "I'm sure that little pinko prick [Lee Harvey Oswald] had something to do with it, but he certainly didn't mastermind anything. He should've shot me, not Jack. I'm the one who's out to get them."

News items about Jack's assassin, and the assassin's assassin, Jack Ruby, were not slow in coming. By the day of JFK's funeral, Bobby knew for certain that Lee Harvey Oswald had Communist ties and had spent time in New Orleans, demonstrating on behalf of the Fair Play for Cuba Committee. He knew that Jack Ruby had strong links to the Mafia and that Oswald had declared himself nothing more than a "patsy." He also knew that the CIA, with his permission and sanction, had hatched a plot code-named Operation Mongoose, whereby leading Mafia bosses had been solicited and employed by the CIA in a futile effort to assassinate Castro and overthrow the Cuban government. Given this intricate pattern of interwoven threads, RFK could not easily have overlooked the distinct possibility that his unrelenting campaign against Castro and the Mob had somehow backfired on his brother.

Over much of the next year, utilizing trustworthy FBI agents, CIA operatives, and personnel from his own department, Bobby conducted an exhaustive private investigation into the true causes behind JFK's assassination. "He could talk about little else," said Ken O'Donnell. "He'd call me late at night and go through the multiple combinations and permutations that could have led to Jack's assassination. He had no faith in the newly formed Warren Commission's investigation, which is why he initiated his own. He suspected the Cubans, the Russians, as well as the CIA, FBI, and Secret Service. He asked if I thought some U.S. government agency might have been involved. He asked the same question of Courtney Evans, the FBI liaison between the Kennedy family and J. Edgar Hoover. I mentioned the Syndicate—the Mob—as a possibility. I'm certain he thought the Mob had been involved. He suspected Carlos Marcello, the New Orleans capo to whom Jack Ruby had ties. But he never satisfactorily resolved the issue. All he kept saying was, 'They should've killed me,' without indicating who *they* were."

Ultimately, because of all the enemies he'd made along the way, Bobby blamed himself for his brother's death. "He felt incredibly guilty," recalled Larry O'Brien, who urged RFK to "drop the matter for the time being and get on with it. We need you to lead us back to the White House. That's what your brother would have wanted."

Although he eventually aborted his personal investigation, RFK never stopped thinking about the probability of an assassination conspiracy. The thought haunted and crippled him. He lost weight, literally shrank in size. His aides in the Justice Department were all aware that he had stopped coming to the office. On the rare occasions that he put in an appearance, he seemed distracted and scattered. The man who time and again told his children that "Kennedys don't cry" cried frequently. Like Jackie, he had difficulty falling asleep. Refusing his physician's offer of a prescription for sedatives, he often climbed into his Cadillac and drove off by himself into the night.

Peter Stanford, owner of a small bar in Arlington, Virginia, remembered Bobby's nighttime visits during the period immediately following JFK's assassination. "He'd drop in three or four nights a week, always alone," said Stanford. "He'd arrive late, order a beer, and we'd chat. He liked the fact that mine was an ordinary, blue-collar bar. Nobody bothered him. He'd reminisce about his childhood, about growing up with his brothers, especially JFK. He discussed Jackie's children, how they'd have to grow up without a father. From the way he spoke, I assumed he saw a lot of Jackie. He told me he couldn't talk to his wife. Ethel, who had lost her parents in a private airplane crash, was so filled with religious fervor that she objected to the teaching of Darwin's theory of evolution at the private school her children attended. Jackie, on the other hand, understood him. She knew exactly what to say to him, because her problems were the same as his."

In truth, Bobby spent more time with Jackie, Caroline, and John Jr. than he did with his own wife and children. Adhering to the Kennedy family's adopted myth of Camelot, RFK increasingly played Lancelot to Jackie's Guinevere, especially when it came to helping raise her offspring. In her memoir, *White House Nanny*, Maud Shaw observed that RFK had become a surrogate father to John and Caroline. He'd show up at Jackie's N Street home early in the morning and sit with the children while they ate breakfast. He played games with them, read bedtime stories to them, spoke to them about their father, constantly reminding them what a "great man" JFK had been. He taught them how to ski and how to swim. On Father's Day at Caroline's school, RFK stood in for his brother. "The sad part," wrote Maud Shaw, "was that the attorney general nearly suffered his own nervous breakdown. Although he didn't believe in self-pity, he always appeared to be in pain. He looked gaunt, wasted. He often wore a leather bomber jacket with the presidential seal embossed on it. The jacket had belonged to his brother. With all the weight he'd dropped, the attorney general barely filled the jacket—he seemed lost in it."

So profound was Bobby's suffering that he told Jackie he didn't see how he could go on with a career in public service. He wanted to leave Washington and start his own law practice, preferably in New York or Boston. Jackie reacted by writing him a most feeling and tender letter, imploring him not to give up, not to quit. She told him she needed him, as did her children. "Now that Jack's gone, Caroline and John need you more than ever," she wrote. "Above all, the country needs you. It is time to honor Jack's memory—not to continue to mourn it. We would both, myself included, be negligent in our responsibilities to that memory if we collapse. Jack would want us both to carry on what he stood for, and died for." Enclosed with the letter, Jackie sent RFK a sheaf of yellow legal pages filled with JFK's scrawl, entitled "Notes made by President Kennedy at his last Cabinet meeting, October 29, 1963." Bobby framed the pages and mounted them in his study at Hickory Hill.

Jackie's letter, written in mid-January 1964, communicated the former First Lady's resolve to save not only Bobby's soul but her own as well. According to Lem Billings, "She seemed to be on the road to recovery. There would be further setbacks and stumbling blocks, but on the whole, Jackie was determined to set her life back in motion."

In late January, Dame Margot Fonteyn, the British prima ballerina, spent a weekend as Jackie's houseguest in Georgetown. As Fonteyn remembered it, Robert Kennedy was around a good deal of the time. And when he wasn't there, he'd be on the telephone with Jackie. "They seemed uncommonly close," said Fonteyn, "no doubt drawn to one another by their shared loss."

When Fonteyn finally found herself alone with Jackie, she expressed her sorrow over the president's death. Jackie said nothing at first. After a while she remarked, "I miss Jack, of course, but mostly I miss him for the children. To be honest, we had our share of problems, and being in the White House didn't exactly help matters."

"What married couple doesn't have problems?" said Fonteyn.

Fonteyn later admitted finding it odd that the former First Lady had spoken so candidly, albeit briefly, to a virtual stranger about her marriage. "I'd met the Kennedys during their tenure in the White House," said Fonteyn, "but prior to that weekend, I hadn't spent much time alone with Mrs. Kennedy. However, when I thought about it, it began to make sense. Better to unburden yourself on someone with whom you're not so familiar than on a friend. A so-called friend will betray you; a stranger won't. Besides, Jackie didn't impress me as someone who would necessarily surround herself with allies. She apparently had difficulty trusting people, especially women."

Jackie disclosed several other closely guarded family secrets during Fonteyn's stay. Just as John F. Kennedy had been a womanizer, he became wary of his wife's frequent meetings with other men. He came to believe she was doing what he was doing. Among others, he suspected his wife of having had an affair with Gianni Agnelli, the Italian business tycoon and principal shareholder of the Fiat Automobile Corporation. As a result, he insisted on having paternity tests performed on both Caroline and John Jr. The test results evidently satisfied him, because he eventually dropped the matter.

The most startling admission Jackie made that weekend involved Bobby Kennedy. The former First Lady told Fonteyn that shortly after the president's autopsy, Bobby had disposed of several dozen slides of his brother's brain matter prepared during the postmortem examination. "He told me," Jackie told her guest, "he didn't want to take a chance on one day having the slides reappear as part of some mawkish exhibition at a place like the Smithsonian. So he dumped them. I can't say I blame him."

A second visitor to Jackie's house that month was Aristotle Onassis. Having resumed his romance with Jackie's sister, Ari had appointed Stas Radziwill, Lee's husband, to head Olympic Airways, one of many corporations owned by Onassis. "In that way," said Pierre Salinger, "he hoped to get Stas out of the picture, though in reality the two men were reasonably close friends. Stas had his own set of girlfriends. The only problem with the arrangement was that Drew Pearson, the syndicated Washington columnist, found out about Ari's visit with Jackie and wrote a scathing article insinuating that Onassis was sleeping with both Bouvier sisters at the same time. The article went on to say that Onassis had been defrauding the U.S. government for at least two decades, avoiding payment of taxes on his business ventures in the States, including real estate and oil refineries."

Reading the column, Bobby Kennedy telephoned Pierre Salinger in California, where he was planning to run for the Senate. "I've known that bastard Onassis for years," RFK told him. "We first met in 1953 at Pamela Churchill's apartment in New York. He was a snake then, and he's still a snake. Other than his bankroll, I don't understand what Jackie sees in him."

Onassis returned to Jackie's house a day later, this time bringing along his teenage daughter, Christina. "My father thinks Jackie looks Greek," Christina told French journalist Pierre Dauphin. "Frankly, I think she looks like a vampire. Her eyes are set so far apart, I can't believe they see the same thing."

Although Jackie leaned heavily on Bobby for companionship and emotional support, she ignored his cautionary warnings about socializing with Onassis. Pierre Salinger correctly surmised that Ari provided her with much-needed business advice and occasional financial assistance. JFK's will had left the preponderance of his assets in trust to their children. Jackie received $200,000 per annum from the estate, plus a paltry $10,000 widow's pension from the government, hardly enough to enable her to live in the style to which she'd grown accustomed. Bobby augmented Jackie's inheritance by instructing Stephen Smith to allot the former First Lady an additional $50,000 per year, the money to be paid in monthly installments by the Joseph P. Kennedy Jr. Foundation. While the extra cash helped, Jackie's finances remained problematic. Aristotle Onassis had no problem making up the difference between the amount of capital Jackie received each month and the amount she needed to pursue a life of luxury.

It is open to debate whether Onassis would have continued to "make up the difference" at this stage had he been aware of an event that ensued shortly after his end-of-January visit to Washington. On the evening of February 3, Jackie and her sister had dinner at the Jockey Club with Marlon Brando and Brando's business manager, George Englund. Lee Radziwill had previously added Englund to her forever-expanding list of lovers, and it had been Englund's idea to arrange the dinner. Brando included several pages on his meeting(s) with Jackie in the first draft of his 1994 autobiography, *Songs My Mother Taught Me*, but an editor at Random House, a friend of Jackie's, insisted on removing the telling passages prior to the book's publication. According to Brando, the three-hour meal involved a good deal of drinking, in the course of which Jackie regaled the group with stories of her 1963 semi-official visit to India. She described her encounter with Prime Minister

Nehru, who taught her how to stand on her head for hours and medi-
tate. The evening's only damper was Jackie's annoyance when she spied
a group of newsmen and photographers outside the restaurant. After
dinner, the two sisters left together and were soon joined at Jackie's
house by their dinner companions. In anticipation of her date with the
sexy movie star, Jackie had sent her children and their nanny to her
mother's house. While Lee and Englund cuddled on a couch, Jackie and
the actor danced and drank. During their dance, Jackie, deeply
attracted to Brando, "pressed her thighs" suggestively into his. They
danced again, then sat down and began to "make out." In Brando's
words, "From all I'd read and heard about her, Jacqueline Kennedy
seemed coquettish and sensual but not particularly sexual. If anything,
I pictured her as more voyeur than player. But that wasn't at all the case.
She kept waiting for me to try to get her into bed. When I failed to
make a move, she took matters into her own hands and popped the
magic question: 'Would you like to spend the night?' And I said, 'I
thought you'd never ask.' "

A week later, Jacqueline left her children behind and spent the weekend at the Carlyle Hotel in Manhattan, where she once more saw
Brando, visiting him at a small Sutton Place apartment he'd borrowed
from a friend. Commenting on Jackie's "boyish hips" and "muscular
frame," the actor went on to say, "I'm not sure she knew what she was
doing sexually, but she did it well."

Having twice consummated her relationship with Brando, Jackie
showed no interest in pursuing him further. Two weekends later, however, she returned to New York and again checked into the Carlyle.
During her stay, she met author Irwin Shaw for breakfast, lunched with
Truman Capote, and ate dinner with Leland and Pamela Hayward (the
former Mrs. Pamela Churchill and future Mrs. Averell Harriman). She
topped off her trip by accompanying Bobby Kennedy (who also spent
the weekend in New York) to the Waldorf Towers to visit ex-president
Herbert Hoover. Suffering from a form of dementia and half blind,
Hoover became confused. "The two of you make a nice couple," he
said. "When did you get married?"

Back in Georgetown, Jackie telephoned Truman Capote (with whom she and her sister had become extremely close friends) and told him that in New York she'd found her true mecca. "Nobody follows me around in New York," she said. "They don't single me out. I get looks, but nothing compared to Washington. Everything about Washington reminds me of Jack. New York reminds me of my childhood and my father. I feel more human in New York." When Capote suggested she consider relocating to New York, she responded, "I'm considering it, Truman. I definitely am."

Jackie also told Capote that her sister wanted to sleep with Bobby Kennedy, and that on a recent trip to the Far East, he'd stopped off in London, where Lee had thrown a party for him. Although Jackie suspected her sister of having an affair with Bobby, she lacked proof. "Well, she said nothing to me about it," the author told Jackie, "and she tells me everything." Privately, however, Capote felt certain that RFK and Lee had been together romantically. To film producer Lester Persky, he commented, "Like all those Kennedy men, Bobby's not one to pass up an opportunity."

Over Easter weekend 1964, several weeks after the former First Lady testified before the Warren Commission, Ethel Kennedy took Jacqueline's children and her own on a ski trip to Sun Valley, Idaho, while Bobby, Jackie, Stas and Lee Radziwill, and Chuck Spalding embarked on a weeklong Caribbean vacation as Paul and Bunny Mellon's houseguests at Mill Reef Estate, overlooking Half Moon Bay in Antigua. Bunny Mellon, Jackie's closest female friend, introduced her visitors to American financiers Jay Gould and Laurens Hammond (inventor of the Hammond organ), both of whom owned homes in Antigua. The group spent their vacation swimming, sailing, shopping, and sleeping. They picnicked and went waterskiing. They went on excursions to English Harbour and Saint John's. They drank and danced at Savoy, a now-defunct, then-happening nightclub owned by Roy Chesterfield, a friend of the Mellons. Jackie and her sister did the twist to a Chubby Checker recording, reminding Chuck Spalding of a 1962 Executive Mansion party at which the sisters performed the same dance routine, incurring a *Washington Post* society page headline that read "Twisting at the White House."

"Everything considered, we had a decent time in Antigua," recalled Chuck Spalding. "One night we barbecued dinner on the beach. Somebody remarked that Jack Kennedy couldn't tolerate barbecue—much as he liked it, it invariably upset his stomach. The mere mention of his brother's name sent Bobby into an instant depression. His entire demeanor changed. When she saw this, Jackie went to him, threw her arms around his neck, and gave him a hug. His face brightened. I couldn't help but notice how close they seemed, and I wondered why in hell Ethel Kennedy had sent her husband on a vacation with Jackie while she remained behind. What could she have been thinking?"

It didn't take much to see that Bobby and Jackie were developing something more than friendship. They held hands, touched, whispered into each other's ears. Every morning they took a long walk together along the shoreline. At night they huddled on a verandah and gazed in wonderment at the starlit sky. "There was definitely something between them," said Spalding. "You had to be dumb, deaf, and blind not to sense it."

While still in Antigua, Jackie presented RFK with a copy of Edith Hamilton's *The Greek Way,* an assemblage of essays on the preeminent figures of Athenian literature and history. Bobby read the volume, discovering in it a philosophy that would enable him to put into perspective the tragedy of his brother's death. "When the world is storm-driven and . . . bad things happen," Hamilton writes, "then we need to know all the strong fortresses of the spirit which men have built through the ages."

Bobby carried *The Greek Way* around with him for much of the rest of his life, underlining key passages, annotating important pages, taking notes, memorizing lines, pulling out his dog-eared copy from time to time in order to read from it to friends and strangers alike. The book became his sacred text. It opened up for him a world of suffering and redemption, a world in which man's destiny was determined by the gods, but also a world in which man struggled on despite the finality of a tragic fate. "The book changed my life," said Bobby. "It gave me hope."

What RFK didn't realize at the time is that Jackie had originally learned about *The Greek Way* from Aristotle Onassis. Handing her a copy of the book, the shipping tycoon had suggested it would help her overcome her malaise and sadness. Jackie, in turn, bought another copy and gave it to Bobby. "Had he been aware of Onassis's involvement," said Larry O'Brien, "it's doubtful he'd even have opened the book."

Chapter 5

◆

DESPITE BOBBY Kennedy's often rough, tough, hard-nosed veneer, Jacqueline Kennedy had always felt compassion and tenderness for him. "I wish you were an amoeba, so you could multiply and there would be two or more of you," she once told him. Jackie's allegiance to Bobby, her willingness to overlook his more obvious faults, did not mitigate the fact that he lacked his brother Jack's finesse—his calm sensibility and measured objectivity. Over the years, RFK had managed to make as many enemies as he had supporters and friends. "Bobby could be a royal pain," said Lem Billings. "You either loved or hated him—there was no in between."

The novelist, essayist, and playwright Gore Vidal, distantly related to Jackie (his mother, like hers, had been married to Hugh Auchincloss), counted himself among RFK's detractors, having practically been tossed out of a White House reception by Bobby when the author, apparently having had a few drinks, became overly familiar with the First Lady. Years after the row with Bobby, looking back on the incident, Vidal said, "As I let the drama idle away in my mind, I suspect that the one person Jackie ever loved . . . was Bobby Kennedy. There was always something oddly intimate in her voice when she mentioned him to me."

At first Jackie's relationship with Bobby had a secretive, rather furtive quality to it. In late May 1964, two months after returning from

Antigua, RFK brought both Jackie and Ethel to a formal dinner cruise around the Potomac River aboard the presidential yacht, USS *Sequoia*. Recalling the event for the December 2007 issue of *Vanity Fair*, journalist Maureen Orth, then still a college student, noted that the guest list included Steve and Jean Kennedy Smith, Red Fay (JFK's undersecretary of the navy), George Stevens Jr. (head of the U.S. Information Agency's motion picture division), and JFK speechwriter (and historian) Arthur Schlesinger Jr. While Orth, a guest of Red Fay, focused on Jackie's resplendent white gown, she failed to notice the romantic undercurrent that evening between Bobby and Jackie. Their poignant glances across the dinner table did not go undetected by Arthur Schlesinger, however.

"I knew Bobby and Jackie had grown close," said Schlesinger. "I knew they'd vacationed in Antigua and that Ethel hadn't gone along. I also knew they were working together to raise funds for the John F. Kennedy Library at Columbia Point in Boston. What I didn't know is that there was apparently more to their relationship than I originally thought."

At one point during the *Sequoia* dinner cruise, the new head of the Kennedy family and his sister-in-law disappeared below deck. They were gone for no more than ten minutes. "I have no idea what transpired between them," said Schlesinger, "but when they returned, they looked as chummy and relaxed as a pair of Cheshire cats."

Red Fay likewise speculated about the possibility of a liaison between Bobby and Jackie. "After Jack's death," he said, "Jackie kind of went into hibernation, and Bobby was with her all the time. I don't know if he became infatuated or not. She was a fascinating woman. Bobby was a controlling individual. If she exercised her charm, she'd be hard to resist."

Inevitably, Ethel Kennedy began to resent the gradually increasing chatter among family, friends, and gossip columnists that her husband was spending too much time in the company of his brother's widow. An article in *New York Express* commented on Bobby and Jackie "being seen together all the time." The *New York Post* quoted one of RFK's secretaries saying that Jackie called the attorney general's office "every day" looking for him. It reached the point where Ethel confronted David Ormsby Gore, British ambassador to the United States during the Kennedy administration and a great admirer of Jackie, and asked what, if anything, he knew about the relationship. She then telephoned Hervé Alphand, the former French ambassador, and posed the same question. Neither Ormsby Gore nor Alphand proved helpful in providing Ethel with the information she sought.

On May 29, 1964, several days after the presidential yacht soirée, on the occasion of JFK's forty-seventh birthday commemoration, Jackie took Caroline and John to Arlington National Cemetery and placed flowers on JFK's grave. After attending a memorial mass for her husband at St. Matthew's Cathedral in Washington, she traveled to Hyannis Port, where, with Bobby and Teddy by her side, she addressed television viewers throughout Europe and the United States, expressing her gratitude for their prayers and condolences in memory of President Kennedy.

Less than a week later, Jackie and Bobby gave a dinner party at the St. Regis Hotel in New York, the purpose of which was to personally thank major contributors to the JFK Memorial Library fund as well as members of the library's executive board and its board of trustees. At evening's end, Bobby Kennedy rose to make what he billed as "an important announcement." After much soul-searching and lengthy discussions with family members and his most trusted advisors, he had decided to resign as attorney general. He planned to make his political stand by moving to New York and running for the senatorial seat currently occupied by Kenneth B. Keating, a stalwart Republican. The idea had taken hold before Lyndon Johnson's declaration, mainly directed at RFK, that he would bypass all members of his Cabinet in selecting a running mate for the upcoming November presidential election. "Let's face it," Bobby had told Ken O'Donnell. "If Johnson had to choose between Ho Chi Minh and yours truly for the vice presidential slot, he'd go with Ho Chi Minh." In the end, Johnson selected Senator Hubert Humphrey of Minnesota as his choice for VP.

Joan Braden, the wife of journalist and onetime CIA operative Tom Braden and an old pal of Jackie's, later recalled the details of a conversation that took place at this time between herself and the former First Lady. "Jackie telephoned and told me about Bobby's desire to move to New York and run for the Senate," remarked Braden. "She said she too planned on relocating to New York and had already placed her N Street townhouse and her weekend home in Virginia on the auction block. She'd been talking about leaving Washington for months, so her decision to go through with it didn't surprise me. Nor did it surprise me to hear, through the grapevine, that Bobby and Jackie were supposedly having an affair."

What did surprise Braden was an unannounced visit she received one evening in early June from Bobby Kennedy, whom she hadn't seen since before the assassination. Recalling the visit, Braden noted that Bobby seemed despondent and vulnerable. "For more than an hour," she said, "he carried on about Jack, intermittently wiping away tears. His brother's death had turned Bobby's life upside down. He thought perhaps my husband, having been with the CIA, might have some idea as to who had been behind Jack's assassination. Bobby suspected such Mob figures as Sam Giancana and Carlos Marcello. I told him I'd ask Tom when he returned from a trip he'd taken to California."

Bobby suddenly asked Braden if they could go upstairs to her bedroom. She went. On the bed, they kissed. Then he took off his tie. He wanted to make love to her.

"I could not go through with it," she said. "He was hurt, silent, and angry. He left in a huff. I watched through the window as he walked under the streetlights toward his car. He held his back very straight, as if he knew I was watching. Afterward, I wondered what had prevented me from going to bed with him. My husband would have understood, even if Ethel would not have. I might add that Tom and I had an open marriage."

On June 19, 1964, a small chartered plane carrying Senator Ted Kennedy, Senator Birch Bayh of Indiana, and three others crashed outside Northampton, Massachusetts, killing two (the pilot and Teddy's aide Edward Moss) and injuring the remaining three passengers. Teddy suffered a number of shattered vertebrae and a punctured lung. Two days later, Bobby and Jackie visited Teddy at Northampton's Cooley Dickinson Hospital. He'd undergone six hours of surgery the day before, but when they got there, they found him propped up in bed belting out an Irish ballad. During a painful three-month convalescence, Teddy received a slew of encouraging get-well cards and letters from Jackie. In one letter, she wrote that her children needed Ted as much as they needed Bobby. She later sent him the leather back brace that JFK had worn after undergoing spinal surgery in New York shortly after marrying Jackie. The package to Teddy included a handwritten note that read in part: "Jack would have wanted you to have his back harness. Wear it in style."

Robert Kennedy's resolve to quit Washington and move to New York hastened Jackie's determination to do the same. To expedite matters, she turned to André Meyer, the French-born director of Lazard Frères, the New York investment banking firm, and asked him to help her find a residence for herself and her children somewhere in Manhattan. Meyer, a longtime financial advisor to the Kennedy clan, had initially met Jackie when she was First Lady. Having donated a $50,000 nineteenth-century Savonnerie rug to the White House, the financier immediately gained favor with his new friend. Now, with his latest assignment in hand, he crisscrossed the city in search of the perfect domicile. After a good deal of to-ing and fro-ing, he located what he considered ideal accommodations. He counseled Jackie to pay the $250,000 asking price for a spectacular fifteen-room (five-bedroom, five-bath) cooperative apartment on the fifteenth floor of 1040 Fifth Avenue, at Eighty-fifth Street. Fourteen of its twenty-three windows overlooked Central Park, the Metropolitan Museum of Art, and the Central Park reservoir, around which she was soon spotted walking for exercise, trailed at a discreet distance by her Secret Service detail.

Jackie spent an additional $125,000 to have the apartment refinished and refurbished, a project that took most of the summer and early fall to complete. While the work proceeded, Jackie and the children resided in a large eighteenth-floor suite at the Carlyle and at a ten-room house rental in Glen Cove, Long Island. By no small coincidence, Bobby leased a weekend house five minutes from Glen Cove. To establish his New York residency in order to run for the U.S. Senate, he purchased a nine-room condominium at 40 UN Plaza, while Ethel remained behind with most of their children at Hickory Hill, evidently choosing to ignore her husband's relationship with Jackie.

Lee Radziwill, whose Manhattan apartment at 969 Fifth Avenue was only a few blocks from Jackie's, gave a "Welcome to New York" dinner party for her sister. According to Chris Andersen's *Jackie After Jack,* Bobby attended without Ethel "and hovered around Jackie like he owned her." One of the dinner guests cited by Andersen noticed that there was a current of "electricity" between them.

Although it is difficult to ascertain precisely when their affair began, it can safely be said that once they moved to Manhattan, Bobby and Jackie's relationship intensified. Film producer Susan Pollock had a friend who occupied a suite opposite Jackie's at the Carlyle. On several occasions, the friend saw Bobby and Jackie return to the suite late at night, then leave together in the morning. "You can look at people and tell if they've been intimate," said Pollock. "My friend could tell. In any case, their affair was an open secret. Everyone knew about it."

Bobby and Jackie spent time together going through Jack's presidential memorabilia and personal belongings for the JFK Library, making available various odds and ends, including Kennedy's Oval Office desk and rocking chair. They flew to Boston together to check on the library's progress and met with I. M. Pei, whom Jackie had chosen as the structure's chief architect. Samuel H. Beer, a former professor of government at Harvard and a member of the JFK Library's executive board, told RFK that Jackie seemed "heavily sedated and ghostlike in appearance." "That's how she articulates," Bobby responded. "She has always spoken that way. It's her Connecticut finishing school accent. She might sound sedated, but I can assure you she's not."

Having raised more than $25 million for the JFK Library fund,

Jackie mounted a final telephone campaign. She convinced the French government to donate $100,000, then turned her attention to select individuals, many having donated funds before. André Meyer coughed up $150,000; Gianni Agnelli gave $250,000; Paul Mellon wrote out a check for $500,000. Although Aristotle Onassis offered the library a donation of $1 million, RFK refused the money, telling Jackie he wanted nothing of "the Greek's ill-gotten gains."

Evangeline Bruce, another contributor to the JFK Library fund and the wife of Ambassador David Bruce, met Jackie for lunch in the early summer. "She seemed thrilled to be living in New York," recalled Bruce. "I asked her if she missed the apparatus of political celebrity afforded by her former status as First Lady. 'Are you kidding?' she responded. 'I remember the hundreds of staged events, the thousands of photos I had to pose for looking empathetic or concerned, the millions of politically opportunistic lies and half-truths that buzzed around my head during my days in Washington. Do you realize I never even voted in a national election before I married Jack?' "

Evangeline Bruce asked Jackie if she intended to campaign for Bobby Kennedy in his bid for the Senate.

"I owe it to him," she said. "I'll do whatever I can to help."

Later that summer, not long after Bobby gave Jackie a surprise thirty-fifth birthday party, she departed on a ten-day cruise of the Adriatic Sea with Texas billionaire Charles Wrightsman and his wife Jayne, visiting Yugoslavia and spending a weekend in Italy with Stas and Lee Radziwill, whose on-again, off-again marriage was apparently on again.

Despite having given thousands of dollars to JFK's presidential campaign fund, Wrightsman had become involved in a bitter dispute with RFK. Their feud had to do with a 1963 federal indictment issued by Attorney General Robert F. Kennedy and the Justice Department against society columnist (and Kennedy family ally) Igor Cassini. Igor, married to the Wrightsmans' daughter, Charlene, had been accused of accepting funds from Generalissimo Rafael Trujillo of the Dominican Republic in exchange for unspecified public relations services. Igor's "crime"—his failure to register as a "foreign agent"—resulted in a

$10,000 fine, a six-month probation, and the loss of his position with the Hearst Newspaper Corporation.

It didn't end there. Following the issuance of the indictment against Cassini, Charlene Wrightsman wrote an impassioned letter to President Kennedy, which began: "I cannot tell you how surprised and shocked I have been by Bobby's harsh and punitive attitude. We always considered ourselves good friends of the Kennedys, and Ghighi [Igor] still cannot understand why the son of a man [Joseph P. Kennedy] whom he considered one of his oldest friends . . . should now be determined to bring him down to total ruin."

JFK forwarded the letter to Bobby and encouraged him to quash the indictment, but the attorney general refused. A month later, Charlene Wrightsman committed suicide by taking an overdose of painkillers and sleeping pills.

"In fact," said Oleg Cassini, Igor's brother, "Ghighi went to the Dominican Republic to speak with Trujillo at President Kennedy's behest. His failure to sign on as a foreign agent was a mere technicality. Bobby's open aggression against him had nothing to do with Trujillo. It had to do with a newspaper column my brother once wrote reporting that JFK, while president, attended a private party in New York at which he danced the night away with Marina Cassini, my brother's fourteen-year-old daughter from a previous marriage. Never one to take a family slight lightly, Bobby always had it out for Ghighi after that."

Oleg Cassini wasn't the sole RFK critic to comment on the Trujillo affair. Charles Wrightsman blamed his daughter's suicide on Bobby, and told Jackie as much during her stay aboard his yacht. "Charlie said some harsh things about Bobby," remarked Jayne Wrightsman, "and Jackie responded in kind. They had a clash of temperaments. She stayed mad a long time. We didn't hear from her again until 1968."

Back in New York following the Wrightsman cruise, Jackie attended a meeting of the Joseph P. Kennedy Jr. Foundation at the Four Seasons, and then drove out to Glen Cove with her children and Bobby Kennedy. Convinced that nobody knew of their romantic involvement, Bobby and Jackie practically flaunted their mutual affection, hugging and kissing on the beach and walking arm in arm into a local restaurant for dinner. Leaving Caroline and John Jr. with Maud Shaw, Jackie went horseback riding with Bobby one afternoon. According to Diana Dubois's biography of Lee Radziwill, *In Her Sister's Shadow,* stable owner Bruce Balding walked in on the couple as they embraced and kissed in the barn after their ride. Although they quickly separated, Balding had virtually caught them in the act.

In August, encouraged by Bobby to participate, Jackie arrived at the Democratic National Convention in Atlantic City, New Jersey. "If one person could upstage an entire political convention, it was Jacqueline Kennedy," observed Arthur Schlesinger. "She and Bobby absolutely stole the show. On the one occasion she appeared at the convention center, she received tremendous applause, almost as impressive as the twenty-two-minute standing ovation accorded RFK when he introduced a commemorative film about Jack. The crowd's response to Bobby and Jackie, and their relative indifference to LBJ, must have driven the president wild. He got it into his head that the two of them would somehow upset his carefully laid victory plans."

If Lyndon Johnson fretted over Jackie's popularity among Democratic Party delegates and devotees, he was just as concerned about the possibility, no matter how real, that an equally popular Bobby might lead a floor revolt and wrest away the party's presidential nomination. He knew that JFK had intended his younger brother to succeed him as president in 1968; he was also cognizant of Bobby's efforts to convince President Kennedy to dump him as his vice presidential running mate in '64. Given the overflow of bad blood between them, LBJ asked J. Edgar Hoover to keep tabs on Bobby during his stay in Atlantic City. Only too happy to comply, Hoover assigned a team of FBI agents to spy on Bobby for the duration of the convention. The only internal memorandum of interest received by Hoover had it that "the subject [RFK] seems to spend all his free time with Mrs. John F. Kennedy. Although it can't be confirmed at this time, they appear to be sharing the same hotel suite."

Courtney Evans, the FBI operative who had formerly served as an official liaison between the bureau and the Kennedy family, found it comical that Hoover would agree to sanction a surveillance operation against RFK. "If anyone seemed capable of perpetrating a 'dirty tricks' campaign, it was President Johnson. Bobby always felt that if pushed to the wall, Johnson would leak the names of the women with whom John F. Kennedy, while president, had been romantically linked, including Judith Campbell Exner, Sam Giancana's girlfriend. It was LBJ, for that matter, who insisted that Hoover replace me as the bureau's liaison to the Kennedys. Johnson felt I'd grown too close to the Kennedy family and that I'd lost my sense of objectivity. Hoover capitulated and kicked me upstairs to an administrative desk job. Not long thereafter, I left the bureau in favor of greener pastures."

In following up on Bobby and Jackie, President Johnson enlisted the help not only of J. Edgar Hoover but also of several of his associates, Jerry Bruno among them. An advance man for LBJ, Bruno received express instructions from Johnson not to let Bobby or Jackie out of his sight. "He was so concerned about them," said Bruno, "as to force Marvin Watson, the convention coordinator, to rearrange the convention schedule so that Jackie's main appearance took place after the balloting. He was absolutely neurotic when it came to the Kennedys."

On the last night of the convention, accorded his own prolonged standing ovation, Bobby introduced a twenty-minute film memorializing his late brother. He concluded his address by quoting a passage from Shakespeare's *Romeo and Juliet:* "When he shall die, / Take him and cut him out in little stars [. . .] And he will make the face of heaven so fine / That all the world will be in love with night, / And pay no worship to the garish sun."

The "garish sun" allusion was clearly intended as a backhanded literary slap to the face of Lyndon Johnson. He and his supporters were galled by the reference. More painful than galling for LBJ was Bobby's disclosure to a *New York Times* reporter that it had been Jackie who had provided him with the passage in question. In retaliation, Johnson declined to attend a convention-ending reception for Jackie organized by Averell Harriman. When asked by *The Washington Post* if she felt slighted by LBJ's failure to appear, Jackie offered one of her typically understated yet wickedly humorous responses. "I'm not even sure he was invited," she said. "And if he was invited, I'm certain he had more important things to do. The last time I looked, he was still president of the United States."

In September 1964, Jackie enrolled Caroline in the second grade of the Convent of the Sacred Heart, a prestigious Catholic girls' school located in a gingerbread mansion on Fifth Avenue and Ninety-first Street. Two of Caroline's cousins, Victoria and Sydney Lawford, attended the same school. Often sad-looking and without friends outside her immediate family circle, Caroline seemed to brighten only when "Uncle Bobby" came to visit, which was apparently a frequent occurrence. Polly Feingold, who worked on RFK's senatorial campaign staff, had become friendly with Bobby's official driver, a white-haired, blue-eyed retired Irish cop named Jim Fitzgerald. One day Feingold overheard Fitzgerald describe how, around midnight, he regularly dropped off his boss in front of Jacqueline Kennedy's Fifth Avenue apartment building, retrieving him again the following morning. "He'd stride out of the building with a grin on his face and a twinkle in his eye," added the chauffeur, implying the obvious.

Barbara Deutsch, a neighbor of Jackie's at 1040 Fifth Avenue, related a similar anecdote. "In those days, I had a French poodle that I walked late at night and again early in the morning," she said. "About three or four times a week, a black Town Car drove up and dropped off Bobby Kennedy in front of the building. He'd always stop to pet the dog, then continue into the building and take the passenger elevator up to Jackie's apartment. I'd often see him again in the morning, climbing back into the car. Now and then he'd leave with Caroline, evidently driving her to school."

Dave Powers emphasized the major role that Bobby Kennedy played in helping Jackie raise her children during their formative years. "From the day of Jack's death," said Powers, "Bobby took them in hand. He never stopped talking to them about their father. That's a very Irish thing to do, to remember the dead by constantly reminiscing about them. Bobby had a way with kids. He knew how to talk to them without talking down to them." Indeed, as Caroline and John grew a bit older, Bobby conversed with them about the civil rights movement. He spoke about the children of Harlem, about their brutal living conditions, about life in the tenements—rats, ill health, clapboard residences without heat or hot water. "Do you realize how fortunate you kids are?" he'd ask. John Jr. vowed that when he grew up, he'd get a job and send his earnings to the poor kids of Harlem so they could buy something to eat.

As for Jacqueline Kennedy, she gradually adapted to her lifestyle as a New Yorker and a single mother. She frequently walked her daughter to school in the morning and picked her up again at the end of the school day. On the way home, they invariably stopped for ice-cream cones or went shopping for clothes at any of a number of children's boutiques on the Upper East Side. On weekends she took both children for bike rides or rowing in Central Park. She took them to the Bronx Zoo, the United Nations, the Museum of Natural History, and to see the *Nutcracker* at Town Hall. Essentially she wanted them to grow up like other cosmopolitan children, rather than as the privileged offspring of a celebrated American president killed at the peak of his power.

The fact remains that Jackie was no ordinary mother. Arguably, she was the most recognizable woman in the world. After arriving in New York, she'd been offered her own newspaper column and her own television show, neither of which appealed to her. "Can you imagine me hosting my own TV show, interviewing Hollywood celebrities?" she asked George Plimpton. Her photograph had appeared on the cover of nearly every major (and minor) magazine in North and South America. "You could visit any continent in the world and mention her name and people knew her," said Larry O'Brien. Andy Warhol, whose *Death and Disaster* series of Jacqueline Kennedy portraits had enhanced his own celebrity, recalled taking her to the Brooklyn Museum of Art one afternoon to see an exhibition of ancient Egyptian art. "As we wandered through the galleries," he said, "every person there seemed to recognize her. They whispered among themselves. You could hear her name in the air: 'Jackie . . . Jackie . . . Jackie . . . Jackie.' That's all you heard. It was totally weird."

Jacqueline Kennedy lent herself to Robert Kennedy's New York senatorial campaign in August, just one month before the primary. She even allowed Caroline and John to participate. The children appeared with their uncle at campaign stops in Brooklyn and the Bronx, posing with Bobby for press photographs and newsreels. Jackie, meanwhile, took part in numerous fund-raisers, including a star-studded affair to which she invited such guests as Paddy Chayefsky, Gloria Vanderbilt, Leonard Bernstein, Lillian Hellman, Mike Nichols, Lauren Bacall, John Kenneth Galbraith, Arthur Schlesinger, and interior designer Billy Baldwin, who had helped decorate the former First Lady's Fifth Avenue residence. Cohosted by attorney William vanden Heuvel in his sprawling Central Park West apartment, the party raised in excess of $1.1 million, a veritable fortune for that period.

Although early statewide polls indicated that Bobby could defeat the Republican incumbent by a substantial margin, Senator Keating was an experienced and popular politician with a substantial following of his own, particularly in upstate New York. Moreover, RFK would have to overcome at least one major obstacle: he was perceived by many as an outsider, a "carpetbagger," exploiting for his own ambitions a state in which he had few roots. Other, less obvious deterrents, especially within the "reform" (or liberal) wing of the party, involved his early support of Senator Joe McCarthy, his questionable dealings with the Mafia, his general use of certain power-mongering tactics during his term as attorney general, and his ongoing feud with President Johnson. Additionally, Bobby was the Kennedy most associated with the political ideology of the father, whose pro-Nazi leanings prior to and during World War II hadn't been forgotten by the large Jewish population of New York City. "Bobby, of course, wasn't a Nazi," said Larry O'Brien, "but he was Joe Kennedy's kid, and Joe Kennedy wasn't exactly popular among the Jewish community."

Having beaten out Samuel Stratton, an independent Democratic congressman (in a landslide, 86.4% to 13.7%), for his party's senatorial candidacy in the New York Democratic primary, RFK kicked off his campaign against Keating at the Fulton Fish Market, then located in Lower Manhattan. A whirlwind of activity followed, the campaign taking him from county to county and town to town. John Treanor Jr., an RFK aide, recalled the euphoria that surrounded the first weeks of the campaign. "The crowds mobbed Bobby," he said. "It was like the second coming of JFK. If anything, the crowds were larger and even more demonstrative than they'd been when Jack ran for the presidency. It was wild. People were ripping at RFK's cuff links, his watch, his clothes, his hair, anything they could grab. After every campaign stop—Buffalo, Albany, Glens Falls, Saratoga Springs, Rochester, wherever—his face would be covered with welts, which often became infected, from strangers reaching for him, scraping and scratching him with their rings and fingernails."

In the frenzy of excitement that greeted Bobby's entry into the race, his Republican Party opponent seemed almost superfluous. Although he referred to Bobby as a "pseudo candidate," Jacob Javits, New York's other Republican senator, candidly admitted that Keating "has a steep hill to climb if he hopes to beat Robert Kennedy." Invoking the spirit of his slain brother at every opportunity, Bobby—like JFK before him—knew how to "play" (or seduce) a crowd. Following in his brother's footsteps, RFK soon demonstrated his propensity for yet another JFK characteristic, namely the intermingling of politics and carnal pleasure.

While Jackie remained behind in Manhattan and Ethel at Hickory Hill, the former attorney general reportedly became involved with beautiful, twenty-six-year-old Natalie Fell Cushing, whose mother, Mrs. John "Fifi" Fell, a New York socialite, had allegedly been one of President Kennedy's many love interests. Married at the time to independent producer Freddy Cushing, Natalie told her wealthy husband that she planned to embark on a road trip with Ethel Kennedy. Instead she joined Bobby on the campaign trail as he made his way around the state. Natalie's good friends Steve and Jean Kennedy Smith were well aware of Bobby's affair with Natalie. The intense but brief entanglement became the talk of Newport, where the Cushings lived in a mansion overlooking the Atlantic. The Cushings eventually divorced.

Ken O'Donnell remembered hearing about the affair from Steve Smith. "Stephen was managing Bobby's senatorial campaign," noted O'Donnell, "and he became increasingly concerned that if word of the affair spread, it would impact on RFK's political future. Ironically, Bobby had faced the same problem while overseeing Jack's various campaigns."

Jackie's mother and stepfather still spent their summers at Newport, so it was only a matter of days before the former First Lady heard about Bobby's little fling. Not surprisingly, she reacted by initiating a flirtation of her own. In the middle of Bobby's race for the Senate, she started an affair with John Carl Warnecke, a San Francisco architect whose keen talent had enabled him to graduate in a single year (1941) from the three-year master's program in architecture at Harvard. Ten years Jackie's senior, Warnecke had been chosen by the then First Lady, in 1962, to redevelop historic Lafayette Square, across the street from the White House. After JFK's death, the president's widow commissioned the architect to design the Kennedy memorial grave site at Arlington National Cemetery. Divorced and the father of three, Warnecke told Red Fay, with whom he'd attended Stanford University as an undergraduate, that he hoped one day to marry Jackie. Although they remained friends, Jacqueline jettisoned Warnecke as her bed partner after less than a month, resuming her romance with Bobby Kennedy. In retrospect, Warnecke represented little more than a rebound romance to a woman whose married lover had taken up with another mistress.

Having reconciled with RFK, Jackie once more became involved in Bobby's bid for political office. Joined by his three sisters—Eunice, Jean, and Pat—she traveled to all five boroughs of New York City, shaking hands, making speeches, signing autographs. "She swallowed her pride and went to bat for Bobby," said Truman Capote. When RFK asked

Jackie to meet with Dorothy Schiff, publisher of the *New York Post,* the former First Lady invited the older woman to lunch at the Carlyle. As a result of their meeting, the *Post* endorsed Kennedy over Keating.

Despite the *Post*'s endorsement, RFK's early lead gradually began to dwindle. Jackie suggested they bolster their lead by asking Lyndon Johnson to come to New York to barnstorm with Bobby. Although he hated the thought of asking LBJ for anything, Bobby went along with the idea. Jackie made the call and convinced Johnson to campaign on Bobby's behalf. Johnson's support did nothing to alter Bobby's all too negative opinion of him. If anything, his disdain for his brother's former vice president deepened. Following LBJ's return to Washington, Bobby told Jackie, "I'm so pleased the president lent us a hand. I can't wait to tell Ethel Bird about it." On a more serious note, he criticized Johnson for not listening to his political advisors. Unlike Jack, who debated every decision with those around him, Johnson sought advice only from Johnson. "He's his own jury and judge," said RFK.

Largely absent from Bobby's campaign was Ethel Kennedy (or "Old Moms," as she called herself), who made several trips to New York but for the most part remained in McLean, Virginia. Her friend Coates Redmon encouraged her to play a more active role, but Ethel refused. "I'm certain her reluctance had something to do with her suspicion that Bobby and Jackie had initiated a sexual relationship," said Redmon. "Her suspicions were well founded. I'm ninety-nine percent sure they were involved, and I'm sure Ethel had caught on at some point. You'd go to dinner parties in New York or Washington, and people would talk. And you could see how it might all have started, and how, after JFK's death, they could have had a mad, morbid attraction to each other, and how this initial attachment continued to grow."

Redmon recalled a weekend during the campaign when Bobby visited his wife and children at Hickory Hill. "I was visiting as well," she reminisced, "and we were in the den looking at family photographs. There was this great snapshot of Jackie, and I commented on it. 'It's the most attractive picture of her I've ever seen,' I said. Ethel looked at it, but didn't utter a word. Bobby took a look. 'She is beautiful, isn't she?' he commented. 'Don't you think she's beautiful, Ethel?' 'She's an attractive woman,' Ethel conceded. 'Thank you for saying so,' replied Bobby. You could have cut the tension in the room with a knife. After another minute or two, Ethel rose and left the room. She wasn't pleased."

After a point, Bobby's wife did little to disguise her pain and anger from other members of the family. Mary De Grace, who worked for a number of years as a laundress for Bobby and Ethel at Hyannis Port, remembered an exchange overheard by one of her coworkers: "Katherine, an elderly maid employed by Ethel, was present one afternoon when Teddy Kennedy, some time after his airplane accident, walked into Ethel's house, approached her and bent over to give her a kiss. Ethel pushed him away and said, 'We'll have none of that Bobby and Jackie stuff in this house.' "

According to Merribelle Moore, a Skakel family friend, the wounded wife "called my brother Frank all the time to discuss the situation. She couldn't understand what Bobby saw in Jackie. She wanted Frank to tell Bobby to stop sleeping with Jackie. But Frank had no intention of getting involved. He told Ethel what she needed to do was find a marriage counselor to help heal her marriage."

In the late fall, Jackie sent a letter to C. Douglas Dillon, secretary of the Treasury, informing him that while her children required ongoing Secret Service protection, she did not, particularly with regard to the graveyard shift, 11:00 p.m. to 7:00 a.m. "It's pointless for them to stand around in the cold all night in front of my apartment building," she wrote. Pierre Salinger suggested that Jackie's real reason for curtailing her overnight coverage had to do with Bobby Kennedy—it meant that he could come and go without having to log in with Secret Service personnel.

Although many of the Secret Service files concerning Jackie during this period seem to have mysteriously disappeared, several of those that remain contain choice tidbits on the former First Lady's relationship with RFK. One set, dated October 18, 1964, reveal that Bobby and Jackie shared a bedroom on at least one occasion in the New York apartment of Steve and Jean Kennedy Smith. Another set, this one undated, states they stayed in a suite occupied by Peter Lawford at Manhattan's Sherry-Netherland Hotel.

Franklin Roosevelt Jr. was amazed that the Bobby-Jackie romance, having progressed as far as it had, remained under wraps as long as it did. "Everybody knew about the affair," remarked Roosevelt. "The two of them carried on like a pair of lovesick teenagers. People used to see them at Le Club, their torsos stuck together as they danced the night away. I suspect Bobby would've liked to dump Ethel and marry Jackie, but of course that wasn't possible. Among other things, I doubt Jackie ever intended to remarry. For all the hope and optimism he engendered among his fellow citizens while he served as president, JFK had been nothing but trouble as a husband—daily assignations and a lifetime of serious venereal diseases. Jackie had no intention of repeating the exercise—not now, at any rate."

In mid-October, Roosevelt accompanied RFK and Jackie to the Plaza Hotel for late-afternoon cocktails with Richard Burton. Bobby had recently befriended the actor. "After a half-dozen Irish whiskeys," said Roosevelt, "Burton began encouraging Bobby and Jackie to get married. This went on for a good twenty minutes. Finally, Jackie managed to change the subject by insisting that Burton, who was thoroughly crocked, recite something from Shakespeare. Burton complied."

It was the same month that the St. Louis Cardinals played the New York Yankees in that year's World Series. Bobby Kennedy was asked to throw out the first ball at the first of three games at Yankee Stadium. Also present was Joe DiMaggio, the great former Yankee center fielder and onetime husband of Marilyn Monroe. Having always held Jack and Bobby Kennedy responsible for Marilyn's accidental suicide, DiMaggio refused to shake Bobby's hand that day, giving rise to a New York *Daily News* sports page headline: "Joltin' Joe—No Fan of RFK's!"

The negative publicity resulting from DiMaggio's snub so soon before the election disturbed Bobby both for its personal and political implications. The following day, he met with Jackie for lunch at the

King Cole Bar in Manhattan. Anticipating his concern over the Yankee Stadium confrontation, she tried to cheer him up by giving him a copy of Alfred Lord Tennyson's "Ulysses," with its prophetic line, "To sail beyond the sunset, and the baths / Of all the western stars, until I die." The poem's line—"Come, my friends. / 'Tis not too late to seek a newer world"—provided RFK with the title for a 1967 volume of his own written work. What particularly pleased him was Jackie's acknowledgment that "Ulysses" had likewise been one of JFK's favorite poems.

On the evening of October 27, just one week before Election Day, CBS-TV in New York offered to broadcast an hour-long debate between Robert Kennedy and Ken Keating. When the senatorial candidates failed to agree on a format, RFK withdrew. On October 26, RFK aides Adam Walinsky and Peter Edelman learned that Keating had purchased a half hour of airtime on the same network and planned to "debate" an empty chair to dramatize his opponent's supposed refusal to appear. RFK immediately called the station and asked to buy an equal amount of time, his half hour to directly follow Keating's. He was rebuffed. He decided to take his request to a higher authority: network president William Paley, who happened to be an excellent friend of Jackie Kennedy. The former First Lady telephoned Paley, in California, and Paley's call to his station in New York promptly netted Bobby his desired airtime.

Meanwhile, somebody in Bobby's camp came up with a plan: Why not have RFK "storm" the television studio during Keating's presentation and challenge him to an impromptu debate? Bobby's advisors were evenly divided as to the advisability of such a tactic. To settle the matter, the candidate telephoned his sister-in-law. "I think it's a fabulous idea," said Jackie. "If I were you, I'd do it."

Bobby Kennedy and his aides arrived at the CBS television studios in Manhattan on October 27 at 7:27 p.m., three minutes before the start of Keating's program. "I'm here to debate Senator Keating," RFK told the uniformed security guard. The guard placed a call, and a network attorney instantly appeared on the scene. As television and newspaper cameras recorded the confrontation, the attorney informed Bobby that his studio time had been reserved for 8:00 p.m. "Senator Keating," he added, "has decided against a face-to-face debate."

"In that case," said Bobby, "I demand that the empty seat be removed from the set and that Keating's remark that I refuse to debate him be struck."

Keating proceeded with his televised "one-man" debate, but ultimately agreed to meet Bobby for an October 30 face-off on *The Barry Gray Show,* a highly popular New York radio program. According to the host, "Bobby looked half Keating's age and seemed twice as energetic. I thought he kicked Keating's ass."

At the last minute Hubert Humphrey, LBJ's running mate, came to town to campaign with Bobby. "I'd never seen anything quite like it," said Humphrey. "We were in one of those motorcades rumbling down Fifth Avenue. . . . And people were just ecstatic. They literally tore at Bobby Kennedy, and I remember women were tossing their shoes into the open car, and at the end of the tour, there was this undergarment— half girdle, half garter belt—on the floor of the car, and I said to Bobby, 'You're a magician. How did you do that?' I'd never seen such excitement as he generated in that particular tour."

Bobby Kennedy won election to the U.S. Senate by some seven hundred thousand votes. A day later, Jackie joined Bobby and Ethel at a family celebration hosted by Steve and Jean Kennedy Smith.

"Well, we did it!" exclaimed Jackie over dinner.

"What do you mean by 'we'?" asked Ethel. "You didn't even vote this year, Jackie."

Indeed, despite her romantic attachment to Bobby, Jackie refused to vote in 1964. She and Bobby had argued the point. The closest she ever came to shedding light on the matter was a brief discussion of the subject in her oral history for the John F. Kennedy Library, in which she observed: "Bobby said I should vote, and I said, 'I don't care what you say, I'm not going to vote.' It was just completely emotional, and it got blown up into I don't know what. It was an emotional decision. It was something a widow would do. It didn't make any sense. But that's what it was, and nobody approved of it. I think all of the rest of the Kennedy family went and voted."

Despite her overall loyalty to the Kennedy clan, Jackie had never been completely comfortable playing the role of family squaw. It hadn't suited her personality while she was still a Kennedy wife; it suited her even less now that she was a Kennedy mistress. She didn't want to fit into the psychological matrix of this raucous, power-driven tribe.

Chapter 6

———— ◆ ————

Mary Harrington, a well-known, well-connected, four-times-married Southern belle and socialite, nicknamed "Magnolia," first met Bobby Kennedy at a Las Vegas nightclub in 1959. "I'd gone to Vegas," she said, "to visit Barbara Marx, an old friend whose husband at the time was Zeppo Marx, the older and less renowned brother of Groucho Marx. Barbara and I were at a show at the Tropicana featuring Frank Sinatra and Sammy Davis Jr. Barbara later married Sinatra, but that night her gaze was firmly fixed on Bobby Kennedy, who was seated in the audience with brother-in-law Peter Lawford."

As Harrington recalled the evening, "Bobby and Barbara took one look at each other, and the next thing I knew, they were off and running. They weren't heard from again until the next morning. Although Barbara always publicly denied having had an affair with Bobby, I can vouch for the fact that it happened. The affair lasted about three or four months. Frank Sinatra always hated Bobby for it—he couldn't stand it that RFK had been there before him."

Whenever Bobby and Barbara saw each other, Mary Harrington accompanied them as a kind of female beard. But before too long, Bobby came to regard Harrington as more than just a convenient camouflage. She had an apartment at the Carlyle in New York, and whenever Bobby came to town, he'd call her up and they would have a drink. "I wasn't attracted to him at first," she continued, "but he gradually grew on me, as I'm sure he grew on many women. He wasn't as hand-some as his brother Jack, whom I'd met on a few occasions, but he seemed much more sincere. When he spoke to you, he looked you directly in the eye. And in contrast to his public speeches, wherein he tended to sound a bit shrill, when he spoke to you individually, he did so in a soft, low tone. It was as if he was caressing you with his voice. In reality, he did better with the ladies than Jack. JFK fucked them, but Bobby made love to them."

By early 1960, RFK began calling Mary more often, saying he could no longer see Barbara Marx because she was becoming so emotional. Then, in March, Harrington came down with phlebitis and wound up in New York Hospital. Bobby sent a note up to her room along with flowers and a gold bracelet from Cartier. His friends soon began drop-ping by to see how she was doing. And then late one night—after vis-iting hours—he showed up himself. Mary later learned that he'd bribed the night-shift nurse to sneak him in. He told Mary he thought he was falling in love with her. Their affair began then and there, Bobby crawl-ing into Mary's hospital bed. Following her recovery a week later, they saw each other an average of twice a week, mostly in New York but also in Washington and Boston. After a while, he became deeply involved in his brother's presidential campaign, and they saw less of each other. They remained close friends, and the friendship endured until the end of his life.

During Christmas vacation of 1964, after Bobby's convincing vic-tory over Keating, Mary Harrington happened to be staying in a house next door to the Kennedy estate in Palm Beach. "It was purely coinci-dental," she said. One morning she peered out her bedroom window on the third floor, overlooking the Kennedy property, and there, sun-bathing in the grass next to the house, was Jacqueline Kennedy, wear-ing a black bikini bottom and no top. A door opened and out walked Bobby Kennedy in a white swimsuit. He approached Jackie and knelt by her side. "As they began to kiss," said Harrington, "he placed one hand on her breast and the other inside of her bikini bottom. After a minute or so, she stood up, wrapped a towel around her breasts and shoulders, and walked toward the house. Bobby followed. I was shocked. It was clear that Bobby was sleeping with his sister-in-law."

The next time Mary Harrington and Bobby spoke on the phone, she chided him for his public display of affection.

"You mean you were watching?" he asked.

"It was inadvertent," she responded. "I happened to look out the guest bedroom window. I wasn't spying on you."

Bobby proceeded to tell Harrington all about Jackie and their relationship—how, as a senator, he divided his time between Jackie in New York and Ethel in McLean, Virginia. It was as though he had two families and two homes. He loved Ethel, he told Mary, but he felt just as strongly about Jackie. To be sure, both women needed him, as did both sets of children. His and Ethel's offspring were thoroughly undisciplined. They raced across the lawn at Hickory Hill, stormed the tennis court, and threw themselves into the swimming pool. They were constantly pushing and shoving one another, getting into fights. They all owned pets of one sort or another: goats, pigs, snakes, rabbits, birds, dogs, cats, mice. Bobby Jr. had a boa constrictor that liked to feast on live rats. Hickory Hill was a pigsty—clothes and toys were strewn everywhere. The furniture was torn and tattered. Yet the place was always filled with houseguests: government officials, friends, relatives, and celebrities. On any given day, a visitor might run into Mick Jagger, Warren Beatty, or retired baseball star Ted Williams. Hickory Hill was a beehive of commotion, a madhouse. The telephone never stopped ringing. Television sets blared in the background. By way of contrast, Jackie's apartment seemed sedate, tranquil, almost solemn. It contained rare, delicate, museum-quality artifacts and antiques. Books, plants, and fresh flowers filled every nook and cranny. Classical music and the songs of Noël Coward were piped into every bedroom, including those of the children. Jackie's visitors included some of the world's leading authors, artists, and statesmen. The family's most frequent visitor was Robert Kennedy. Caroline and John Jr. were as attached to Uncle Bobby as they would have been to their own father had he still been alive. RFK, in turn, felt the same love toward his nephew and niece as he did for his own children.

Yet for all the attention Bobby bestowed upon Jackie and her children, he remained essentially a part-time lover and surrogate dad. To fill
the void, the former First Lady continued to spend a good deal of time
with André Meyer, attending the theater, opera, and art gallery open-
ings with him. She was a regular at the elderly financier's Friday afternoon cocktail parties in his apartment at the Carlyle. Cary Reich,
Meyer's biographer, surmised that the old man had fallen in love with
Jackie. "Jackie constantly toyed with him," said Reich. "What drove
him to distraction was that breathless, little-girl-lost manner in which
she addressed him. 'André, what should I do? I don't know what to *do.*'
She was a very intelligent woman but also somewhat superficial. She
carried on like this in front of Meyer's wife [Bella], his family, and the
other women who came to visit him on Friday afternoons. The other
women were extremely jealous of Jackie. The reason was obvious: Jackie
received all of Meyer's attention, whereas the others received none."

Another of Jackie's elder gentlemen-in-waiting was Dr. Henry Lax,
a Swiss-born Park Avenue physician whose patient list included not
only André Meyer, at whose apartment she first met the internist, but
also Aristotle Onassis. Jackie soon became Lax's patient as well.

Renee Luttgen, an office assistant and also a companion to the doctor, recalled how "coquettish" and "flirtatious" Jackie could be, playing up
to the doctor with that "insufferable" ingénue voice. "She would appear
at the office as if stepping onto a stage," claimed Luttgen. "Everything—
the smile, the gestures, the words—seemed artificial and carefully
rehearsed. She would wear those large oval sunglasses on top of her head.
When I opened the office door, she would strike a pose as if she expected
a TV news team to pop out of the woodwork. She and Henry were close,
but in front of me she always called him 'Dr. Lax.' She consulted him on
everything, from her strenuous daily exercise regimen to personal
finances. She asked some very frank questions about sexual physiology,
claiming she'd been brought up a Catholic and had never learned about
female sexual gratification. Henry drew the female anatomy on a sheet of
paper and then traced it with his finger in the palm of her hand, explaining how everything worked. I seriously doubt she didn't already know."

Although Henry Lax and Jackie never indulged in a physical relationship, the physician told Renee Luttgen that she'd admitted having a one-time tryst with André Meyer. "It apparently wasn't overly satisfying for her," said Luttgen. "Nevertheless, Meyer possessed all the qualities Jackie admired in a man. He was much older, extremely powerful, and very affluent."

According to Luttgen, the former First Lady similarly spoke to Dr. Lax about her affair with Bobby Kennedy. "I don't know the details," remarked Luttgen, "but she seemed to adore him. Politically he was an idealist, and because he was married without the possibility of a divorce, he became the unattainable object of her desire."

Being a single woman once again, Jackie represented a tremendous threat to Ethel Kennedy and Bella Meyer, as well as to all the married women in her social circle. With her personality, fame, and beauty, she had only to enter a room full of couples, and conversation came to a sudden halt. Her electrifying aura stopped the room cold, as men of every description rushed over to speak to her and to bask in her reflected glory. Those who didn't approach were intrigued but also intimidated. She intimidated men and made women jealous. It took a certain kind of man to become romantically involved with somebody as famous as Jacqueline Kennedy.

One such man was Aristotle Onassis, whose audacity, tenacity, and wealth finally won Jackie over, at least to the extent that she willingly entered into a liaison with "the Greek." In early February 1965, the former First Lady joined Ari aboard the *Christina* on a five-day cruise to Nassau. Although she had no intention of embarrassing Bobby Kennedy politically by becoming involved with Onassis, Jackie realized that if she didn't accede to Ari's sexual demands, she risked losing his friendship and patronage. She had thwarted his advances long enough.

John Karavlas, the second captain of the *Christina,* recalled an incident that took place after the yacht reached Nassau. "We'd anchored off the island the night before," he said. "In the morning, I was summoned by the first captain. He wanted to consult with Onassis about a dinner party that was being given aboard the yacht that night, but he couldn't find the tycoon. Nor could he find Mrs. Kennedy. He asked me to check the ship—maybe they were still asleep. I checked every stateroom, every deck—no Onassis, no Mrs. Kennedy. Then I heard sounds coming from a small, flat fishing vessel Onassis kept tied to the side of the *Christina.* I approached the railing, peered over, and there in the shipping vessel was a nude male posterior rising and falling, rising and falling. It was Onassis. He was on top, and Mrs. Kennedy was beneath him. They were making love."

Onassis sensed the crew member's presence. "What do you want?" he shouted.

"I was just looking for you, sir."

"Well, you found me," said Onassis.

When they arrived back in New York, Onassis told Johnny Meyer, an aide and confidant, about his tryst with Jackie. "You'll be happy to know I finally bagged the queen," he boasted, in a manner that Meyer considered nothing short of disgusting. "Bobby," he went on, "just sees me as the rich prick moving in on his brother's widow. Sooner or later, it'll come to a test of wills."

Although he was twenty-five years older than Robert Kennedy (and twenty-nine years Jackie's senior), Aristotle Onassis demonstrated many of the same characteristics as his younger rival. "Ari could be very pushy, but he also had a great deal of charm," remarked Johnny Meyer. "If he couldn't get his way by being nice, he'd resort to bullying, a tactic also utilized by RFK. Both men were controlling figures. And both men hated each other. Onassis couldn't be critical enough of RFK. He was so positive Bobby had killed Marilyn Monroe that he hired a private investigator to document the murder. The P.I.'s findings were inconclusive."

Two weeks after Jackie returned from her sojourn to Nassau with Aristotle Onassis, she accompanied Bobby Kennedy for a few days at the opulent estate of socialite Audrey Zauderer (today Audrey del Rosario) in Round Hill, the most exclusive section of Montego Bay, Jamaica. Kathryn Livingston, a New York magazine publisher and editor, spoke to Zauderer years later about the visit: "When I began the conversation, Audrey, always an extremely private person, seemed eva-

sive—consciously or unconsciously—about the subject of Bobby and
Jackie's relationship. Everybody was talking about it. 'Jackie came down
with John-John and the nanny [Maud Shaw],' she said, 'and I had to
put up with all those Secret Service people.' And Bobby? 'Bobby also
came,' she said. 'He came alone, without Ethel.' She went on like this
for a while, saying nothing of great import. I finally came out with it
and asked bluntly, 'Well, do you think there was a romance between
Jackie and Bobby?' And she stopped and flashed this little smile as if I'd
finally hit on it. She gave a very strong nod of her head, indicating yes.
'Yes?' I asked. 'You're saying they were involved romantically?' This time
she mouthed the word: 'Absolutely!' "

Another witness, Maud Shaw, who had become friendly with Evelyn Lincoln, wrote JFK's former private secretary that even though
Bobby and Jackie "had separate bedrooms, they kept dodging in and
out of each other's boudoir, making no secret of their dalliance. I have
seen this happen in the privacy of Mrs. Kennedy's New York residence,
but I was shocked they were so blatant in front of Mrs. Zauderer."

Bernard Hayworth, a German screenwriter vacationing at the
Round Hill Resort, located down the beach from Audrey Zauderer's
estate, recalled seeing the group at dinner one evening in the resort's
dining room. "That's all the guests could talk about: Bobby and Jackie,
Jackie and Bobby. None of us knew at the time that they were having
an affair, just that they were vacationing together in the area. I might
have seen an article or two about them in one of the tabloids, but I considered it nothing more than newspaper talk. Then, late one afternoon,
I was lazying around on the beach. And right at that moment, Bobby
and Jackie Kennedy appeared. The sun was beginning to set. It was
dusk. I don't think they saw me at first because I was down at the end
of the strand. Bobby laid out a blanket on the sand. Jackie doffed her
beach jacket, walked to the water's edge, and went in for a swim—just
sort of glided off like a water bird of exotic origin. There was something
very regal and wondrous about her. She returned after about fifteen
minutes, dried herself off, and lay facedown on the blanket next to
Bobby. He began massaging her back and kissing her neck. I felt like an

intruder, so I stood up to leave, and that's when he saw me. He froze, and so did I. After what seemed an eternity, he started massaging Jackie again. I departed. I have no idea what transpired after I left, but I can well imagine."

"Bobby Kennedy didn't need sex as a daily fix the way his brother Jack did, but he knew how to get it when he wanted it," said Morton Downey Jr. "Like his father and brothers, he could be rather brazen when it came to women. His relationship with Jacqueline Kennedy, however, wasn't solely based on sex. Unlike most of the other women in his life, he had deep feelings for Jackie. But with this and a few other exceptions, sex was a macho thing for Bobby, as if he had to prove himself. I never knew him *not* to have girlfriends on the side. He was sexually active during his younger years, during his term as attorney general, and during his entire senatorial period. Bobby and Ethel were close, but this didn't preclude his fooling around when the opportunity presented itself."

Downey, who achieved minor notoriety during the 1980s by hosting a confrontational television talk show, was the son of the Irish tenor who became Joseph P. Kennedy's best friend. The Downeys lived most of the year in Palm Beach, not far from the Kennedy homestead, and, in addition, owned a home in Hyannis Port. Mort Jr., who had grown up with Bobby, moved to Los Angeles in 1963. He and RFK kept in close contact. When RFK ran for president in 1968, Downey was by his side.

As Mort Jr. recalled, one of RFK's shorter-lived flings during his days as attorney general involved the actress Kim Novak. "Kim represented Bobby's answer to Jack's affair with Angie Dickinson," said Downey, "except Novak was better-looking." In late 1961, RFK helped Novak procure travel documents for a monthlong trip to Russia. When she returned to the States, Bobby visited her in her suite at the Plaza in New York. Mel Finkelstein, a press photographer and confidant of the actress, confirmed that while RFK and Kim "were making love in her hotel room," a fire alarm went off. A few minutes later, the telephone rang in the suite, and a desk clerk asked them to vacate the premises. Bobby, who had no desire to be spotted in the hotel lobby with a Hollywood actress on his arm, ducked into a rear stairwell and made his way to the front exit, where he learned that somebody had accidentally set off the alarm. He and Novak kept in touch by telephone and letter, but never saw each other again.

"There was a side of Bobby that was attracted to celebrities and the high life," continued Downey. "He enjoyed going to fancy restaurants. He loved visiting Hollywood and attending Hollywood parties. One such party took place at the home of Tony Curtis, and half the men there were dressed in drag. 'If I'd known,' said Bobby, 'I would've brought J. Edgar Hoover.' "

When he visited Los Angeles post-1963, RFK usually stayed with pop singer Andy Williams and Claudine Longet, Andy's young, very pretty Paris-born wife. He sometimes brought Ethel along. The two couples spent a good deal of time vacationing together and visiting each other on both coasts. In the mid-1960s, Andy Williams had his own weekly television variety show, while Claudine was following the path of an aspiring actress, procuring occasional TV and feature film parts. Not surprisingly, it turned out that Bobby and Claudine were secretly seeing each other on the side. Or perhaps it wasn't so secret.

According to Downey, Bobby told him he'd become involved with Claudine as a result of his anger toward Jackie, who insisted on maintaining her relationship with Onassis.

"I don't know how," said Downey, "but Bobby had discovered that Jackie wasn't just keeping company with Onassis—she was sleeping with him. RFK had created this rationale whereby Jackie was cheating on him with Onassis, and this in turn gave him license to do the same. Never mind that Jackie was single and Bobby wasn't. One day I said to Bobby, 'You're becoming more and more like Jack.' In a way, I think this notion pleased him."

Pierre Salinger, who along with Sammy Davis Jr., Paul Newman, Joan Collins, Anthony Newley, and Peter Lawford, had invested in a posh L.A. nightspot called the Factory, concurred with Mort Downey regarding RFK's attraction to Hollywood stars and starlets. "He was great pals with Shirley MacLaine and Mia Farrow," said Salinger. "Mia was then married to Frank Sinatra. During a phase when Sinatra was on location in New York making a film, Bobby came to the Factory with Mia Farrow and a bunch of friends. Bobby liked to dance. He and Mia spent the entire evening on the dance floor. When Sinatra, who already loathed RFK, read about it in the gossip columns, he allegedly ordered his lawyers to serve Mia with divorce papers."

Salinger happened to be present at the Factory the night that RFK, Ethel Kennedy, Andy Williams, and Claudine Longet came in. At one point during the evening, Salinger noticed the two couples had switched partners. "Bobby and Claudine were heavily engaged with one another, and so were Andy and Ethel," said Salinger. "It surprised me that nobody in the press picked up on this juicy tidbit and nothing appeared in print."

Yet another budding actress with whom the senator spent time was Candice Bergen, whom he met in 1965. Increasingly rattled by Jackie's come-lately affair with Aristotle Onassis, Bobby asked the blond actress, then nineteen, to accompany him to a dinner party at the former First Lady's New York apartment. Candice, who resided in an apartment on East Sixty-eighth Street in Manhattan, seemed unaware of any romantic bond between RFK and Jackie. George Plimpton, another guest at the dinner, recalled that Candice—at the time a professional photographer as well as an actress—and Jackie—once the "Inquiring Camera Girl" for the *Washington Times-Herald*—chattered away about cameras and lenses. "If Jackie harbored any jealousy, she didn't show it," said Plimpton. "Of course, she may simply have been feigning indifference. She'd always been a supreme actress. Just for reasons of self-survival, she had to be. Look at her marriage to John F. Kennedy."

Bobby and Candice continued to see each other. In Paris, on one occasion, Senator Kennedy was the guest of honor at the home of Hervé Alphand. Among the other guests that evening were actresses Shirley MacLaine and Catherine Deneuve. Bobby brought Candice Bergen, who was in Paris shooting a film. "The party was lively and gay," remembered Alphand. "We ate and then danced. Bobby and Candice looked very comfortable together."

Before leaving Paris, Bobby and Candice dined again, this time without the crowd. Idle commentary on their rendezvous found its way into the local society pages. "U.S. Senator Robert F. Kennedy," reported Edgar Schneider in *Paris-Presse,* "could not resist the pleasure of once again seeing the beautiful Candice Bergen. Tired of official banquets and political meetings, Kennedy decided that nothing could be more agreeable to end his Paris stay than an intimate dinner in a cozy place in Saint-Germain-des-Prés. So Bobby very candidly asked Miss Bergen to share his last evening."

The same article went on to say that Bergen had brought along her small dog, a Yorkshire terrier, which she kept under the table while the couple ate. RFK, a true canine fan, fed the dog scraps from his dinner plate. As the couple finished their dessert, Kennedy bent over and scooped up the dog, indelicately stuffing it inside his suit jacket, then headed for the street to catch a cab.

Like RFK's relationship with Jackie, his liaison with Candice Bergen caught the attention of Ethel Kennedy. Her friend Coates Redmon insisted that Bobby's wife "must have taken note, because RFK and Candice made little effort to hide what they were doing. I don't know why Ethel remained so passive about the situation, at least outwardly. I had the feeling all the Kennedy wives, including Rose, closed their eyes to these extramarital affairs. Female liberation hadn't yet become a popular movement in the U.S. If it happened today, I wonder if Ethel's reaction would have been the same."

"Bobby and Candice weren't being furtive; their actions were obvious," said Truman Capote. "I was in Switzerland at the time, and I happened to read about it in some local Swiss newspaper, so you can imagine. And I knew them both. Candice had that Waspish, preppy look that appealed to all the Kennedy men. And like Shirley MacLaine and Mia Farrow, she struck me as rather bright. Bobby wasn't as much into bimbos as his two brothers were. He had lengthier, more serious affairs. He tended to be a bit more selective. That's not to say he never had one-night stands, but in general he seemed to prefer bona fide relationships."

Whatever else one might have thought of RFK, it has to be said that there was a schismatic aspect to his character and personality. It seemed almost as if Bobby and Robert F. Kennedy were two different people, with contrasting ideas and conflicting values; playful and amorous on the one hand, arch and earnest on the other. Of the original quartet of Kennedy brothers, RFK was the most religious, thus the most like his mother. But like his father, he was a prisoner of his own sexuality. Bobby's priest, one might conclude, must have had a field day whenever RFK went to confession.

"For all his 'serious' affairs," said Larry O'Brien, "Bobby still, on occasion, enjoyed a good roll in the hay."

Indeed, during a spring 1965 barbecue at Hickory Hill, according to Jerry Oppenheimer, author of *The Other Mrs. Kennedy,* a biography of Ethel Kennedy, RFK took off on a motorcycle with Polly Bissell, a recent Radcliffe College graduate he'd hired to work in his Washington senatorial office after meeting her at the Martha's Vineyard home of writer William Styron. Television journalist Douglas Kiker, a guest at the cookout, told Oppenheimer that Bobby and his blond companion were clad only in bathing suits as they rode to a nearby wooded area and parked the Harley.

They were interrupted when a McLean police car drove up. As Kiker heard it, when RFK saw the patrol car, he hiked up his trunks and darted into the trees, leaving Bissell to fend for herself. Only after the officers escorted Bissell back to Hickory Hill did Bobby emerge to make his own way back. Bissell later told Kiker that she and Bobby were "merely friends." Their intention had simply been to go on a short sightseeing trip.

A McLean, Virginia, police report, however, filed on May 25, 1965, signed by Patrol Officer Charles Duffy, stipulated that a man and woman were spotted a half mile from Hickory Hill, "copulating in public." The report went on to note that the man, on seeing the two officers approach in their car, ran into the woods, leaving the young woman and a motorcycle behind. "She identified herself as a houseguest of Senator and Mrs. Robert Kennedy," continued the report. "She rode the motorcycle back to Hickory Hill, and we followed. The man was never identified. No summons was issued and no arrests were made."

Despite all his wanderings, and despite his romance with Jacqueline Kennedy, it was common knowledge that Bobby always came home to his wife. Even though she was no glamour girl, and though she lacked Jackie's panache and allure, Ethel had her ways. She knew how to raise the roof. During the mid-1960s, she and her husband attended a party in Washington to mark the resignation of McGeorge Bundy as national security advisor to Lyndon Johnson. "Ethel Kennedy wowed them with the frug the other night," a newspaper account of the shindig began, referring to a popular dance of the sixties. She evidently "wowed them" with her outfit as well. Washington journalist Joe Alsop recalled that while the other ladies at the party showed up in their best floor-length chiffon and peau de soie, Ethel wore Courrèges boots and a minidress of shiny black-and-white vinyl with rhinestone shoulder straps. The festivities lasted until dawn, and Ethel cut up the dance floor. "She was no great beauty, but she had a good figure and a great pair of legs. She was very devoted and loyal to Bobby. In her eyes, he could do no wrong."

The women in his office were younger, the film actresses he coveted were prettier, Jacqueline Kennedy was more creative, but RFK cherished his wife for reasons that only a few people outside the domain of their union could understand. Marie Ridder, a friend and journalist, noted that those who were close to Bobby knew how much he needed Ethel. "I remember being on a private plane with them," said Ridder. "Ethel was a nervous flier because her parents and a brother had perished in separate airplane crashes. But you could see how happy Bobby was to have her there with him. The whole time, he kept his hand on her shoulder. There were rumors about other women. I was on another flight with Bobby when Candice Bergen got on, and I presume he had a flirtation or even an affair with her. But I don't think it meant much to him. I can't comment with any degree of authority on his relationship with Jackie, because I never saw them together in a private setting. I heard he loved her, but Ethel remained his life's partner. They were devoted to each other."

In March 1965, Maud Shaw informed Jacqueline Kennedy that she planned on spending her annual monthlong spring vacation in Sheerness, England, visiting her elderly brother and sister. She knew that Jackie intended on passing part of May and June in London with Caroline and John, and she wondered if the children could spend a few days with her and her family in Sheerness. To her surprise, the former First Lady responded that starting in the fall, her services would no longer be needed. Jackie suggested the nanny retire and remain in Britain. To drive home the point, she presented Shaw with a retirement present: a leather-bound photo album of the children.

On March 22, Shaw wrote to Evelyn Lincoln: "I had planned on going to England with the children in May, but Mrs. Kennedy has just told me she will not need me to return to the States. I must say it was a bit of a shock."

While Jackie stayed with her sister and her sister's children, Tina and Anthony, at Stas Radziwill's home in London, Caroline and John spent a week with Maud Shaw and her siblings. While in London, Jackie had lunch with Evangeline Bruce, who happened to be visiting her sister at the same time.

"Jackie felt her children had outgrown Maud Shaw," said Bruce. " 'Miss Shaw's good with young children,' Jackie told me, 'but I want someone more attuned to their present needs.' However, I soon learned she terminated the nanny because she discovered the woman had contracted with both British and American publishers to write a tell-all about her seven and a half years with the family. The book [*White House Nanny*] appeared later that year. Jackie feared it might disclose compromising information concerning her relationship with Bobby Kennedy. She considered it an invasion of privacy, since Shaw (like all her other employees) had signed a nondisclosure agreement promising not to write about the Kennedys. Jackie enlisted the help of Sol Linowitz, the chairman of the board of Xerox Corporation, and threatened to sue the publishers of the book. In the end, she let the matter drop."

Jackie had similar concerns about a volume, *The Pleasure of His Company,* being prepared for publication by Red Fay, which she suspected might reveal the names of some of JFK's extramarital partners, replete with salacious details. She contacted Fay and pleaded with him not to publish the book. A compromise was struck, whereby Fay agreed to let Bobby Kennedy read and edit the potentially embarrassing manuscript prior to publication.

Even more aggravating to Jackie was William Manchester's *The Death of a President,* sections of which were about to appear in *Look* magazine. "For reasons I will never understand," said Manchester, "Jacqueline Kennedy, who had personally chosen me to write the book, suddenly decided to oppose its publication. I suppose she felt it contained too much hard-edged material on her marriage to the late president, and she was determined to stop the presses unless I agreed to surrender total editorial control. Of all people, she even turned to J. Edgar Hoover for help, and before I knew it, I was being trailed by a team of FBI agents."

Jackie also forced Bobby Kennedy to intervene. A number of RFK's senatorial staff members and advisors, including Ed Guthman, Burke Marshall, John Seigenthaler, Frank Mankiewicz, and Richard Goodwin, likewise became involved, reading the manuscript and offering suggestions for cuts and revisions. When Manchester agreed to make certain changes but not others, Jackie sought an injunction to prevent the volume (and related magazine excerpts) from appearing in print. While Bobby's loyalty and love for his sister-in-law led him to blindly support her, no matter how unreasonable or irrational her demands, he warned her that her war against *The Death of a President* was pure folly and would in the long run only damage her public image. She rebuffed his advice and insisted that he continue the campaign to contain Manchester.

"Bobby, whom I'd always liked and admired, began to physically harass me," recalled Manchester, referring to an encounter with RFK in the lobby of a New York hotel. "He went totally insane. He blocked the way so I couldn't get around him. He was yelling and screaming so ferociously that he literally foamed at the mouth. 'You'd better comply with Jackie's wishes,' he shouted, 'or I'll see to it that your fucking book never comes out!' "

Although Manchester ultimately agreed to make the requested alterations, as well as to contribute a large percentage of the book's profits to the John F. Kennedy Library, Jackie was still grumbling about the situation in June 1965, when she and her children traveled from London to Runnymede, England, the site of the signing of the Magna Carta in 1215. It was there that Queen Elizabeth dedicated a national monument in honor of President Kennedy, a ceremony attended by Prime Minister Harold Macmillan, U.S. secretary of state Dean Rusk, RFK, and Ted Kennedy, the latter three having been flown from the United States aboard a 707 provided by Lyndon Johnson. Afterward, the group joined the queen for tea at Windsor Castle. Over the next few days, Bobby and Jackie took the children on several London tours, stopping at Whitehall, Buckingham Palace, and the Tower of London, where John Jr. managed to get stuck in the mouth of an old cannon and had to be pulled to safety.

While still in London, Caroline and John posed for the camera of Sir Cecil Beaton. Pleased with the photographs, Jackie must have been less enthused by Beaton's description of her in his *Diaries,* published in the late 1970s, as an "oversized caricature of herself." To his friend, British aristocrat Edith Roades, he said, "Mrs. Kennedy complained nonstop for more than an hour about all the books that were being written about her and the late president. She then began to wax poetic about Senator Robert F. Kennedy, with whom she appears to be much in love. He reciprocated by doing everything in his power to please her. I thought if he ever became president, she would once again reign as First Lady."

Chapter 7

◆

FOLLOWING HER return to the States from England with a new governess in tow, Jacqueline Kennedy took the children on a late June 1965 vacation to Hawaii. Renting a large house at Diamond Head in Honolulu, she enrolled Caroline in a hula class for youngsters and hired a local college student to teach both children the rudiments of surfing. Wandering into the surf by himself one afternoon, John Jr. got caught in the undertow only to be rescued by a vigilant Secret Service agent. A day later, the same agent again saved the boy, this time by yanking him out of a bonfire that neighbors had started on the beach.

Jackie, Caroline, and John Jr. were joined in Honolulu by a nephew of Hugh Auchincloss, John F. Nash, who had six children of his own. Peter Lawford also visited, bringing along his brood of three. Ten-year-old Christopher Lawford, Peter's son, penned an autobiography forty years later in which he wrote about inadvertently spotting Aunt Jackie in the buff as she emerged from a shower stall. More startling was Peter Lawford's recollection of Jackie viciously slapping her daughter across the face when she discovered that the child had smeared her lips and cheeks with globs of ruby lipstick, the tube supplied by one of the Nash children.

"It was misplaced rage," said Lawford. "Jackie was angry because Bobby Kennedy had telephoned her in Honolulu and demanded that she publicly relinquish the federal monies which had been appropriated to maintain an office in New York to help process John F. Kennedy's presidential papers. Bobby became concerned about how it would look if Jackie continued to receive public funds, particularly considering the family's wealth. She was infuriated. 'What other sacrifices must I make to satisfy this lousy clan?' she asked. She eventually agreed to the forfeiture, but only after Aristotle Onassis reassured her that he would pick up her office expenses, which in turn enraged Bobby. 'I don't want the Greek's money used in connection with Jack's papers,' he barked. 'Then you pay for it,' Jackie told him. She was right. Bobby could be very dictatorial. Now that he'd established himself as an elected official, he was focused on his own public image. Everything the family did—or didn't do—reflected on his burgeoning political career. It was clear that as early as 1965, he had presidential aspirations."

Putting the family's finances on the back burner, Jackie flew to New York, after which she took the children to Canada, where they visited Montreal and Toronto. In July she celebrated her thirty-sixth birthday with the entire Kennedy clan at Hyannis Port. She traveled to Virginia to spend time with Paul and Bunny Mellon, and turned up at Hammersmith Farm in Newport to help her mother plan the construction of a new windmill residence on the Auchincloss property—the previous windmill having burned to the ground.

In August she went to Boston with Bobby Kennedy to celebrate Cardinal Cushing's birthday and returned to Newport for a dinner given by Senator and Mrs. Claiborne Pell. While still in Newport, she and George Plimpton put together an end-of-summer party for Caroline Kennedy, which involved adults disguised as pirates and a buried treasure chest. Bobby Kennedy gave Caroline a puppy. Caroline promptly bathed the dog and groomed its fur with her mother's toothbrush.

"Jackie put on a happy face," said Plimpton, "but seemed out of sorts. It had nothing to do with her toothbrush. It had to do with Bobby Kennedy. There seemed to be some undercurrent of anger."

Taki Theodoracopulos, a budding author who had become Lee Radziwill's newest companion, strolled into the Sherry-Netherland

Hotel in Manhattan one day in early September, accompanied by Peter Lawford and one of Lawford's girlfriends. The three were planning to have lunch, but as they walked toward the hotel restaurant they noticed Bobby Kennedy and Jackie seated close together at the end of the bar. The bar at the Sherry-Netherland had always been one of their favorite hideaways. "Peter and Bobby were on the outs," said Taki, "so it didn't particularly surprise me when Peter turned to his girlfriend and, in a loud voice, said, 'See, I told you—the son-of-a-bitch is doing her.' "

Having temporarily reconciled, Bobby and Jackie were next seen together at a dinner party given by the wealthy Charles and Jane Engelhard. At Bobby's behest, the former First Lady attended an October reception at the United Nations for Pope Paul VI. The same month, she and New York attorney William vanden Heuvel rented Manhattan's Sign of the Dove restaurant and "Killer Joe" Piro's band for a midnight buffet and early morning dance in honor of John Kenneth Galbraith. According to Galbraith, "Although they were no longer involved, Jackie invited John Warnecke to the affair. Jackie was all smiles that night, especially when Bobby Kennedy put in a brief appearance. She looked at him the way a lover beholds his or her beloved. The thing about Bobby was that he portrayed himself as something of an altar boy, and everyone, including the press, bought into it. The real Bobby Kennedy was anything but an altar boy."

A few days later, Bobby accompanied Jackie to Bernardsville, New Jersey, in the middle of Essex Fox Hounds Club country, where she had recently leased a small farm, a place she could go to "get away from it all." From time to time, when his senatorial duties permitted, RFK spent weekends there with her and her children. A few years later, she gave up the rental property and purchased a renovated farmhouse on ten acres down the road from her Bernardsville friends and neighbors the Murray McDonnells, an Irish Catholic clan as large and prosperous as the Kennedys. Jackie boarded her horses and ponies with the McDonnells, taking them out for carefree rides through the woods. On Sundays she took part in the weekly fox hunts organized by the club. Bobby remained an occasional weekend visitor.

C. Douglas Dillon, who lived nearby and had sponsored Jackie's membership in the Essex Hounds, recalled his shock when he showed up unannounced at Jackie's rented house one Saturday morning only to discover Bobby and the former First Lady "smooching" in the backyard. "I must have been pretty thick," he said, "because I frequently encountered them at parties and on public occasions in New York. It never dawned on me that they were anything but devoted friends, brought closer by the death of John F. Kennedy. But when I saw them together that day at Jackie's weekend retreat, everything suddenly began to make sense."

Carl Killingsworth, an NBC-TV public relations executive, originally met Jackie at a New York dinner party given by her friend Kitty Carlisle Hart. Kitty, who was on the board of the American Red Cross, had asked Jackie if she wanted to visit a Veterans Administration hospital in Queens that housed American soldiers injured in Vietnam. Encouraged by Bobby, Jackie spent an afternoon at the facility conversing with the wounded and dying. At Kitty's dinner, Jackie discussed her visit and how moving an experience it had been. It seemed to Killingsworth that Bobby Kennedy had made his sister-in-law more politically aware, particularly concerning America's military presence in Vietnam, which the senator had begun increasingly to oppose. By the same token, he piqued her interest with his special concern for the problems of the poor and the disenfranchised. Jackie frequently accompanied him on visits to public housing projects to raise funds and draw attention to the cause.

"I became a fairly close friend of Jackie's," said Killingsworth. "She'd call up, and we'd go to the ballet or a movie, and invariably wind up at P. J. Clarke's for burgers or omelets at the Brasserie. Mike Nichols came along now and again. Others who often joined us were Truman Capote and Leonard Bernstein. Jackie appeared to prefer the company of men as opposed to women. She didn't have many female friends. She once told me men were less petty than women. Women held grudges, men didn't. The odd thing is that Jackie herself rarely forgave anyone she felt had betrayed her."

After a point, it struck Killingsworth that Jackie almost never brought up Camelot or President Kennedy. By way of contrast, one of her favorite subjects was Robert Kennedy. The first time Killingsworth went to her Fifth Avenue apartment, he noticed that there wasn't a single photograph on display of JFK. The only photo in her living room was a large framed portrait of Bobby Kennedy, which sat on top of her piano. It was inscribed: "To Jackie, my love. Always, Bobby."

Not knowing whether to say anything, Killingsworth finally pointed to the picture and suggested, "Jackie, looking at that photo, people might get the wrong impression."

"Frankly," Jackie responded, "I don't care what people say about me. I'd jump out the window for Bobby."

In January 1966, Washington attorney Clark Clifford, former chairman of President John F. Kennedy's foreign intelligence advisory committee and then an advisor to President Johnson, received a telephone call from J. Edgar Hoover, whom he'd known since the days of the Truman administration. The FBI director asked Clifford to drop by his office at his earliest convenience.

When Clifford arrived, Hoover ushered him into an adjacent office where a movie projector and screen had been set up.

"What's all this?" asked Clifford.

"You'll see," retorted Hoover.

After Hoover and Clifford sat down, the lights dimmed, and an attendant turned on the projector. Clifford found himself watching a silent three-minute black-and-white film showing deceased actress Marilyn Monroe committing a sexual act upon a man whose face was just out of range of the camera.

"There was no question in my mind that the woman on her knees performing fellatio was Marilyn Monroe," said Clifford. "I had no idea as to the identity of her partner."

When the film ended and the lights came on again, Clifford looked over at Hoover. The FBI director had a smug expression on his face. "Do you want to watch it again?" he asked.

"I think I've seen enough," said Clifford.

"Did you recognize the couple?" inquired Hoover.

"I recognized Marilyn Monroe," responded the attorney. "How could I possibly identify the other person in the film? We never see the man's face."

"We have reason to believe that it's Robert Kennedy," said Hoover.

"How can you possibly know?" asked Clifford. "How do you know it's not President Kennedy? Wasn't he also involved with Marilyn? For that matter, it could be anyone."

Hoover explained that the film had been taken with a hidden camera planted in the actress's bedroom during the period shortly before her death when she was consorting with Bobby Kennedy, not Jack. The bureau had been given the film in 1965 by a former aide to Teamsters union boss Jimmy Hoffa, RFK's number one target during his term as attorney general.

"My guess," continued Hoover, "is that Hoffa meant to blackmail Robert Kennedy in order to get the Justice Department off his back. We also know that Joe DiMaggio offered Hoffa a large sum of money for the film, but the transaction never took place. I called you in because I thought you might want to discuss the matter with your friend, President Johnson."

"What does Lyndon Johnson have to do with it?" asked Clifford. "Even assuming it's Robert Kennedy in the film, why would the president want to become involved?"

"I'm not sure," said Hoover. "All I know is that the president has his own grievances against Senator Kennedy. He ought to be apprised of the film's existence, don't you think?"

Knowing that Hoover had always resented the former attorney general, Clifford surmised that the FBI director hoped to use the film to ruin RFK politically—and he hoped to accomplish this feat at the highest possible level. Although Clifford had no intention of delivering the film to President Johnson, he told Hoover he'd give the matter some thought.

Several months after viewing the film, Clark Clifford encountered

Jacqueline Kennedy at a Manhattan dinner party given by *Vogue* editor Diana Vreeland. "At one point in the evening, Jackie took me aside," recalled Clifford. "She looked me straight in the eye and asked if I knew anything about 'a certain film' involving Marilyn Monroe and Bobby Kennedy engaging in a sexual act. I have no idea how she'd gotten wind of it or if she knew that J. Edgar Hoover had shown me the film. I imagine she had her spies throughout Washington, and very little escaped her scrutiny. In any case, I wasn't going to implicate myself in the affair. I told her I knew nothing about it. I don't think she fully believed me, but she let it slide, and we returned to the dinner table. She never brought it up to me again, and I have no specific knowledge of what became of the film."

In February 1966, again following the advice of Bobby Kennedy, Jackie enrolled five-year-old John Jr. in kindergarten at the St. David's School on East Eighty-ninth Street, a five-minute walk from her Manhattan apartment. A Catholic school for boys, St. David's catered mainly to the sons of old, moneyed New York families but managed to include among its roughly three hundred students a substantial mix of boys on scholarship from a diversity of backgrounds. The heterogeneous environment at St. David's appealed to Jackie, who didn't want either of her children to become overindulged or spoiled.

Although generally well liked by fellow students, John went through an initial period of adjustment. During his second week of classes, he bloodied the nose of a classmate who insisted on calling him John-John. When the school headmaster asked Jackie to come in to discuss the incident, she brought Bobby Kennedy along. Uncle Bobby admonished the youngster: "use your mouth and brain, not your fists." The boy's mother took the matter a step further by insisting that John begin seeing the well-known child psychiatrist Erik Erikson. Eventually Caroline went to see him as well.

RFK continued to mentor Jackie's children at every turn, often flying in from Washington to attend parent-teacher conferences with Jackie or standing in for his slain brother on parent visiting days. As she'd previously done for Caroline, Jackie made a point of bringing John to school in the morning and picking him up in the afternoon.

"Jackie's presence at Sacred Heart or St. David's invariably drew a crowd," noted Carl Killingsworth. "She stopped traffic. People gawked. Parents, students, teachers, pedestrians—even policemen—stopped in their tracks and stared. She attracted reporters and paparazzi. Ron Galella began his merciless pursuit of Jackie at this juncture, popping out of the bushes in Central Park or from behind parked cars on Fifth Avenue. As sophisticated as New Yorkers are supposed to be, they couldn't resist the celebrity of Jacqueline Kennedy. It was like the Second Coming."

During Caroline's first year at Sacred Heart, Jackie arrived after school one day with Adlai Stevenson, former American ambassador to the United Nations during the Kennedy administration. Stevenson accompanied Jackie and Caroline for ice cream sodas that afternoon. He proceeded to go on several additional outings with the former First Lady and her children, including a ferry ride to the Statue of Liberty and a trip to Coney Island for hot dogs and amusement park rides. In his own self-effacing fashion, Stevenson demonstrated more than a passing interest in Jackie. The more he saw of her, the more attracted he became. When she sensed that he had developed a romantic attachment, Jackie retreated, sending him a series of playful but off-putting notes. Angered by her methodology, Stevenson told *Washington Post* owner Katharine Graham, with whom he was rumored to have had an affair, that Jackie was "a royal tease, the temptress of her age."

Jackie had the same problem with Robert Lowell, the celebrated American poet married at the time to literary critic Elizabeth Hardwick. Having initially forged a distant friendship with Lowell in 1964 when he sent her a copy of his most recently published volume of poetry and an edition of the Greek philosopher Plutarch's *Lives* (which she subsequently gave to Bobby Kennedy), Jackie soon began to correspond with the poet. During 1965 and early 1966, they saw each other occasionally, brought together by mutual friend Blair Clark, a politico who in former days had been close to Jack Kennedy. In a letter to Lowell, who lived down the block from the Café des Artistes, on the West Side of Manhattan, Jackie remarked how fortunate she was to have "a friend across Central Park," which became the title of a later Lowell poem. The friendship was consecrated as an official piece of gossip when a picture of the couple appeared on the front page of *Women's Wear Daily* on December 1, 1965. They were photographed leaving the theater on the opening night of *Hogan's Goat,* a play by William Alfred. Within days, Lowell was telling friends that he intended to divorce Hardwick in order to marry Jackie Kennedy.

"Lowell was completely taken with Jackie," said Blair Clark. "I don't know how much she encouraged him, but she evidently didn't realize that he was a manic-depressive, that he took lithium, and was in and out of mental hospitals. When I saw how obsessed with her he'd become, I told her that in my opinion he was going into another of his manic spins, and that she ought to be careful. The obsession acted as a triggering device. I was close to him, and was brought in whenever he had an episode. I recognized the signs. He had a fixation on her. She bedazzled him. She had a way of dangling men like marionettes; they danced at her feet. She liked Lowell, but only as a personality, someone with whom to chat about literature once in a while."

Lowell, in fact, did suffer a manic-depressive episode, and over Christmas 1965 wound up at McLean Hospital near Boston. Jackie wrote him there, thanking him for an Alexander the Great biography he'd sent her, and telling him that at his suggestion she'd begun reading the works of Juvenal and Cato. Unwilling to deal directly with the subject of his illness, she added that he was wise to "go away" over the holidays—as if he had gone on vacation rather than into a mental institution.

When Lowell returned to New York after a month at McLean Hospital, a stay that included a dozen sessions of electroshock therapy, he again contacted Jackie. On one occasion, he invited himself up to her Fifth Avenue apartment and for more than two hours read to her from a newly completed sheaf of poems. In February 1966, he invited her to join him for a weekend at a small inn outside Boston. She turned him down.

Carl Killingsworth recalled the incident that put an end to Jackie's friendship with the poet. "In late February 1966," he said, "Rudolf Nureyev gave a party for some friends at the Russian Tea Room in New York. I was there. Jackie brought Lowell. There were a few others. We were eating and drinking when the subject of Sidney Kaye came up. Kaye owned the Russian Tea Room. Someone innocently mentioned that Kaye happened to be Jewish. This set off Lowell. He began spouting off against the Jews. 'If I'd wanted Jewish food,' he said, 'I'd have gone to a delicatessen.' And so on. It got worse. It turned out Lowell was a virulent anti-Semite. Jackie couldn't take his rant any longer. She stood up and excused herself. 'I don't feel well,' she announced. 'I'm going home.' I went outside to help her catch a cab. As she slid into the backseat, the only thing she said was, 'That man is an absolute fool.' As far as I know, she never spoke to Lowell again, though Bobby Kennedy, whom she'd introduced to Lowell, remained on friendly terms with him."

Robert David Lion Gardiner, the eccentric New York heir, first encountered Jackie Kennedy at the Manhattan home of Lady Jean Campbell. In March 1966, he invited her to visit him at home on his privately owned islet, Gardiners Island, off the coast of Long Island. After dinner, which was also attended by Gardiner's wife (former British model Eunice Bailey Oates) and several others, they were having coffee and cognac in the wood-paneled den. As Gardiner later told the story, Jackie took out a pack of cigarettes and looked around for a light. She saw a gold cigarette lighter on the coffee table. The lighter belonged to Mrs. Gardiner. After lighting her own cigarette, Jackie slipped the lighter into her pocketbook. Gardiner witnessed the entire transaction but was uncertain what to do.

"What was I supposed to do?" he reminisced. "I suppose I could have said, 'Mrs. Kennedy, can I please have my wife's lighter back?' I mean, I was absolutely convinced she knew precisely what she'd done. I didn't want to make a fuss, because this was a former First Lady, possibly the most renowned female figure in the world."

Several uncomfortable minutes later, Gardiner reached into a humidor he kept on top of a nearby bureau. He removed a cigar, cut off the tip, and asked, "Have any of you seen my wife's gold cigarette lighter? Did you, Mrs. Kennedy? I believe you were the last one to use it."

Jackie shrugged. "I have no idea where it went," she said.

The lighter left the house with Jackie and was never returned to its rightful owner. Gardiner retaliated by spreading stories about the former First Lady, accusing her of kleptomania and other petty crimes. The gossip soon reached the ears of Aristotle Onassis, who asked Jackie what she knew about the cigarette lighter. In response, she said that she'd accidentally placed the lighter in her pocketbook and didn't realize it until some time after the get-together.

"Where's the lighter now?" inquired Onassis.

"I have no idea," responded Jackie. "I haven't seen it in weeks."

To put an end to the incident, the Greek shipping magnate sent Gardiner a personal check for $5,000, accompanied by a threatening note that read in part: "Enclosed you will find a check to cover the cost of your wife's cigarette lighter. . . . Should you persist in spreading malicious innuendo about Mrs. Kennedy, I will be forced to retain counsel in her behalf in order to litigate for slander."

At some point, the lighter seems to have mysteriously reappeared; after Jacqueline Kennedy's 1994 death, it was auctioned off at Sotheby's in New York as part of her multimillion-dollar estate.

Chapter 8

———◆———

IN EARLY 1966, Jacqueline Kennedy became involved in the establishment of an international fund for the preservation of the historic artworks of Florence, Italy, many of which had been damaged by a rash of recent floods. She enlisted the help of Bobby Kennedy and Robert McNamara, encouraging them to make available what contributions could be raised immediately through official channels. She was named honorary chairwoman of CRIA, the Committee for the Rescue of Italian Art, an already existent philanthropic group whose resources she combined with those of her own newly founded organization.

"Once Jackie undertook a project, whether it was the JFK Library or the artworks of Italy," said Robert McNamara, "she stuck with it to the bitter end. With regard to the Florentine floods, she thought nothing of calling me three or four times a day. Angie Novello, Bobby Kennedy's personal secretary, told me Jackie called his senatorial office all day, every day. She solicited all her friends, including Aristotle Onassis. She even convinced Lyndon Johnson to make an out-of-pocket donation. She raised millions. She single-handedly saved the art treasures of Florence. And when she was done with Florence, she turned her attention to the artworks of Venice, a city that is slowly sinking into its own waterways."

On a quick under-the-radar trip to Europe, Jackie spent a few days at the alpine ski chalet of John Kenneth Galbraith in Gstaad, Switzerland, before traveling to Rome to meet with some of the leading members of CRIA. While in Rome, she met with Valentino, a coutourier then little-known outside his own country, whose chic creations she had discovered several years earlier in New York. During their latest get-together, Jackie told the designer that she would use him as her chief dressmaker provided he agreed to two stipulations. First, he would have to contribute a sizable sum of money to CRIA. Second, all bills related to his fashion work on her behalf had to be sent to the Joseph P. Kennedy Jr. Foundation in Manhattan. Valentino consented. When his exorbitant bills began arriving at Kennedy headquarters, Steve Smith contacted Bobby Kennedy, who pointed out that his wife, mother, and sisters did the same thing—why shouldn't Jackie? The other complainant was Rose Kennedy, who accused her "self-indulgent" daughter-in-law, the president's widow, of spending ten times as much on her wardrobe as anyone else in the family. When Bobby communicated his mother's lament to Jackie, the former First Lady commented, "What does she want? I'm already a Kennedy family captive. My children and I are permanently deprived of the pleasures of anonymity. To please Rose, must we also be as parsimonious as she?"

Over Easter vacation 1966, Jackie took her children to Córdoba, Argentina, to stay at the cattle ranch of Miguel A. Carcona, whose three grown daughters had often socialized with Joe Kennedy's three eldest sons. While there, John Jr. added a stone to a mound of rocks collected years earlier by his father. The next day, at a private beach, Jackie was photographed changing into her bathing suit. The professional photographer, hidden amidst a clump of bushes, published the seminudes in *Gente,* an Argentine magazine with a large male readership. Refusing to comment on the incident or the snapshots, Jacqueline returned to New York, dropped off her children, and several days later set off on a long-planned trip to Spain as the guest of the Duke and Duchess of Alba, as well as Angier Biddle Duke, currently the American ambassador to Spain.

Attempting to exert more control over the European press than she had in South America, Jackie insisted that no photo or quote could be released without her express consent. Any news item had to be cleared with Nancy Tuckerman, Jackie's personal representative in New York.

"I told her," said Angier Biddle Duke, "that it would be virtually impossible to control the European press, particularly because there was so much interest in her. And sure enough, shortly after her arrival the newspapers and magazines were crammed with stories on her relationship with Antonio Garrigues, Spain's ambassador to the Vatican."

Garrigues, sixty-two, a handsome widower with eight children, had long been a friend of the Kennedys. He and Jackie had last seen each other during her recent trip to Rome. Now that he was squiring the former First Lady around Madrid, journalists somehow assumed he and Jackie were on the verge of announcing their engagement.

"Jackie quickly grew tired of the many reporters that followed her around from dawn to dusk," noted Duke. " 'This is worse than when I lived in Georgetown after Jack's assassination,' she complained. She was particularly cloyed by the dozens of questions the press posed about Garrigues, whom she regarded as little more than a good buddy. Of course, she knew how to handle the media. God knows, she'd had enough practice. But I think she expected us to shield her from the press, and that simply couldn't be done."

From Madrid the group traveled to Seville, where Jackie was received by the Duke and Duchess of Alba and installed in the lavish Palacio de las Dueñas. In her bedroom suite, she found the latest copy of *Women's Wear Daily,* which contained a front-page story linking her to Antonio Garrigues. Garrigues, for that matter, had been designated by the American embassy to accompany Jackie to the International Red Cross Ball, a glamorous charity event for 2,500 guests, among them Prince Ranier and Princess Grace of Monaco. It would be hosted by the Duke of Medinaceli in the courtyard of Casa de Pilatos, his capacious villa in the center of Seville.

A few hours prior to the start of the event, Jackie telephoned Angier Biddle Duke and informed him that she couldn't possibly permit Antonio Garrigues to escort her to the ball. There had already been far too much newspaper talk about them.

Duke tried to reason with the former First Lady, pointing out that it was too late to strike Garrigues's name from the guest register without creating a major furor.

"I couldn't fully comprehend Jackie's objection," said the ambassador. "After all, in recent years she'd been falsely linked to countless men. I kept pressing her for an explanation. 'Angie,' she finally said, 'I'm involved with two other gentlemen at the moment, both of whom I value and respect. I'm not going to sabotage my happiness for the sake of a stupid party.' "

Although Jackie didn't divulge the identities of the "two other gentlemen" in her life, Duke had his suspicions. The names Bobby Kennedy and Aristotle Onassis were all too familiar to anyone who knew Jackie. To save face, he phoned Garrigues himself and asked if he minded escorting his wife, Robin Duke, to the ball, instead of Jackie. He provided some vague excuse for the switch. Garrigues reluctantly agreed. To further protect his charge, Ambassador Duke called a press conference the following day. "I want to make it crystal clear and completely understood," he announced, "that there is no basis in fact in rumors of an engagement or any other romantic link between Mrs. Kennedy and Ambassador Garrigues."

Although she had toyed with the thought of cutting short her visit to Spain, Jackie chose to stay, and almost immediately her vacation began to improve. She attended the bullfights in Seville. She donned the traditional Andalusian riding habit (black-trimmed red jacket, flowing chaps, flat broad-brimmed hat), mounted a horse, and took part in Seville's annual country fair. "To visit Seville and not ride horseback," she informed a reporter, "is like not coming at all." She then returned to Madrid and went to a farewell dinner party in her honor at the American embassy, where she was seated between Prince Juan Carlos de Bourbon, who later became the king of Spain, and the country's minister of industry, Gregorio Lopez Bravo, a rising political star. To her immense relief, Antonio Garrigues, who'd also been invited, sent his regrets—he couldn't be there because he'd been called back to the Vatican for an important meeting with another ambassador.

On returning to her apartment in New York, Jackie found two imposing floral arrangements waiting for her. Both, she told Truman Capote, were accompanied by almost identically worded greeting cards. The first read "Welcome Home" and had been signed by Bobby Kennedy; the other card contained the same message but bore the signature of Aristotle Onassis.

In June Jackie took Caroline and John to San Francisco, and from there on a return trip to Hawaii. As they'd done in 1965, Peter Lawford and his children joined Jackie, renting a house next door to the $3,000-per-week three-bedroom residence Jackie had leased in Kahala from Senator Peter Dominick of Colorado. John Warnecke, also vacationing in Hawaii, dropped by for a visit. Another visitor, John Sperling, a close friend of Lawford's, developed something of a crush on Jackie. "I told her," said Peter Lawford, "that John was divorced and therefore available, which is more than one could say for Bobby Kennedy."

In early July, Aristotle Onassis arrived in New York to see Jackie, then flew with her to Hammersmith Farm in Newport, where they bumped into Joan Braden. "I'd met Onassis once before," recalled Jackie's old friend. "That meeting took place at a dinner party in London a few months after JFK's assassination. Ari wasn't a handsome man, but he seemed charming and worldly. And he obviously possessed the means to be able to look after Jackie. I felt they made a promising couple, and I made my sentiments known."

Onassis returned to Greece, while Jacqueline stayed behind in Newport to attend the wedding of her younger half sister Janet Jennings Auchincloss and Lewis Rutherfurd, a descendant of Peter Stuyvesant. Dick Banks, a portrait artist living in Newport and an acquaintance of the Auchinclosses, remembered how Jackie's presence nearly ruined the wedding ceremony. "The town was one big gridlock," he remarked, "full of reporters, photographers, and tourists, all gathered to catch sight of Jackie and her children. Little Janet [Janet Jennings Auchincloss] broke down in tears. As usual, Jackie upstaged everyone and stole the show. 'I shouldn't have come,' she told me. It wasn't her fault. Her mere presence at any event was enough to turn it into a freak show."

Two months later, she attended a second wedding, this one for Pamela Turnure and Robert N. Timmins, chairman and chief executive officer of a successful Canadian brokerage firm, at St. Ignatius Loyola Church in Manhattan. Turnure had followed Jackie from Washington to New York, where she worked on President Kennedy's administrative papers, a project that was being financed by Aristotle Onassis. Jackie not only organized the Turnure wedding, she gave a reception for the couple in her Fifth Avenue apartment.

Pierre Salinger, a guest at the Turnure nuptials, was completely perplexed by Jackie's commitment to Pamela, who had served as her White House press secretary. "I mean, Pamela had originally been Jack Kennedy's girlfriend," he remarked. "Jackie knew about it but for some obscure reason never held it against her. Another oddity connected to the Turnure wedding had to be Bobby Kennedy's arrival at the reception. In one room you had JFK's former mistress, and in the other you had Jackie's current lover. If this arrangement didn't speak to the tenor of the times, the sexual climate of the sixties, I don't know what did. It all began to seem so very incestuous."

Considering the surge of public scrutiny into the private life of Jacqueline Kennedy in the years following JFK's assassination, it seems almost inconceivable that more did not appear in the press about her romance with Bobby Kennedy. Equally dismaying was the fact that so many members of the Kennedy family's inner sanctum were aware of the affair. Chuck Spalding, who remained close to the clan, told John F. Kennedy biographer Nigel Hamilton that Bobby and Jacqueline Kennedy were involved almost to the end of Bobby's life, and that their liaison had helped restore the former First Lady's emotional health. It had done the same for Bobby. "For the first year or year and a half after Jack's death," said Spalding to another biographer, "Bobby was not very happy. But a few years after the assassination—from 1965 through 1968—he felt a sense of completion. He attributed his recovery to his relationship with Jackie. Bobby and Jackie were extremely close. I ought to know—I went on vacations with them. I was there with them."

Truman Capote felt he understood the romantic bond that grew between Bobby and Jackie. In a series of videotaped interviews with Capote conducted by film producer Lester Persky in 1976, Capote defended the union, describing it as "perhaps the most normal relationship either one ever had. There was nothing morbid about it. It was the coming together of a man and a woman as a result of his bereavement and her mental suffering at the hands of her late, lecherous husband. In retrospect, it seems hard to believe that it happened, but it did."

Capote, whose closest ally for several years was Lee Radziwill, recalled Lee's almost daily updates on the affair. "It was passionate," testified Capote. "But it was fraught with incalculable difficulties: his career, her renown, his marriage, her affairs with other men, including Onassis. There was something sad about it. What was sad is that the affair was doomed. Because of who they were and what they represented, sooner or later it had to end. At the same time, it was the impossibility of the relationship that made it so poignant and strong. Not that Jackie had any illusions about RFK. Like his father and brothers, Bobby was addicted to sex and got it where and whenever it was offered to him."

In his book *Nemesis,* British journalist Peter Evans presents Eunice Shriver as another inner sanctum member with knowledge of the affair. Citing a conversation between Eunice and Ethel Kennedy, Evans quotes Shriver as saying to her sister-in-law, "Well, what are you going to do about it—Bobby's spending an awful lot of time with the 'widder.' " According to Evans, Ethel offered no response. Her silence, the journalist observes, "said it all." It wasn't that she was afraid to speak up or that she had simply become another Kennedy wife "living in fake ignorance about her man." Ethel may have been naïve, but she wasn't *that* naïve. In fact, Ethel had reached the same conclusions as Truman Capote about her marriage. With all their children, her husband's Catholicism, and his concern with the Kennedy legacy, she realized that their marriage was largely intact. Above all, she knew of Bobby's overriding desire to pursue the presidency in 1968, and she recognized the importance of remaining on solid terms with the "widder." Jackie remained the Kennedy family's most powerful political force, their ticket to retaking the throne. If Bobby's affair with the former First Lady was the price Ethel had to pay, she was prepared to accept it. Even so, she knew her limitations. Whenever Jackie visited Bobby at home in Hyannis Port, Ethel would jump up and leave the room.

Aristotle Onassis maintained his own view of Jackie's relationship with Bobby Kennedy. "It disturbed him," said Onassis aide Johnny Meyer. "At the same time, it titillated him. He used to compare Jackie to his former wife, Tina, whom he divorced when he discovered she'd become friendly with Stavros Niarchos, Ari's main competitor in the shipping trade. I have to give Jackie credit for telling Ari the truth about her romance with Bobby Kennedy. She could just as easily have lied about it. Most women would have denied the affair, but, then, Jacqueline Kennedy wasn't most women."

Onassis once boasted to Johnny Meyer that he could "bring down" RFK by going public with details of the senator's affair with his sister-in-law. "I could bury that sucker," said Onassis, "although I'd lose Jackie in the process. But can't you just see the headlines?"

Meyer was present during one explosive exchange between Jackie and Ari, in which the latter proclaimed, "Your boyfriend's a little prick," to which Jackie responded, "That doesn't describe him anatomically."

One of Ari's favorite stories about RFK referred back to March 1965, when the Canadian government offered to name its highest unclimbed mountain peak (13,900 feet) after President John F. Kennedy. In recognition of the honor, the National Geographic Society suggested that Bobby accompany its party of mountaineers in their initial assault of the Yukon mountain, which was to be named Mount Kennedy. Always the daredevil and sportsman, Bobby readily accepted the challenge and soon joined Mount Everest veteran Jim Whittaker (an RFK friend) and several other seasoned climbers on the six-day expedition.

According to Ari's version, which he based on conversations with others present on the occasion, Bobby never joined the expedition but instead was flown by helicopter to a spot only a few yards from the summit. As a *National Geographic* camera crew recorded the senator's progress, he made his way up the last twenty feet to reach the mountain's highest peak, where he planted an American flag, a PT-109 tie clip, a Kennedy family flag, and a copy of JFK's 1961 inaugural address. Bobby then crossed himself and said a few words about his "arduous ascent."

Onassis routinely ended his Mount Kennedy saga with the words, "Now, there's an American hero for you. Well done, Robert Kennedy!"

Florida senator George Smathers recalled having lunch with Bobby Kennedy in Washington in the summer of 1966. RFK spoke at length about one of his latest senatorial endeavors, the Bedford-Stuyvesant project, an ambitious plan he'd devised to refinance and rehabilitate one of Brooklyn's (and the nation's) most dangerous impoverished neighborhoods. "Bobby was appalled by the degree of poverty that existed in contemporary America," said Smathers. "After becoming a senator, he went on a walking tour of Appalachia. He couldn't believe the number of families he found living under the worst imaginable conditions in abandoned vehicles and dilapidated shacks. Whether it was Appalachia or Bedford-Stuyvesant, Bobby wanted to get everything done at once. RFK advisor Dave Hackett reported that they'd visit Bed-Stuy on a Monday morning, and Bobby would meet with real estate developers and local contractors and explain what needed to be done; when he returned three days later, he became annoyed because nothing had been accomplished. He couldn't fathom why it should take more than a day or two to tear down and then restore whole blocks of shops, lofts, and low-rise office buildings, as if it could all be done with the wave of a magic wand."

Over lunch that afternoon, Smathers asked Bobby why he'd aborted his personal investigation into his brother's assassination.

"Because every time I pump the FBI or CIA for information," RFK responded, "I end up with a death threat in the mail. So does Teddy. I don't care about my own life, but I do care about my brother's. My using the CIA in conjunction with the Mafia to go after Castro may have led to Jack's death. One in the family is enough."

For his part, Smathers supported the theory that there had been a conspiratorial plot between organized crime and the CIA, or, more accurately, a renegade faction of the CIA. Smathers had little faith in the findings of the Warren Commission. "Gerald Ford, the future president, was an FBI mole," said Smathers. "He was on the commission but reported everything back to J. Edgar Hoover." Despite the FBI director's disdain for the Kennedys, Smathers firmly believed that it was the CIA—and not the FBI—that had worked with the syndicate to assassinate Kennedy. "In 1957 JFK and I spent a few days in Havana," continued Smathers. While there, they were introduced to crime figures Meyer Lansky and Santos Trafficante, both of whom controlled Cuba's hotels, casinos, and nightclubs, creating an exuberant after-hours atmosphere. "Trafficante set us up in a hotel suite with several choice ladies of the night. Only later did I realize how stupid we'd been. It wouldn't have surprised me to learn that we'd been filmed through a one-way guest-room mirror. The opportunity for blackmail, particularly after Jack became president, pointed to the foolishness of our little adventure. Jack could never resist temptation. His name cropped up in 1963 in connection with the so-called Profumo debacle, in which an international vice ring nearly brought down the British government. He'd been linked to one of the women involved in the case. Had he lived, Jack would've been dragged through the mud. And then there was the matter of Mary Pinchot Meyer, his last mistress, who was murdered in 1964 while walking along the towpath in Georgetown. Had he been alive, that case also would have come back to haunt Jack."

RFK, long his brother's bagman, almost certainly knew of the meeting in pre-Castro Cuba between Jack and Trafficante, as well as all the rest of JFK's sordid dealings. Ultimately, according to Smathers, Bobby's decision to discontinue his investigation into his brother's assassination probably had less to do with the Mafia and more to do with his and Jackie Kennedy's madcap affair following Jack's death.

"At least, that's what Ted Kennedy told me," noted Smathers. "One of Bobby's fears was that somebody would eventually leak information on the affair to the press. Too many people were in on the secret. Exposure in the media would have ruined any chance Bobby might have had of following in Jack's presidential footsteps. Frankly, between the CIA and Bobby's interlude with Jackie, it's a wonder that none of it had already been exposed in the press."

Conceptual artist Larry Rivers became friendly with Jackie in the spring of 1966. "I met her either through George Plimpton or photographer Peter Beard, who was dating her sister, Lee. I soon began attending dinner parties at Jackie's beautifully appointed Fifth Avenue apartment. On occasional weekends, she visited Plimpton in the Hamptons, and Beard at Montauk, Long Island, where he owned a converted lighthouse. Once or twice, she stayed at Andy Warhol's weekend house on the Island. She was engaged at that time in several fund-raising ventures, one for the refurbishment of the New York Public Library at Forty-second Street, and another for the preservation of the New York Metropolitan Opera House. When she asked you to donate funds, it was impossible to turn her down. You saw her coming, and you whipped out your checkbook. She had numerous acquaintances within the titled European community, and she seemed particularly adept at hitting them up for bread as well."

Rivers couldn't recall how he learned of Jackie's relationship with Bobby Kennedy, only that it surprised him. "I knew she and Aristotle Onassis were involved, and that he helped her out financially. But I couldn't see what benefit she derived from Bobby, which led me to conclude that theirs might have been a real love match."

In her own way, suggested Rivers, Jackie could be very tough minded. She was extremely bright. Her chief attribute, aside from her physical beauty and ability to bewitch, had to be her sense of style. She was the "It" Girl of her generation. She was hip. She was cool. She'd meet Rivers for lunch at La Côte Basque. She'd be wearing her Chez Ninon navy blue Balenciaga coat, a camellia bloom on one shoulder and a Coco Chanel handbag dangling from the other. Everyone who

Jackie, her suit stained with blood, stands with Bobby, holding her hand, as they watch the casket of her slain husband, President John F. Kennedy, placed in an ambulance at Andrews Air Force Base, Maryland, near Washington, D.C., November 22, 1963. The body of the president was flown from Dallas, Texas, where he was fatally shot earlier in the day. At right are Evelyn Lincoln and Kenneth O'Donnell of the White House staff. Mrs. Lincoln was the late president's personal secretary. (Associated Press)

Jackie and Bobby walk hand in hand at the funeral of the late President John F. Kennedy on November 25, 1963. (Bettmann/CORBIS)

During a party at the Manhattan home of movie executive Arthur Krim, Marilyn Monroe stands between Bobby (left) and John F. Kennedy, May 19, 1962. The party followed a fund-raiser at Madison Square Garden celebrating the president's birthday, where Monroe famously sang "Happy Birthday, Mr. President." (Time & Life Pictures/Getty Images)

Actor William Holden standing on a roof terrace, 1960. He and Jackie enjoyed a brief affair during her marriage to JFK. (Getty Images)

Marlon Brando, 1968. Brando was Jackie's first lover following President Kennedy's assassination. (Esther Anderson/CORBIS)

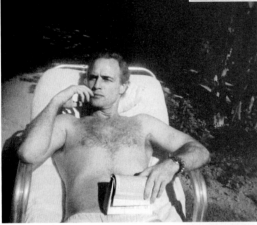

Architect John Carl Warnecke explains a model for the restoration and development of Lafayette Square across the street from the White House to then First Lady Jackie Kennedy in 1962. Several years later, the two would have a short-lived affair. (Bettmann/CORBIS)

Jackie holds JFK Jr. while Bobby looks on.
(Copyright, Estate of Stanley Tretick)

Jackie waits with her brothers-in-law,
Senator Edward M. Kennedy (D-Mass.)
and Attorney General Robert F. Kennedy,
in Bobby's office at the Justice Department
before making her first public statement
since the late president's assassination.
(Bettmann/CORBIS)

Jackie saying good-bye to
Bobby and his wife, Ethel,
at her Georgetown home.
It was during this period
that Bobby and Jackie were
romantically involved.
(Bettmann/CORBIS)

Jackie, President Lyndon B.
Johnson, and Bobby at
the 1964 Democratic
Convention. (Steve Schapiro)

Bobby and Jackie wishing "bon voyage" to former British ambassador to the United States Lord Harlech and his wife as they leave for London aboard the *Queen Mary,* March 1965. Lord Harlech was a close friend of the late President Kennedy and was rumored to have had a romantic attraction to Jackie. (Bettmann/CORBIS)

Jackie ends her visit to the colorful fair of Seville, Spain, in April 1966, enjoying a horseback ride through the fairgrounds. (Bettmann/CORBIS)

Jackie smiles broadly after surprising Bobby as he paraded up Fifth Avenue in the 1966 St. Patrick's Day parade. (Bettmann/CORBIS)

Jackie walks with her two children,
Caroline and John, at JFK Airport,
on their way to Switzerland.
(Bettmann/CORBIS)

Bobby at his Hickory Hill home
with Ethel and several of their
children. (Steve Schapiro)

Jackie and Bobby at a party,
1967. (Ron Galella)

Jackie and Bobby at an event where 650,000 feet of news and videotape footage of the former president was donated as a joint gift from CBS News and NBC News to the John F. Kennedy Presidential Library and Museum, May 1967. (Time & Life Pictures/Getty Images)

Bobby campaigns in the 1968 presidential race in California. (Steve Schapiro)

Bobby and Ethel, after winning the Democratic Party primary in Indiana, 1968. (JP Laffont/ Sygma/CORBIS)

Bobby meets with the "Boiler Room" girls, all of whom worked on his staff during his 1968 run for the presidency. Mary Jo Kopechne, who died at Chappaquiddick in a car driven by Ted Kennedy, is at far left. (Source unknown)

Jackie visits Bobby's presidential campaign headquarters in New York accompanied by Roswell Gilpatric in June 1968. Their affair had become a matter of public record earlier that year, when he left his wife and joined Jackie on a trip to see the Mayan ruins in the Yucatán region of Mexico. (Bettmann/CORBIS)

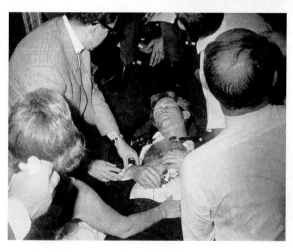

Clutching rosary beads, Senator Robert F. Kennedy lies mortally wounded on the floor of the Ambassador Hotel in Los Angeles after being shot by Sirhan Sirhan, following his victory speech in the California primary election. Ethel is at lower left. (Bettmann/CORBIS)

Jackie and future husband Aristotle Onassis walking together. (Ron Galella)

Bobby and Jackie on a 1966 family ski trip. (John Bryson/Sygma/CORBIS)

was anyone would come over to the table and pay their respects. But when you were in her company, she gave you her full and undivided attention. She focused on you and you alone. Other New York eateries she frequented included the Colony, La Caravelle, Le Mistral, and Orsini's. One night Rivers took her to the Copa, where they met up with film director Mike Nichols and actor Alan Arkin. As far as Rivers could tell, Nichols had a terrible crush on Jackie. It was one-sided. She wasn't physically attracted to him. She kept him at a distance, but did so with such skill and delicacy that he kept coming back for more. At one juncture, he said, "Taking her anyplace is like going out with a national monument."

Rivers recalled a mid-1966 dinner party that Lee Radziwill threw for her sister, a function that had become something of an annual tradition. Jackie arrived in a white silk Valentino evening gown and white mink jacket, escorted by Bobby Kennedy and Averell Harriman. Others at the party included Mike Nichols, classical music conductor Leopold Stokowski, film producer Sam Spiegel, Leonard Bernstein, Sammy Davis Jr., Arlene Francis, Bunny Mellon, Brooke Astor, George Plimpton, Pierre Salinger, and Franklin D. Roosevelt Jr.

"Just as we were about to sit down for dinner," said Rivers, "the door opened and in walked Aristotle Onassis. You could have knocked me over with a feather. Lee, a former lover of Ari's, had invited him without telling Jackie. Nor apparently had she informed Onassis that Robert Kennedy would be there that night. It might have been Lee's idea of a joke, although neither RFK nor Onassis saw any humor in it. She might have acted out of pure jealousy, angry that Jackie had stolen Ari away from her. Whatever the motive, it marked the first time I ever saw a look of panic cross Jackie's face, as the two men stood there gawking at each other. Nobody said a word. Finally, the always-irreverent Franklin Roosevelt Jr. spoke up. 'I guess you boys know each other,' he said. Jackie spent the rest of the evening attempting to divide her time and attention equally between her two pursuers."

Rivers ultimately felt sorry for Lee. "Being Jackie Kennedy's younger sister was tantamount to finishing last in the Kentucky Derby," he said.

"No matter what Lee did, she couldn't win." According to her friends, she was very pretty but always appeared to be in a foul mood. Without a true vocation, Lee constantly searched for something to do. One month she wanted to become an actress; a month later she considered herself an interior designer. She was a hypochondriac, constantly going to doctors and complaining that she wasn't feeling well. The main reason that she and Stas Radziwill left England and resettled in the United States was that the royals and their equivalent shunned them socially. Lee was perceived as an affected arriviste, an upstart, whose sole claim to fame was her familial tie to Jacqueline Kennedy; Stas Radziwill's only claim to legitimacy was his standing as Jacqueline Kennedy's brother-in-law.

A week after Lee's party for Jackie, Larry Rivers attended a reception at attorney Roy Cohn's Manhattan townhouse. "Roy Cohn loathed Bobby Kennedy as much as Jimmy Hoffa and J. Edgar Hoover combined," observed Rivers. "Cohn and Kennedy had both worked for Senator Joe McCarthy, so there was a long history of enmity between them. Cohn also represented Aristotle Onassis, whom he happened to admire. He knew I was friendly with Jackie, so he began spouting off. He insisted Bobby Kennedy had bisexual tendencies and was having a go of it with Rudolf Nureyev at the same time he and Jackie were involved. I took his gay accusation as nothing more than vicious gossip. He terminated his rant by saying RFK had far more foes than friends and one day would meet the same end as his brother Jack."

In order to see Jackie on a more regular basis, Aristotle Onassis rented an apartment on East Sixty-fourth Street in Manhattan. "She doesn't seem to mind Bobby Kennedy dropping in at all hours," Ari told Johnny Meyer, "but when I visit her apartment, she tells me the doormen are talking."

The doormen at 1040 Fifth Avenue *were* talking, but not exclusively about Aristotle Onassis. Sam Murphy, a spring and summer replacement for one of the building's regular doormen (injured in a 1966 automobile accident), remembered seeing RFK on a fairly frequent basis: "I worked the overnight shift for most of those six months—11:00 p.m. to 7:00 a.m.—and I'd see Senator Kennedy an average of three times a week; that is, when Mrs. Kennedy and her children were in town. The senator usually arrived late at night and left early the next morning. As I understood it, he commuted back and forth to Washington. As for Aristotle Onassis, I saw him only two or three times during that period. On the occasion or occasions I did see him, he'd arrive weighted down with all sorts of presents, presumably for Jackie, Caroline, and John Jr. He was very generous in terms of tips. I'd hail a cab for him on Fifth Avenue, and he'd hand me a twenty-dollar bill."

Kenneth McKnight had been a chief administrator with the U.S. Commerce Department during the days of Camelot. In July 1966, he received a telephone call from his longtime friend Chuck Spalding asking if he might be interested in working for Senator Robert F. Kennedy. Following their conversation, Spalding arranged a meeting between the two men at RFK's senatorial offices in Washington.

"I'd met Jack and Jackie Kennedy several times, but never Bobby," said McKnight. "My appointment with RFK, well known as a taskmaster who kept long hours, had been scheduled for 8:00 p.m. When I arrived, the office was open, but the office staff had evidently gone home. The place was empty. I wandered down a corridor past cubicles and closed office doors to Bobby's personal suite at the far end. The door was ajar. I peeked in and there, on a sofa, sat Bobby Kennedy, and straddling his lap, her arms around his neck, was Jackie Kennedy. When they saw me, they disengaged and stood. I apologized for barging in on them. Jackie smiled. To my surprise, she remembered my name. 'How are you, Ken?' she asked. 'How have you been?' She introduced me to the senator and left the room."

In the course of his meeting with RFK, McKnight brought up the name of Sargent Shriver, whom he'd known from his term in the Department of Commerce. "I had no idea Sarge had been relegated to Bobby's shit list," recalled McKnight. Shriver had made the grievous mistake of volunteering to run President Johnson's poverty program.

Working for Johnson was looked upon by RFK as a sinful indication of disloyalty toward the Kennedys. It earned the sinner the senator's eternal wrath.

"The one word that wasn't part of RFK's vocabulary," said McKnight, "was the word *compromise*. In his view, you were either for or against the Kennedys. There was no in between."

RFK and McKnight spoke for nearly an hour, after which Bobby walked the visitor back up the hallway to the front entrance. There, as he extended his hand, RFK said, "By the way, Ken, nothing you saw or heard tonight leaves this office. Is that understood?"

"If I hadn't agreed," McKnight said later, "I honestly believe he would've murdered me then and there."

Several days later, McKnight heard from Chuck Spalding, who wanted to know how the meeting had gone.

"Not so well," said McKnight. "I saw something I probably wasn't supposed to see."

"In other words, Jackie was with him?" said Spalding.

"You know about them?" asked McKnight.

"Everyone knows about them," responded Spalding. "That's the problem."

In September 1966, Jackie invited Diana Vreeland and a few other friends to her house for dinner. Jewelry designer David Webb had fashioned a necklace of pink coral for the former First Lady, which she wore that evening with a matching pink jumpsuit. Bobby Kennedy arrived in time for dessert, bringing along William vanden Heuvel and Yevgeny Yevtushenko, the internationally renowned Russian poet. Recalling the dinner party, Vreeland said, "Jackie impressed Yevtushenko with her sweeping knowledge of European and Russian literature. He couldn't get over it. I saw him again in New York the following year, and he was still singing Jackie's praises. 'She ought to be teaching literature at a university,' he said. 'Well,' I told him, 'why don't you arrange for her to come to the University of Moscow?' And I'll be damned if he didn't do just that. A few months later, she received an invitation from the president of a Soviet university to come and teach for a year. Of course, that wasn't exactly in the cards for Jackie."

In October Jackie received a telephone call from Simon Wiesenthal, the Austrian Nazi hunter to whom she'd been introduced by Evangeline Bruce during a brief visit to Paris in 1965. "Jackie gave money to the cause and couldn't have been more supportive," claimed Wiesenthal. His telephone call to Jackie had to do with Fritz Stangl, former commandant of the Treblinka concentration camp, who had been hiding away in São Paulo, Brazil. Through Wiesenthal's intervention, the Brazilian authorities had apprehended Stangl. The local governor, however, notified Wiesenthal that Stangl could be detained for no more than seventy-two hours. This meant he would be set free before he could be extradited to Germany to stand trial for an array of war crimes, including mass murder. After speaking with Wiesenthal, Jackie contacted Bobby Kennedy. RFK went above the governor's head and convinced a leading Brazilian official to extend Stangl's detention long enough to have the extradition phase of the case heard in court. Returned to Germany, placed on trial, Stangl died of a heart attack six months after being sentenced to life in prison.

Just when Jackie's relationship with Bobby seemed to be going well, she heard about Margo Cohen, an RFK Washington office employee who, according to Kennedy advisor Peter Edelman, had "fallen in love" with the senator. Unable to ascertain the extent of RFK's relationship with Margo—or even if there really was a relationship between them— Jackie imagined the worst. She and Bobby had recently taken Caroline and John Jr. to Serendipity in Manhattan for ice cream floats, and Bobby had struck Jackie as acting "remote and distracted." As she often did when she felt compromised or neglected by RFK, Jackie turned her attention to Aristotle Onassis, visiting him at his Avenue Foch town house in Paris. When she returned, knowing it would get back to Bobby, Jackie told Ted Kennedy that she was considering marrying Onassis, "sooner rather than later."

An item in the November 15, 1966, edition of *Paris Match* reported that during Jackie's sojourn with Onassis, opera diva Maria Callas, Ari's "official" companion, had appeared unannounced at her paramour's home. A row ensued. As Onassis described it for the benefit of Johnny Meyer, "The two of them nearly came to blows. I had to separate them." Before Maria left, she called Jackie a "geisha girl," a sobriquet originally bestowed upon Jackie by Truman Capote.

Lilly Lawrence, the daughter of Reza Fallah, head of the Iranian Oil Syndicate, had known Onassis for years. "Jackie was the most money-hungry woman I ever met," she said. "She and Ari had that much in common. She lusted after money, and he possessed it. She craved the kind of lifestyle that only he could provide. She wanted security, both for herself and her children. Whenever Ari saw her, he handed her an envelope full of cash. He was used to paying for sex. He enjoyed the company of call girls. Never one to mince words, he used to say, 'It's a straightforward transaction. There are no strings attached. You pay them and they spread their legs. If you want something special, you pay them a little extra.' The last thing Bobby Kennedy wanted was to have Jackie get married to Ari. It would have blackened her name, as well as that of the Kennedys. Jackie threatened Bobby with the possibility that she and Ari might wed in order to keep Bobby in line. It didn't always work."

In early December, Jackie dined at Le Pavillon in New York with Bill Walton, up for the day from Washington, and the Hervé Alphands, who had flown in from France. Bobby Kennedy joined them. When asked what he'd done during the previous summer, Bobby described a dangerous kayak trip he'd taken down the Salmon River ("The River of No Return") in Idaho. Jackie listened and then said, "Oh, Bobby, you're *so-o-o-o* reckless." She proceeded to tell her dinner companions that the most important thing to her about a man "is that he must weigh more and have bigger feet than I do." When approached for an autograph by another diner, she replied with a smiling, breathy "No—thank you."

As if Onassis alone didn't suffice, Jackie finally "evened the score" with Bobby by indulging in a fling of her own, seeking revenge in the arms of the talented *New Yorker* cartoonist Charles Addams. Twenty years Jackie's senior, Addams divided his time between a Greenwich Village apartment and a home he owned in Sagaponack, Long Island. Like so many of her lovers, Addams was a married man. Although she let Bobby find out about it, Jackie acted in such a way as to keep news of the affair under wraps. Addams, unfortunately, began to brag to friends about being with the former First Lady. "Being in bed with her," he told one pal, "is like living in a fairy tale." The fairy tale ended for Addams when Jackie heard from George Plimpton that Addams had been indiscreet.

"Charlie couldn't stop talking about Jackie," said journalist Doris Lilly. "From one minute to the next, she cut him dead. I remember dining with him in a New York restaurant when Jackie walked in. She had to pass our table to reach hers. Charlie smiled and gave her a little wave of the hand. She stared straight through him as if he didn't exist. 'What a bitch!' I thought to myself, just as Charlie spat out the words. 'What a bitch!' he said. 'What a fucking bitch!' "

Chapter 9

◆

BOBBY KENNEDY was so busy and preoccupied at times that often he was oblivious to much of what was going on at Hickory Hill. His children were always a priority, but being head of the entire clan meant that he didn't always exercise control over his own household. Within the family circle, he was criticized for spending more time with Jackie and her children than he did with Ethel and his own. Sid Mandell, an Associated Press photographer, remembered being brought up to Hickory Hill for an exclusive picture-taking session with Bobby and the children. An impromptu touch football game was organized with the entire family, even the toddlers, taking part. "I took five rolls of film," said Mandell. "The minute we were done, RFK walked into the house, grabbed his briefcase, and was driven off in a waiting car."

In preparation for a January 1967 political trip to Europe, Bobby had a member of his staff prepare a half-dozen letters to Ethel, one of which he sent her each time he reached a new European capital. "As far as I know," said Dave Powers, "though he signed them, he didn't write the letters himself. Meanwhile, he telephoned Jackie three or more times a day, as much to keep tabs on her whereabouts as to get some much-needed advice on how to deal with the various European leaders on his itinerary."

"Like his brothers, Bobby Kennedy gave the impression of being a family man," said Pierre Salinger, "but this was predominantly the result of an effective public relations campaign. In reality, the Kennedys were only interested in power and politics. They didn't go in for snuff-boxes, Fabergé eggs, or Persian rugs. They weren't interested in fine furniture or great art. They spent their money on buying votes, whether it was to get JFK into the Oval Office or Teddy and Bobby into the Senate. Given the vast sum of money they spent on politics, they could have gotten Andy Warhol elected president."

Indeed, the Kennedys were chintzy when it came to their personal lives. They never tipped. Their homes were always in need of repair. The interior of all their houses looked like the inside of a Howard Johnson motel. Their household employees—gardeners, drivers, cooks, and maids—were undocumented illegals, mostly from the Dominican Republic, and were paid the minimum hourly wage. Members of the family never carried cash with them. They charged everything and took months, sometimes years, to repay their debts. They went to Stop & Shop supermarkets in search of bargains. They spent generously on clothes, but this had more to do with outward appearance—a necessary feature of the political arena—than it did with any intrinsic interest in fashion.

A charter member of the so-called Shop till You Drop club, Jacqueline Kennedy was the sole exception to the parsimonious attitude that marked the rest of the clan. In early February 1967, after she and Bobby had once again patched up their relationship, she took him to A La Vieille Russie, the expensive Russian antique shop on Fifth Avenue, where she showed him a little eighteenth-century decanter that she hoped he would purchase for her.

Anna Stigholz, a salesclerk at the store, remembered the couple. "Senator Kennedy ogled the decanter for a minute or two before asking how much it cost. 'It's sixty thousand dollars,' I told him. 'Did you say sixty thousand dollars?' he asked. 'Yes,' I remarked. 'It once belonged to the tsar. It's a valuable piece.' He practically laughed in my face. He took Mrs. Kennedy by the arm and led her to the front door."

They wound up at the Collector's Corner, an antique shop on Madison Avenue and Seventy-fifth Street, from which Jackie occasionally bought small items at moderate prices. Ernest Lowy, proprietor of the shop, recalled a visit by the former First Lady in late February, shortly before she came in with the senator. "I had a two-foot-high jade Buddha from India that interested her," said Lowy. "The sales price was twelve thousand dollars. She asked me to hold on to it for a few weeks. When the couple came in, she pointed to the Buddha. 'How much?' she asked. 'Twelve thousand,' I said. Senator Kennedy winced. He then took out his checkbook. 'I'll give you two thousand now, and you can send an invoice for the remainder to the Joseph P. Kennedy Foundation,' he said. I later found out that Mrs. Kennedy had set him up by first taking him to A La Vieille Russie. Twelve thousand dollars must have seemed a good price to the senator compared to the sixty thousand he would have had to lay out for the decanter. Jackie used a bit of basic psychology to get the item she really wanted."

The showcase Buddha wasn't Bobby's only gift to Jackie that year. She needed a new car. Bobby's initial response to her request took the former First Lady by surprise. "Why don't you turn to the Greek?" he told her. "Maybe I will," she retorted. In order to get RFK to spring for the automobile, Jackie practically had to bribe him by promising to go on the stump if and when he ever ran for president. "You'll never win without me," she said. He bought her the car.

On February 26, 1967, Bobby Kennedy ran into Katharine Graham at a dinner party at the Georgetown home of Joseph Alsop. Two weeks earlier, *The Washington Post* had published a snippy, gossipy story about Jackie. Always quick to defend his sister-in-law, RFK took Katharine Graham to task for permitting the article to run.

"He cornered me and then gave me a lecture," recalled Graham. " 'Why did you run that terrible piece on Jackie?' he said. 'You, of all people, ought to know better. Your husband [Phil Graham] committed suicide. So you must realize how painful it is to lose a spouse. Hasn't Jackie suffered enough?' I thought bringing up my late husband was hitting below the belt, and I told him as much. 'Besides,' I added, 'owning the paper doesn't necessarily give me license to censor or edit articles according to my individual taste or whim. I don't have time to read half the stories that appear in the *Post*. I wasn't even aware of the Jackie story until after it ran.' 'Come off it, Kay,' he snapped. 'Don't give me that crap. If you don't know what your newspaper has to say, then who does?' "

Feeling contrite about his outburst, particularly with regard to his Phil Graham reference, RFK sent Graham a letter of apology. "I obviously upset you and I hadn't meant to," he wrote. "I had just seen Jackie the day before the Alsop dinner and she was so upset and really crushed and I thought to myself that here was a girl who hadn't committed any great crime but who day after day is attacked and pilloried in all kinds of scandalous ways."

Kay Graham accepted Bobby's apology, although it struck her as bizarre that he would use the word *girl* to describe Jacqueline Kennedy, one of the most formidable women of her time.

In March, Ethel gave birth to Douglas Harriman Kennedy, her tenth child. Apprised of the birth, Jackie Kennedy said to Ken O'Donnell, "One more, and Bobby can field his own football team."

The joy of giving birth was marred for Ethel by her gnawing suspicion that Bobby and Jackie were still involved in an affair that had started as a result of their shared loss but which had grown into a romance based substantially on their shared passion. Something was going on. The situation threatened to get out of hand. The backroom gossip among members of the household staff at the compound in Hyannis Port reached its peak in the spring of 1967. The place was abuzz with talk about the affair. Ethel felt threatened by Jackie. In April the FBI informed the president's widow that they had been informed of a possible kidnap plot against Caroline Kennedy. The former First Lady immediately contacted Bobby Kennedy. Bobby spent the next two weeks by Jackie's side, moving into her New York apartment.

Family retainer Mary De Grace recalled how upset Ethel became during this very trying period. According to De Grace, Mrs. Robert Kennedy took out her frustration on her residential staff at Hickory Hill and at the compound. She instituted a whole new set of household rules and regulations. Full-time employees would continue to receive gratis meals, but those who wanted something to drink other than coffee or tea had to provide for themselves. In addition, she placed a blank notebook near the front door. Employees were now required to sign in and out, recording their times of arrival and departure. Anyone who made a personal call during work hours had to pay for his or her use of the phone. Employees were allotted one fifteen-minute coffee break in the morning and another in the afternoon. Anyone who exceeded the time limitation had to make it up by working overtime. Fines were assessed for various misdeeds, such as breaking a plate or saucer. The employees, many of whom already disliked Ethel, soon began to loathe her.

Toward the end of April, an incident took place that ended Mary De Grace's long-term employment with Robert and Ethel Kennedy. "My job as laundress," she noted, "involved washing and ironing shirts, underpants, towels, pillowcases, and the like. The washing machine ran from the minute I arrived at seven-thirty in the morning until after I left at five, when one of the maids took over. The larger items—sheets, blankets, and draperies—were customarily sent out. Anyway, one day Ethel came into the laundry room and began bitching about her laundry bills, accusing me of sending out too many things to the cleaner. 'You must be in cahoots with the laundry man,' she said. 'My laundry bill so far this year comes to more than seven hundred dollars, and you're going to pay for it!' I told her she could wish with one hand and shit in the other and see which hand got filled up first. Then I threw down the iron and walked out the door. That was the last time I ever spoke to her."

Mary De Grace later went to work for Jackie Kennedy at Hyannis Port, an experience she far preferred to toiling for Ethel. "No matter how many maids Ethel Kennedy had on hand, her house was always a pigsty," she said. "Jackie's house seemed much more in order. Of course, there weren't as many kids. Jackie was always pleasant to me. She had a smile, and whenever she saw me, she'd say, 'Hello, how are you doing?' I'm not sure she meant it or truly cared, but she at least went through the motion. Ethel couldn't have cared less about the help so long as you

did your job and kept your mouth shut. Nothing in Jackie's house suggested ostentatious wealth. She had a canopied bed, but her house was
very tastefully decorated in a Cape Cod style. The only sign of wealth
was her wardrobe closet. She had a double closet crammed with expensive designer clothes. And there were maybe fifty pairs of shoes, which
seemed a lot considering that she spent so little time at Hyannis Port. I
suppose she came up only so her kids could socialize with their cousins.
At the same time, it gave Jackie an opportunity to spend more time with
Bobby Kennedy."

In early May 1967, Jackie took Caroline and John Jr. out of school and
flew with them to Acapulco to spend several weeks with Lee Radziwill
and her children. At one point during their stay, a powerboat carrying
a half-dozen Mexican photographers caused Jackie's and Lee's sailboat
to capsize. The press seemed to be everywhere, creating a major problem not only for Jackie and Lee but also for the Secret Service agents
assigned to look after Caroline and John.

Besides having to cope with the press, Jackie and Lee were forced to
contend with each other. As usual, there was a strain in their relationship. Jackie's usurpation of her sister's relationship with Aristotle Onassis had created ongoing problems between them. The cause of their
latest row was Lee's newly launched acting career. Several months earlier, Truman Capote had introduced Jackie's sister to Milton Goldman,
a theatrical agent whose client list included such talents as Laurence
Olivier and John Gielgud. Not the least concerned that Lee had no
demonstrable acting ability or experience, the agent recommended her
for the role of Tracy Lord, the wealthy, egocentric heroine of Philip
Barry's frothy comedy *The Philadelphia Story*, which had been scheduled to open the 1967 summer program at Chicago's Ivanhoe Theater.

"When Madame Queen Jackie heard about her sister's thespian
plans," said Capote, "she flew into a rage. Didn't Lee realize, she said,
that they were merely using her? Didn't she understand how embarrassing all this would be? Never mind that Madame Queen was sleeping
with her very married brother-in-law and concomitantly with none

other than Aristotle Onassis, and that both were paying big money for her services. That didn't count. All that mattered at the moment was that her younger sister was about to make her theatrical debut. Jackie couldn't take it."

Jackie, it turned out, had been right. The reviewers were merciless. "Lee's golden egg," wrote one theater critic of Lee's performance; "pathetic, lamentable, and sad," moaned another. Commenting on the shocking pink, purple, and chartreuse Yves Saint Laurent gown Lee herself had chosen for her role, the *Chicago Tribune* reviewer observed that she looked "like a dog's lunch." Even Truman Capote, who had flown to Chicago that July to hold Lee's hand, winced as he watched his creation make a fool of herself.

The only encouraging voice belonged to TV talk show host and film producer David Susskind, who had publicly denounced Bobby Kennedy when he ran for senator, declaring him "a power-driven carpetbagger." Susskind felt that if Lee were cast in a serious film role, she could give a credible performance. He wanted to do a remake of the 1944 Otto Preminger film *Laura,* with Lee to take over Gene Tierney's title role, the rest of the cast to include George Sanders, Robert Stack, Arlene Francis, and Farley Granger, and John Rich to direct. Rehearsals were set for London in the fall of 1967. Within days, Susskind came to his senses. "To put it bluntly," he said, "Lee Radziwill, or Bouvier, the name she used professionally, could not act. Not only couldn't she get a line across, she couldn't move. And no amount of coaching could unlock her talent, because she had none. The film was never released. A taped 1970 version aired on ABC-TV in the States, as well as in England, receiving universally disastrous reviews. It ended Lee's stage and film career, and it nearly ended mine. What amused me most was a one-line telegram I received from Jackie Kennedy, which read, 'I could have told you so.' "

Returning from Acapulco, Jackie and her children traveled to Newport News, Virginia, where Caroline Kennedy christened the USS *John F. Kennedy,* a mammoth $230-million aircraft carrier. Lyndon Johnson attended the opening ceremony, as did Bobby and Teddy Kennedy.

Robert McNamara gave the dedication address. Describing the event for its fashion-conscious readership, *Women's Wear Daily* portrayed Caroline as a "budding mini trendsetter." *The Boston Globe* reported that some fifty media photographers "swarmed across the carrier's deck and surrounded Caroline and John, their cameras madly clicking away. Admiral Thomas Moorer, former commander of the Seventh Fleet, tried in vain to chase the photographers away. Mrs. Kennedy intervened. 'It's an official occasion,' she told the admiral. 'I don't mind them taking pictures of my kids. What I object to are the photographers that hang out in front of my apartment building in New York, waiting for Caroline and John to come home after school.' "

On May 30, 1967, news arrived that the wife of David Ormsby-Gore (Lord Harlech) had been killed in an automobile accident in North Wales. Jackie and Bobby Kennedy flew to England for the funeral services. Clark Clifford, also a close friend of the former British ambassador to Washington, accompanied the couple on the trip over. "The three of us stayed at the Dorchester Hotel in London," recalled Clifford. "We'd booked three junior suites. It soon emerged that the two of them were sharing her boudoir; his served only as a decoy. I can't say it bothered me that they were shacking up together, though it seemed a bit odd that they would do so under such a somber occasion."

Two weeks later, while RFK journeyed to Delano, California, to meet with Cesar Chavez, founder and head of the UFW (United Farm Workers), Jackie returned to London, this time with John and Caroline. After a few days in England, they went to Ireland on what was to be a six-week vacation, the highlights of which were a day of horseback riding in Waterford, a meeting with Irish president Eamon de Valera, the Irish Sweepstakes, and a visit to the Kennedy ancestral home at Dunganstown.

They spent most of the summer with the Murray McDonnells, Jackie's New Jersey neighbors, and their eight offspring, at Woodstown House, a fifty-three-room mansion in Waterford. Once it became known that there were Kennedys in town, the press arrived in droves, camping out on the periphery of the McDonnell property. Jackie did what she'd grown accustomed to doing: she telephoned Bobby Kennedy and complained about the press. RFK called Ireland's Department of External Affairs and explained that his sister-in-law and her children were on vacation and wanted nothing more than to be left alone.

An incident took place several days later that proved potentially much more hazardous than the presence of press photographers. Late one afternoon, without telling anyone, Jackie set off by herself to go for a swim. After walking a half mile to a deep channel of water behind a stretch of rolling sand dunes, Jackie slipped into the sea. Once in the channel, she found herself caught in a fast-moving undercurrent that was sweeping her away from land. The water was numbingly cold. What Jackie didn't know was that John Walsh, a member of the children's Secret Service detail, had noticed that she was missing from the house. Guessing that she'd gone swimming, he hurried in the direction of the dunes. Scanning the sea, he spotted her in the distance and could tell that she was in trouble. A former Navy SEAL, Walsh, who stood six foot five, plunged into the water and swam after Jackie. He finally reached her, grabbed hold of her torso, and hauled her back to shore. She sat next to him in the grass spitting and coughing up water for the next half hour.

Walsh was rewarded for his valor. On the basis of a letter Jackie wrote to Thomas T. Hendrick, special assistant to the secretary of the Treasury, Walsh received the Secret Service Agency's highest honor, and in 1968 he took over as head of the Secret Service detail assigned to protect Jackie's children.

"If truth be told," Jackie later informed Pierre Salinger, "Mr. Walsh deserves a better fate than to be anointed chief den mother to a couple of young, at times misbehaved kids."

Back in the States from Ireland, Jackie and her children spent Labor Day weekend at the Kennedy compound in Hyannis Port. Caroline and John then returned to New York to begin the new school year, while Jackie flew to Athens to be picked up by Aristotle Onassis and taken for a five-day stay at Skorpios, his private island an hour by air from the

Greek mainland. According to Johnny Meyer, Onassis proposed to her during the visit—she "put him off" by insisting she had to wait until at least five years after JFK's assassination to consider remarriage.

It is anyone's guess whether her trip to Skorpios bothered RFK. "He mentioned it only in passing," said Ken O'Donnell. "His main concern seemed to be that the media didn't report on her affair with Onassis, which he felt would hinder his political ambitions. Reality had probably set in by this point and replaced any passion he still felt for Jackie. I think he loved her, but he understood and accepted the limitations of their romance. They couldn't marry, so eventually she would marry somebody else. He also understood that she was super-high maintenance. She could marry virtually anyone, but there weren't many men around who could afford to take her on. Onassis stood atop a very short list. Bobby hadn't yet announced his candidacy, but by September 1967, he had made up his mind to run for president. He wanted Jackie to wait until after the '68 election before she made any definitive declaration. Out of respect for Bobby, she agreed to wait."

Fortunately for Bobby, instead of focusing on Onassis, the press brought up another gentleman's name in connection with Jackie. In the months after his wife's death, Lord Harlech had been prominently mentioned as a possible future husband for Jackie. She had seen him during her stay with the McDonells in Ireland, and he had visited her during an October trip to the United States. The rumors were further fueled by magazine editor Leo Lerman's disclosure in the London *Observer* that Lord Harlech had always been interested in Jackie. Once, Lady Pamela Harlech had found a newspaper snapshot of Jackie in a bathing suit hidden behind one of the photographs of her that she'd given her husband after they were married. Lerman added that Harlech's wife had long been jealous of the former First Lady, never missing an opportunity to denigrate her supposed rival. For his part, Lord Harlech issued a stern denial—"We're only good friends"—that, unhappily, coincided with Jackie's announcement that she was planning a private trip to the Far East, and that Lord Harlech would go along.

The press treated the early November 1967 journey to Cambodia and Thailand as though it were a prematrimonial honeymoon. When it was revealed that Southeast Asian expert Michael V. Forrestal would also be making the trip, as well as Washington journalist Charles Bartlett and his wife, the press surmised that she had decided to import her own witnesses and probably intended to marry Lord Harlech in Cambodia.

Few of the journalists assigned to cover the junket realized its true purpose. Rather than an erotic jaunt on the part of two lovers, it was a carefully orchestrated semipolitical mission, discreetly sponsored by the U.S. State Department and camouflaged as a personal vacation. Washington had some notion that Jackie might be able to stem the escalating anti-American tide in Cambodia—a by-product of the war in Vietnam—and perhaps work her magic on Prince Sihanouk, Cambodia's chief of state, in a manner comparable to her well-known involvement with the French and Charles de Gaulle during her husband's term in office. Cambodia had broken off diplomatic relations with the United States. Secretary of Defense Robert McNamara devised the idea of sending Jackie. The plan had been cleared with Lyndon Johnson. Averell Harriman worked out the details and logistics of the visit. Lord Harlech, a skilled and seasoned diplomat with myriad connections in Southeast Asia, seemed an ideal candidate to accompany Jackie. Since he knew her personally, and since rumors about them abounded, his presence made the trip seem even more personal in nature.

Before she assented to the mission, Jackie discussed the matter with Bobby Kennedy. Convinced that if she succeeded it would boost her reputation as a political operative, thereby enhancing the family name and his own chances for the presidency, RFK gave her his blessing. What he hadn't counted on was that the press would misconstrue the expedition's purpose and see it only as a prelude to a Jacqueline Kennedy–Lord Harlech marriage ceremony.

Leaving from New York, Jackie stopped over in Rome for three days, got together with Lord Harlech and Michael Forrestal, and with them made the twelve-hour flight to Thailand. The Bartletts joined them in Thailand, and the entire group flew on to Phnom Penh International

Airport in Cambodia, where Prince Sihanouk awaited their arrival with a welcoming speech. Scrutinizing an advance copy of the speech, Lord Harlech came across a comment bound to create controversy. What the prince planned to say was that had President Kennedy lived, there would have been no Vietnam War. While such a statement remained a matter of pure speculation, its utterance would have been an offense to the current administration. Harlech advised Jackie to appeal to Sihanouk to eliminate the passage. The request was made from the airplane by two-way radio. The prince consented. In return, Jackie agreed to add a line to her arrival address, affirming that "President Kennedy, had he been alive, would have loved to visit Cambodia."

"I don't get politics," Jackie later told Lord Harlech. "It's such a petty and seedy business."

The ancient temples of Angkor Wat provided Jackie with the highlight of her trip. For the better part of a week, she and her companions wandered through the ruins, taking photographs and collecting souvenirs. She did her utmost to ignore Sihanouk's nonstop flow of anti-American rhetoric. "My brother-in-law, Robert Kennedy, shares your views on the war," she said at one point. "But he's not yet the president. If he decides to run, and if he's victorious, the war will end."

The remark must have satisfied the Cambodian leader, because he invited Jackie and her travel party to lunch at his summer villa in Sihanoukville, where they fed and rode the royal elephants. He also decided to rename a boulevard after JFK, and he asked Jackie to preside over the ceremony. A U.S. Air Force jet then flew the group—without Lord Harlech, who returned to England—back to Thailand. King Bhumibo and Queen Sirikit (often referred to in the press as the "Jackie of the Far East") installed the travelers in the royal palace at Bangkok. Following a gala reception, the group attended a performance of the Royal Ballet. The next day, while Mrs. Bartlett nursed a head cold, Jackie, Charlie Bartlett, and Michael Forrestal visited the famous Temple of the Emerald Buddha. Before she left Bangkok for home, Jackie went shopping for gifts for her children.

If the long and sometimes tiresome journey wasn't a complete political success, it nevertheless seemed a worthwhile endeavor. "I don't know if anything I said made the slightest impression on Prince Sihanouk," Jackie told Robert McNamara after returning to the States. "He holds us totally responsible for the war. He doesn't like America or Americans. I did my best to convince him that we're not so bad. I doubt I altered his opinion. But he did name a street after Jack, and that's at least a step in the right direction." As for Lord Harlech, the journey represented a personal defeat. Having apparently entertained the notion that he and Jackie might somehow become a couple, he soon realized that her interest in him was purely platonic. For him, the trip was in effect the final act of a nonexistent romantic drama.

Arthur Schlesinger attended a meeting at Hickory Hill in late October 1967, the purpose of which had to do with the prospect of Bobby Kennedy running for president in 1968. Stephen Smith and Ted Kennedy were present, as were Ken O'Donnell, Larry O'Brien, Ted Sorensen, and other Kennedy supporters. New York politician Allard Lowenstein had come up for the day. Lowenstein felt certain that Lyndon Johnson could be beaten in the '68 Democratic Party primaries. Because of the Vietnam War as well as the recent instances of racial violence in the inner cities, LBJ's popularity with the voting public had reached an all-time low. An October 1967 nationwide poll conducted by *The Washington Post* indicated that if Johnson were to seek reelection, he would narrowly win his party's nomination but be beaten by his Republican opponent in the presidential election.

"Lowenstein felt Bobby should run," said Arthur Schlesinger. "I had my doubts. I didn't think it would be possible to unseat an incumbent in the primaries. Besides, Bobby was young, nearly forty-two, the same age as Jack when he ran in 1960. He had plenty of time. Even if LBJ lost the election in '68, and we faced two terms of a Republican administration, RFK would have been well within the age parameters for a president. And if LBJ won, Bobby could've run in 1972."

Jack Newfield, a New York journalist and friend of Robert Kennedy, likewise attended the meeting. In contrast to Schlesinger, he felt that

Bobby would do well to enter the race. "We needed a spokesperson—all of us who had supported John Kennedy, who were sick and tired of the war and the empty promises and who wanted a change," he said. "During the fall of 1967, with more and more body bags coming back from Vietnam, I told Bobby again and again that he *had* to run. Johnson's politics of division and deadlock no longer worked. Ethel Kennedy felt the same way. She wanted it more than Bobby did. But Ted Kennedy, Stephen Smith, Arthur Schlesinger, Ted Sorensen, and a lot of the other political pros said 'no way'—the public would claim he was opportunistic and that it was a personal thing against Johnson. The Democratic Party would be so split and there would be so much antagonism that the Republicans would ultimately be swept into office."

Unable to decide, Bobby approached the one person whose judgment he trusted above all others: Jackie Kennedy. He saw her several weeks after the Hickory Hill meeting on his way back from another visit with Cesar Chavez in California. Jack Newfield hired a car service and met him at the airport. As they drove into Manhattan, RFK said to Newfield, "I wish they'd never renamed the damn airport after my brother. It pains me every time I fly into New York."

Newfield sat in Jackie's living room while she and Bobby discussed the pros and cons of his entering the race. Eugene McCarthy, Democratic senator from Minnesota, had just announced his own candidacy. Better known for his poetry than his politics, McCarthy represented little more than a protest entry. According to Jackie, he couldn't be taken seriously. When Bobby asked whether she thought he should enter the fray, Jackie responded: "Well, there's a good deal of anti-Johnson sentiment out there. If I were you, I'd make a stand. But I'd wait a few months before announcing. And when you do run, you must be authentic. You must be yourself. Don't try to be Jack."

Newfield noticed how attentively Bobby followed his sister-in-law's words. "It was as though the Oracle of Delphi had spoken," said the journalist. "I'd heard many times from many people that they were lovers. I couldn't tell. But I could see they were extremely committed to each other. If she'd told him not to run, I don't think he would have.

On the other hand, I believe she told him what she thought he hoped to hear. I'm not convinced she wanted him to run—she wanted him to do what she thought would make him happy."

Newfield also wondered about Jackie's advice to Bobby about carving out his own identity. RFK's youth, appearance, and general bearing made him a reasonable facsimile of the dead president. Framed by an unruly shock of hair, long a Kennedy trademark, Bobby's face (though a bit narrower) was a haunting reminder of JFK's. Bobby's mannerisms, among them the one-hand-in-the-pocket stance while delivering a speech, aped those of his brother. Other similarities included the New England accent and Bobby's frequent exhortations calling for the creation of a New Frontier. Many of Bobby's pet phrases as uttered during his entire political career—such as "I need your help" and "We've got to get the country moving again"—came straight out of the JFK playbook. Above all, Bobby yearned to complete the work his brother had begun during the three years of Camelot.

The essential difference between Bobby and Jack was their overall style. The coolness, confidence, and calm that characterized JFK did not come easily to RFK, whose image has often been compared to that of the Grand Inquisitor. Even during his 1964 senatorial campaign, he demonstrated a stridency and pushiness that his detractors typified as "ugly and dictatorial." The struggle for Bobby entailed becoming more like his dead brother, not less, particularly if he hoped to emerge victorious in '68. Pierre Salinger recalled a conversation he had with RFK in January of that year. Adhering to Jackie's directives, Bobby had postponed his decision to enter the race. "I told him," said Salinger, "that he couldn't afford to delay too long. I told him he needed to soften his image. I said we could hire a public speaking coach, which is something we'd done with great success for Jack. Selling Bobby to the public was not unlike selling cans of tuna following a botulism scare. Nobody dislikes tuna; it just has to be demonstrated it wouldn't harm anyone." The subsequent transformation surprised even Bobby, who jokingly quipped, "Once I win the presidency, I can go back to being ruthless again."

Informed by Johnny Meyer that Bobby had hired a public speaking coach, Aristotle Onassis issued a quip of his own. "The only thing JFK and RFK have in common," he said, "is Jacqueline Kennedy."

On December 10, 1967, Jackie accompanied Bobby Kennedy to a formal Democratic Party fund-raising dinner at the Plaza Hotel in New York. Humorist Art Buchwald sat at their table and spent most of the night chatting with them. "I asked Bobby whether he intended to run for president," recalled Buchwald. " 'That depends on what Jackie wants me to do,' he responded with a smile. I guess he was kidding, though I suspect she had a definite say in the final decision. From what I'd heard, some of his advisors wanted him to run, others not. What do you do in a situation like that? Ultimately Bobby had to make up his own mind."

Jackie was thirty-eight years old and fast approaching middle age. From a personal point of view, reasoned Buchwald, it would be difficult for her to sit back while Ethel Kennedy filled her shoes as First Lady. For more than four years, she had served as America's "official widow," a position she never wanted and never enjoyed. "What would become of her if Bobby entered the White House?" wondered Buchwald. "Obviously, the only position open to her would be that of Queen Mother, an equally unwelcome role. I believe she found herself in an almost impossible situation. She didn't need or want to serve the nation as Queen Mother, but she also didn't want to deny Bobby his opportunity to occupy the White House. She had lovers, many more than people realized, but the only man she loved was Bobby Kennedy."

In researching his biography of Aristotle Onassis, British journalist Peter Evans unearthed a letter written about this time from Jackie to Ari, which began: "When death ends one dear relationship, it often creates another sweeter still." The letter, with its reference to the assassination of JFK, is, according to Evans, an attempt on Jackie's part to explain to Onassis why she would always be devoted to RFK. He would always be more to her than her husband's brother. "There was a time," read the same letter, "when Bobby meant more to me than life itself."

Chapter 10

◆

ETHEL KENNEDY'S relationship with Bobby, as their friends attested, had always been one of pupil and teacher. She learned from him and conducted her life predominantly to suit his needs. His interests became hers. She was more religious than her husband, and she attempted (not always successfully) to raise the children according to the teachings and dictates of the Catholic Church. After eighteen years of marriage, her love for her spouse seemed almost unconditional; it would be fair to say that she adored him. Like most of the other Kennedy wives, Ethel tended to ignore her husband's infidelities, the sole exception being his abiding and complex affair with Jackie Kennedy. By virtue of her romance with RFK, Jacqueline remained Ethel's chief tormentor, her arch nemesis. It was no accident that Ethel failed to invite her sister-in-law to Bobby's forty-second birthday party on November 20, 1967, a birthday celebration that, tragically, turned out to be his last.

"The possibility of a divorce never entered Ethel's mind," said Ken O'Donnell, "but you can well imagine how much the thought of Bobby's affair with Jackie must have bothered her. The thing is, she had no intention of confronting Jackie personally about the relationship. That would have been too demeaning. I'm not certain to what extent or how often she verbalized her innermost feelings to Bobby. Basically, she resorted to the same tactic so often employed by Jackie in dealing with JFK's rampant womanizing. Both women utilized a sense of humor in dealing with their respective spouses."

Ethel demonstrated an innate ability to poke fun at her errant husband. Whereas Jackie once seated Jack between two of his lovers at a White House dinner party, Ethel came up with her own version of the sit-down supper. In mid-January 1968, she arranged a dinner for fifty at Hickory Hill. The guest of honor that evening was astronaut John Glenn, the future Democratic senator from Ohio and a close friend of the Kennedys. Carefully arranging place cards for her guests, Ethel sat twenty-four women at one table and twenty-five men and herself at another. To drive home her point, RFK's wife wore a particularly low-cut evening gown. Even Bobby managed to find humor in his wife's somewhat less-than-subtle message.

Like most Kennedy men, when it came to relations with the opposite sex, RFK generally allowed himself to be guided by a well-defined and hypocritical double standard. "Had Ethel been involved with another man," remarked George Plimpton, "I'm certain Bobby would have murdered them both—and probably gotten away with it."

As for sixty-one-year-old Aristotle Onassis, although he would have preferred to wed Jackie sooner rather than later, he understood that were such a marriage to take place, it would most likely have to be put off until after the '68 election. "She's worth the wait," Ari informed Costa Gratsos, his legal representative in Athens. "There's something mystifying about her. She's willful and provocative. She possesses a carnal soul. She looks Greek but behaves like an American princess." The shipping tycoon never explained what he meant by "behaves like an American princess," though one can readily imagine it had something to do with her insatiable lust for spending.

In early February 1968, Onassis approached a friend, David Karr, a former public relations specialist from Washington, and asked him to plant an item in Drew Pearson's syndicated *Washington Post* political column. Pearson had been the first journalist to report on Joseph P. Kennedy's pro-Nazi leanings during his term as American ambassador to Great Britain. In 1961 he wrote that Ted Sorensen, and not JFK, had actually written *Profiles in Courage*. Two years later, he rattled on about Lee Radziwill's affair with Aristotle Onassis. An old acquaintance of Pearson, Dave Karr now gave the columnist a new Onassis tidbit, this one alleging that the Greek's relationship with Maria Callas was "on the rocks," and that the shipping magnate had recently "been seen" in the "cozy company" of Jacqueline Kennedy. The same column went on to accuse the Warren Commission of "not doing its job," adding that Robert Kennedy had also "dropped the ball" by failing to fully investigate his brother's murder. Pearson's story concluded with a question: "If Lee Harvey Oswald was simply a patsy, as he claimed, then who murdered President Kennedy?" The reason he planted the article, Onassis told Costa Gratsos, is that he wanted Bobby Kennedy to know "I'm still very much around—and I'm not going away."

The article angered Jackie more than it did RFK. To further complicate matters, she had recently started dating someone new. Born in New York in 1906, Roswell Gilpatric had earned a law degree from Yale and served the Kennedy administration as undersecretary of the Air Force and as deputy secretary of defense. Tall and dapper, Gilpatric and his wife lived at River House, a prestigious co-op apartment building overlooking the East River in Manhatttan. His affair with Jackie became a matter of public record on March 6, 1968, when he left his wife and joined Jackie on a ten-day trip to see the Mayan ruins in the Yucatán region of Mexico.

"I knew JFK when he first entered politics as a Massachusetts congressman," said Gilpatric, "and I met Jackie when she became First Lady. By coincidence, I'd been friendly with a man named John G. W. Husted Jr., a stockbroker from Connecticut who'd been engaged to Jackie before she married JFK. She broke up with him by dropping her engagement ring in his suit jacket pocket at the airport following a weekend visit he'd paid her in Washington. So my initial impression of her, before we met, was somewhat negative. But as I got to know Jackie, I came to appreciate her. She and Jack used to host informal get-togethers at the White House, which I attended. I also saw her at the Hickory Hill seminars, the glorified gatherings at McLean that featured

different speakers each month and which invariably resulted in somebody getting thrown into the Hickory Hill swimming pool by Ethel. In
addition, Jackie came out to my place on the Eastern Shore of Maryland one weekend during the White House years. We were only friends
at that point. The relationship evolved slowly after the assassination."

The strange thing about the Yucatán trip is that Jackie spoke candidly to Gilpatric of her relationships with Bobby Kennedy and Aristotle Onassis. She alluded to both, acknowledging that while she had
"great feelings" for Bobby, she was leaning toward the possibility of
marrying Onassis. During her Mexican sojourn, she called Ari in Paris.
She told Gilpatric that he wanted to set a wedding date. "All this transpired while she and I were having our little tryst," said Gilpatric. "In
fact, the minute I returned to New York, my wife served me with
divorce papers."

Covering the Mexican trip for *Women's Wear Daily,* journalist Agnes
Ash recalled that Jackie and Gilpatric indulged in "a lot of smooching
and hand-holding. They weren't shy. They were carrying on in full view
of the press. Of course, Jackie became indignant when we wrote that she
and Gilpatric were practically petting in public. She already had it out
for *WWD,* because over the years, we'd reported on how much she spent
on clothes. Jackie did her best to have me banned from the group.
Roswell Gilpatric, on the other hand, was very civil. It wasn't an official
government-sponsored trip, but the Mexican police were out in force.
Jackie also had several Secret Service agents in tow, including John
Walsh, who usually looked after Caroline and John Jr. I remember one
outing to the pyramids when Walsh, who towered over the rest of us,
was forced to ride along on a small donkey while everybody else rode
horseback. I reported the incident in *WWD,* and the next day Walsh
took me aside and said if I didn't watch myself, I might end up in a
Mexican jail."

Somehow Rose Kennedy got hold of a prepublication copy of Agnes
Ash's final article on the trip, which included photographs of Jackie and
Gilpatric cuddling and hugging during one of their daily outings. Rose
telephoned John Fairchild, editorial director of *WWD,* and asked him

to cancel the piece, claiming it would have an adverse effect on Jackie's children. "Her request seemed rather odd," said Ash, "considering that Caroline and John were too young to care about the periodical." Fairchild ran the last of Ash's articles, but agreed to "kill" the potentially embarrassing photographs.

While still in Mexico, Jackie received a phone call from RFK. Bobby told her he'd made up his mind to enter the presidential sweepstakes, regardless of the fact that the public would probably label him an "opportunist." Eugene McCarthy had emerged victorious from the New Hampshire Democratic primary, which no doubt influenced Bobby's decision—if he intended to win his party's nomination that summer, he could no longer procrastinate.

What, if anything, RFK might have said to Jackie about Roswell Gilpatric is not known. Bobby had always admired Gilpatric, long an outspoken critic of the Vietnam War. Realizing that he was on the verge of announcing his candidacy for the top spot on the Democratic Party ticket, RFK must have sensed that his romance with Jackie had reached an end point. She, too, understood that press and public alike would be scrutinizing Bobby with such intensity that their affair could not continue. Their love would endure, but practical necessity would force them to revert to what they had been before JFK's death: the dearest and closest of friends. Bobby's main concern with regard to Jackie at this point was to make certain she didn't "run off" with Aristotle Onassis until after the election.

At nine in the morning on Saturday, March 16, 1968, with Ethel by his side, Robert Kennedy entered the caucus room of the Old Senate Office Building in Washington to announce his bid for the presidency—not "merely to oppose any man, but to propose new policies . . . and because I have such strong feelings about what must be done, and I feel that I'm obliged to do all that I can." (In 1960, with Jackie by *his* side, John F. Kennedy had announced his presidential candidacy from the same spot in the same room.)

A day after his announcement, Bobby Kennedy flew to New York to take part in the St. Patrick's Day parade up Fifth Avenue. Marching behind members of the New York City Police Department, near the head of the March 17 procession, RFK was heckled by a group of Irish patriots as a traitor and friend of Hanoi. Others shouted, "Go back to Boston!" and "Get a haircut!" He received a warmer reception from Jackie, who had returned from Mexico the night before. As the parade passed 1040 Fifth Avenue, he caught sight of his sister-in-law leaning out an open window, blowing kisses at him. The streets were crammed with brass bands, motor-driven floats, firemen, students, babies, dogs, and spectators. Several teenage girls ("Bobby-soxers") broke through the police barricades, raced over to Kennedy, and embraced him. A cheer went up as he waved to the crowd.

That evening, accompanied by a group of friends, Jack Newfield among them, Bobby and Jackie dined at La Grenouille, a trendy French restaurant on East Fifty-second Street. As Charles Masson, the restaurant owner's son, later related the story to a writer for *Vanity Fair,* Bobby disrupted La Grenouille's sedate ambience by making a total spectacle of himself. "He was very drunk," noted Masson. Sampling his appetizer, RFK began to complain. In a shrill voice, he said, "This vichyssoise is canned." Masson's father approached the table with his wife, who also worked in the family-owned establishment. Taking great pride in his culinary skill, he said to his wife, "Will you kindly tell Senator Kennedy how I prepare the vichyssoise?" And she did, step by step, at the end of which RFK yelled, "I don't give a damn what you say—it's canned."

He wasn't done. Ordering raspberries with vanilla ice cream for dessert, RFK noticed that one of the raspberries had a blemish on it. He rose to his feet, held up the raspberry, and proclaimed, "At these prices, it's unacceptable for a restaurant to serve rotten raspberries."

Hearing this, the restaurant owner returned to the table. He'd endured enough. Slamming down his fist, he bellowed, "Just because there's one rotten Democratic senator doesn't mean all senators are bad! Now please get out of my restaurant."

Jack Newfield attributed RFK's poor behavior that evening to his having had too much to drink in an Irish bar following the St. Patrick's Day parade. "After dinner," said Newfield, "he brought Jackie home. I think he spent the night with her, because the next morning he called me from her apartment. He seemed morose. If I had to hazard a guess, I'd say this must have been their last romantic occasion together. After that night, Bobby became immersed in the presidential campaign, while Jackie turned her attention to more immediate concerns."

Newfield remembered an incident that took place at Hyannis Port the following weekend. The family had gathered at the compound to discuss campaign strategy. Ethel was there, and so was Jackie. In the middle of the discussion, Jackie offered some words of encouragement. "Won't it be wonderful when we're back in the White House?" she asked. To which Ethel replied, "What do you mean '*we*'? You're not running. This is our moment in the sun."

Although inured by this time to Ethel's often rude bluntness, Jackie knew that if Bobby were to become president, Ethel would indeed be anointed First Lady. If Jackie basked in the reflected glory of RFK's run for the roses, she nevertheless had to come to terms with reality. Her future lay outside the domain of Washington politics, whereas Ethel's lay within. Ethel, not Jackie, would become the proverbial power behind the throne. For all the love that had flowed between them, Bobby and Jackie were no longer a couple. That facet of their relationship was behind them. It was done.

In his book *The Kennedy Women,* author Laurence Leamer reports that Jackie spent "many hours" by herself the following day, walking the familiar grounds of the compound, "from the horse barns . . . to the beach on Squaw Island," where she, Jack, and the children had stayed one summer. That evening she visited Joe Kennedy, the stroke-addled, aphasic patriarch of the clan. She told him she'd done a lot of thinking that day. She then told the old man she loved him—and would always love him.

On March 31, Lyndon Johnson shocked the nation by announcing on television that he would neither seek nor accept his party's nomination for another term in office. By dropping out of the race, Johnson appeared to have paved the way for an RFK victory. As mystified as the rest of the nation by LBJ's withdrawal from the race, Jackie suddenly began to question Bobby's presidential quest. On April 2, she accompanied Arthur Schlesinger to a dinner party at the home of Diana Vreeland. "Do you know what I think will happen to Bobby?" she said to Schlesinger. "The same thing that happened to Jack. There is so much hatred in this country, and more people hate Bobby than hated Jack. That's why I don't want him to be president . . . I've told Bobby this, but he is fatalistic, like me."

Jackie's lament about a violent America was made only two days before the assassination of Martin Luther King Jr. in Memphis, Tennessee. Having entered the Indiana primary, Bobby was campaigning in Indianapolis on April 4 when an aide informed him that King had been fatally shot. That evening he broke the news to a shocked crowd gathered outside an Indianapolis housing project, where he'd been scheduled to deliver a speech. Ironically it had been Bobby, as attorney general, who had authorized the FBI wiretap on King's private telephone line, a deed he'd performed at the request of J. Edgar Hoover. King's murder reminded RFK of his brother's untimely death. "Will this crap never end?" he said to Jack Newfield.

Coretta Scott King, wife of the fallen black leader, spoke to Bobby a day after her husband's assassination. She wanted to know if he could persuade Jacqueline Kennedy to join him in Atlanta for the funeral on April 7. Although Jackie would have preferred to meet with the family after the funeral, she agreed to attend out of devotion to Bobby. Arriving the day of the funeral, the former First Lady met privately with Mrs. King. Overcome by her own feelings of despair and depression, Jackie would tell RFK that she had lost complete faith in the country. "America is going to the dogs," she said. "I don't know why you want to be president."

Bernard Fensterwald Jr., the attorney for James Earl Ray, the man convicted of King's assassination, later noted that Jackie Kennedy and Coretta Scott King "were in the same boat. Mrs. King resented her husband for all his womanizing but molded herself after Jackie. Her per-

formance at the funeral was right on cue. Both women played the mar-
tyr role to perfection. In both cases, their performance served a noble
purpose. In my humble opinion, neither one of them was as distraught
as they appeared. The only difference is that Mrs. King didn't turn
around and get married to Aristotle Onassis."

Fred Dutton, an attorney who'd previously worked in JFK's White
House, had accepted RFK's offer to serve as his campaign manager. Senator Ted Kennedy, as close now to Bobby as Bobby had been to Jack,
served as chief troubleshooter for the campaign. Dutton and Teddy
agreed that of all the Kennedys, none was more vital to the family's political interests than Jacqueline Kennedy. As the guiding light of the JFK
Library and as a genuine American heroine whose name carried univer-
sal appeal, she could almost single-handedly make or break the clan's
manifold efforts to secure Bobby's victory. Given Jackie's past sacrifices,
even Ethel had to grudgingly admit that she was "as much a Kennedy"
at this point as any of them. Her ongoing, behind-the-scenes political
advice to Bobby helped shape the preponderance of his campaign strategy. Jackie had come a long way since her earliest days with JFK.

"Jackie's very special," Ted Kennedy told Ken O'Donnell. "She's
iconic." There were moments, he admitted, when he would stare at her,
drinking in her dark beauty. He found her "incredibly alluring." When
she married Jack, Ted told his brother, "You've got yourself the world's
most ravishing woman." When JFK died, Teddy held her in his arms
for "what seemed an eternity." She had a devastating effect on all the
Kennedy men. From the beginning, Bobby and Teddy constantly vied
for her attention and approval. Sensitive to Ethel's feelings, Teddy
refused every opportunity to discuss Jackie's love affair with Bobby.
"Some things are better left unsaid," he remarked on one occasion, a
tacit acknowledgment that he knew of their liaison but didn't wish to
comment on it.

One of Jackie's self-appointed tasks on behalf of the RFK campaign
was that of major fund-raiser. She went back to many of the same tried-
and-true contributors from whom she'd solicited funds in the past. "I

have my pride," she told Evangeline Bruce, "but not when it comes to raising funds for Bobby." Although she feared for his safety, she felt compelled to help in any way she could. She flew to Palm Beach and stayed at the estate of Charles and Jayne Wrightsman, with whom she had squabbled several years before; they wrote out a huge check. She located new donors as well. She approached Felix Rohatyn, André Meyer's partner at Lazard Frères, and talked him into making a sizable contribution; attracted to Rohatyn, she would have a short-lived affair with him in the late 1970s. She invited actor Gregory Peck to accompany her to the Wildenstein & Co. gallery in New York and cajoled him into handing over a large sum of money. She contacted architect I. M. Pei and philanthropist Doris Duke, arguably the wealthiest woman in the world, and took them to dinner at a Chinese restaurant. Just as Jackie was about to bring up Bobby's campaign, she heard a clicking sound from behind a nearby coatrack. Photographer Ron Galella had prevailed upon a waiter to sneak him into the restaurant, and he was now frantically snapping away with his camera. The evening broke up quickly, but not before Jackie managed to extract generous donations from her dinner guests.

Although Galella used Jackie to advance his career as a paparazzo, he remained one of her primary detractors. "She was the biggest hypocrite of them all," he claimed. "Rich, haughty, and a snob, she kept a secret scrapbook filled with press photographs of herself." Galella learned of the supposed scrapbook's existence by dating one of Jackie's household maids. What neither the maid nor Galella knew was that Jackie possessed a half-dozen personal scrapbooks put together for her by a newspaper clipping service based in Tampa, Florida.

The only scrapbook she compiled on her own, a thick leather-bound volume with the letters *RFK* embossed on its spine, contained several hundred newspaper and magazine snapshots of Bobby Kennedy that she had painstakingly arranged as a tribute to her brother-in-law.

With Bobby no longer a romantic consideration in Jackie's life, Aristotle Onassis traveled to New York to visit the former First Lady. They were seen together at El Morocco, 21, and the Oak Room at the Plaza. Thanks to Jackie's maid, Ron Galella seemed to know exactly where they would be and at what time they would be there. When one of his photographs of the couple appeared on the front page of the *New York Post,* Jackie heard from her friend Joan Braden.

"Jackie, if you marry that man, you're going to fall off your pedestal," she said.

"Better to fall off than to get frozen to it," countered Jackie.

Roswell Gilpatric also read the *Post* that day. "Jackie and I were still dating," he recalled, "but I entertained few illusions. I certainly couldn't afford to maintain the lady in the style to which she'd grown accustomed. Onassis could. I don't believe she loved him. I think she admired him. He was self-made, self-taught, self-assured, and rich as hell. Jackie had always been drawn to men like Onassis. In a violent and turbulent age, he could protect her and her children. Which is not to say that I didn't have regrets. I would have wanted to marry her myself. But then so too would a lot of men."

Bobby, involved in a grueling political campaign that took him and his team of advisors and aides to a different city and state almost daily, filled his few off-hours by launching into a new affair of his own. Mary Jo Kopechne, twenty-seven, had blond hair, blue eyes, and a pretty face. Born in Forty Fort, Pennsylvania, she graduated from Caldwell College and for a year taught elementary school in Montgomery, Alabama. In 1963 she went to Washington and accepted a secretarial position with Senator George Smathers. It was through Smathers that she met the Kennedys. Later she worked for Joe Dolan, legal advisor to RFK. When Bobby became a senator, she transferred to his secretarial pool, sharing a Georgetown townhouse with four other women her age, all of them members of Bobby's staff. During his run for the presidency, this enclave became known as the Boiler Room Girls.

"Although she no longer worked for me," said George Smathers, "Mary Jo and I stayed in touch. I'd become her father confessor, so to speak. She was young, sweet, and impressionable. When she informed me that Bobby had invited her to join him as a secretary on the presidential campaign plane, I warned her against it. I knew Bobby, and I knew that he would take advantage of the situation. And that's precisely what happened. It didn't matter to him whether Ethel was also on the plane. They'd check into hotels at night, and Mary Jo would be given her own room. It didn't take much for Bobby to excuse himself from a strategy meeting for a few minutes and go visit Mary Jo in her room. Nobody was the wiser for it. It reminded me a little of Jack when he campaigned for the presidency in 1960, except that Jackie wasn't around most of the time."

As history has informed us, the Mary Jo Kopechne story ended on a most tragic note. At 11:15 p.m., on July 18, 1969, slightly more than a year after RFK's assassination, Senator Ted Kennedy drove Kopechne from a beach party for the Boiler Room Girls to the ferry on Chappaquiddick, an islet off Martha's Vineyard. Ted's 1967 Oldsmobile went off a bridge and sank in a shallow ocean-fed pond. Teddy escaped, returned to the hotel on Martha's Vineyard where the group was staying, went to his room, and placed a number of telephone calls. One of the first went to Jacqueline Kennedy in New York. He then called his cousin, Joe Gargan, who had arranged the weekend party as a way to thank the Boiler Room Girls for their loyalty and allegiance to RFK. Gargan later told a friend, a lawyer named Eugene Girden, that Teddy had asked him to say he—and not Teddy—had been at the wheel of the car when it went into the water; Gargan flatly refused. More than nine hours elapsed before Teddy called the Massachusetts State Police to report the accident. The delay suggested that the senator from Massachusetts had been inebriated at the time of the mishap.

An autopsy revealed that Mary Jo Kopechne had survived for up to an hour in a small air pocket that had formed inside the car. Had Ted Kennedy reported the accident at once, her life might have been saved. For his role in Mary Jo's death, Ted Kennedy received a slap on the wrist: a two-month suspended sentence. Teddy, Joan, and Ethel Kennedy attended Mary Jo's funeral. Evidently Ethel had no idea that the dead girl had been her husband's last mistress; Jackie learned of their affair, but only long after the fact. Joan Kennedy, seemingly more upset than anyone, suffered a miscarriage one week after the funeral. Ted Kennedy spoke on national television, blaming his failure to take action in the case on "a jumble of emotions." A cursory investigation by the Massachusetts District Attorney's office proved inconclusive. The DA's case files on Ted's involvement mysteriously disappeared a year later and were never recovered. Mary Jo's death by drowning very likely cost Ted Kennedy any chance he might have had of ever being elected president of the United States. He ran in 1980, but failed to win his party's nomination.

Only thirteen states participated in the Democratic Party primary process in 1968. Indiana's May 7 primary was the first such contest Bobby Kennedy entered. He won by some fifteen percentage points, enough of a margin to bring an exuberant smile to his face. He won the Washington, D.C., primary, held the same day, even more decisively. "We're on our way!" he told his staff.

A day after RFK's victory, Aristotle Onassis turned up in New York, retrieved Jackie, and flew with her and John Jr. to Palm Beach aboard an Olympic Airways jetliner. Tipped off to the couple's arrival, local society photographer Bob Davidoff drove to West Palm Beach Airport to meet the plane. "I drove my car right onto the tarmac and sat there waiting for them," explained Davidoff. "The plane landed, and Jackie stepped off with John Jr. She allowed me to take a few photographs, then slipped into a waiting limousine and was driven off. I knew Onassis was still aboard and was waiting for me to disappear so he could disembark. There was a second limo parked on the tarmac waiting for him. I had my grown son Ken with me, and we were determined to sit there all day if necessary. Finally a female flight attendant exited the plane and approached me. 'I hope you took some nice pictures of Mrs. Kennedy,' she remarked, 'because she was our only passenger of note.' I told her I was hoping to get a photo of Aristotle Onassis. 'Oh, but he's not here,' she said. 'He's not on the flight.' 'Well, if it's all right with you, I'll just wait around,' I responded. 'I have nothing better to do.' 'Suit yourself,' she said. She returned to the plane and quickly came out again. This time she said that Ari's brother was aboard, but not Aristotle Onassis. I knew perfectly well that Onassis had a sister but not a brother. 'No problem,' I told her. 'I'll stay put and see what develops.' "

A few minutes elapsed and Aristotle Onassis appeared, dressed in his customary black business suit. Davidoff went up to him and, while they were conversing, his son took photographs. "You fellows are very persistent, but unfortunately I'm not the person you want," said Onassis. "I'm only his brother. Ari's in Athens at the moment. He asked me to accompany Mrs. Kennedy and her son to Palm Beach."

"That's strange," said Davidoff in response, "because I met and photographed Aristotle Onassis once before when he was with Maria Callas. You not only look exactly like him, you sound like him as well."

"We're practically identical twins," murmured Onassis as he walked in the direction of his limousine.

Onassis, Jackie, and John Jr. spent several days at the Wrightsmans' but made no public appearances. They returned to New York, where Jackie dropped off her son before joining Onassis aboard the *Christina* for a short cruise to the Virgin Islands. On May 17, with Jackie again ensconced in her Fifth Avenue apartment and Robert Kennedy on the campaign trail, a correspondent for *The Times* of London interviewed Onassis at a cocktail party at the Hotel George V in Paris. Asked his opinion of the former First Lady, he said: "Mrs. Kennedy is a totally misunderstood woman. Perhaps she even misunderstands herself. She's being held up as a model of propriety, constancy, and so many of those boring American female virtues. She's now utterly devoid of mystery. She needs a small scandal to bring her alive—a peccadillo, an indiscretion. Something should happen to her to win our fresh compassion. The world loves to pity fallen grandeur."

The comment, which was reprinted in every major international newspaper, including *The New York Times* and *The Washington Post,* rankled Bobby Kennedy to such an extent, claimed Pierre Salinger, that he placed a direct call to Onassis and threatened to have his oil tankers permanently banned from American ports, along with their owner, if he didn't immediately cease and desist from making public statements about Jackie. He feared, not for the first time, that the Greek was about to create a scandal of his own either by announcing his and Jackie's imminent betrothal or by disclosing that she and Bobby had been ardent lovers for a number of years.

Besides contacting Onassis by phone, RFK dispatched Ethel and Joan Kennedy to their sister-in-law's apartment to discuss the situation. "Given Ethel's dispassion for Jackie, I don't know how he convinced her to go," said Pierre Salinger. "But she consented and went. The two of them—Joan and Ethel—sat with Jackie in her magnificent living room and pleaded with her not to marry Onassis. If she found it absolutely necessary to marry him, then she mustn't do so until after the November election. Such an action with all the negative publicity attached to it would irrevocably damage Bobby's chances for the presidency."

Bobby was the next visitor. Interrupting his campaign to fly to New York for a face-to-face with Jackie, he arrived at her apartment with Jean Kennedy Smith, who was closer to the former First Lady than any of her sisters. "From what I heard," continued Salinger, "Jackie was very sweet about it, assuring them she had no intention of marrying Onassis until after the election, if she married him at all. Bobby seemed dubious. He entreated Jackie to speak to the Greek and get him to stop making controversial pronouncements in the press. Jean Smith concluded the discussion by saying, 'I'm sure Ari's the sweetest fellow on earth. He's certainly the wealthiest fellow on the planet. Your association with him might be taken the wrong way. And Bobby might not get a second chance.' "

Pierre Salinger had a subsequent conversation with RFK about the possibility of Jackie marrying Onassis: "I asked Bobby what he planned to do about their nuptials should he win the presidency. 'She'll marry that man over my dead body,' he responded. 'I'll deal with it when the time comes.' "

Chapter 11

◆

To the dismay of practically everyone who knew him, Robert Kennedy campaigned for the presidency essentially without benefit of security, the same way he'd campaigned for his senatorial seat. Eschewing the Secret Service detail to which he was entitled, as well as local police representation, he resorted to such private "bodyguards" as ex-FBI agent Bill Barry and former professional football player Roosevelt (Rosey) Grier, neither of whom he would allow to carry a gun.

Although on the face of it all this seemed quite extraordinary—and dangerous—he obviously had his reasons. In the first place, he wanted to appear fearless, not at all cowed or intimidated by the assassination of his brother; second, his personal style entailed reaching out to the people, placing as few obstacles as possible between himself and the crowd; and third, he had long since lost any faith he might once have had in the Secret Service—after all, look at what had happened to Jack. "If someone wants to get me, they'll get me, with or without the Secret Service," he said over and over again. As president-elect, JFK had issued practically the same statement.

Despite the Secret Service Agency's failure to protect John Kennedy, Bobby's decision to campaign without benefit of proper security made little sense. Anonymous death threats against him were so plentiful and commonplace that J. Edgar Hoover would have had to establish a special unit to properly investigate the origins of the dozens of letters that passed across his desk. After Bobby announced his candidacy, his hate mail increased tenfold. The hard-core right-wing press had issued a call to arms: "RFK Must Die!" shrieked the headline of one Bible Belt periodical. In Washington, D.C., the FBI arrested a man who had been impersonating RFK, checking in and out of hotels, using forged identity papers, charging thousands of dollars to Kennedy's personal account. Another arrest took place at New York's JFK International Airport: a homeless man carrying a concealed .44 handgun had followed RFK to his departure gate before being apprehended.

"When I read accounts of the two arrests—the one in New York, the other in Washington—I couldn't help but recall Jackie Kennedy's dire words of warning to me about Bobby," said Arthur Schlesinger. "Indeed, death seemed to be everywhere in the air."

"There was a kind of madness to the campaign," recalled Ken O'Donnell. "Bobby would sit in the back of the plane wrapped up in Jack's old topcoat, as if communing with his dead brother. On the ground, he insisted on riding around in an open convertible, which is how JFK got killed. When the motorcade stopped, Bobby would invariably hop out and disappear into the crowd. Whenever I warned him of the possible danger, he'd respond, 'These are my kind of people.' I couldn't take it anymore. I called Jackie one day and asked her to speak to Bobby about reinstating his Secret Service coverage. 'I've already tried, Ken,' she said. 'He won't do it.' "

"I sometimes thought that Jack Kennedy had come back and was again running for president in the person of his younger brother; a sort of reincarnation," said Larry O'Brien. "Bobby had so many of Jack's mannerisms. For example, when he walked along, he'd thrust a hand into the side pocket of his suit jacket. He also shared Jack's love of danger. Nothing intimidated him. I remember eating lunch with him at some truck-stop diner outside Omaha, Nebraska, where he'd entered the May 14 primary, the first one after Indiana. We were discussing the likelihood of Richard Nixon being named the Republican Party presidential candidate that summer. Across the aisle at another booth sat four of the roughest, toughest-looking hombres I'd ever seen. They started mouthing off at us. They were drunk. Two of them stood up and ambled over to our booth. They were looking for a fight, but Bobby didn't take shit from anyone. 'Why don't you fellows simmer down and go back to your seats,' he said in a subdued but forceful voice. And I'll be damned if that's not exactly what they did. Unfortunately, it was Bobby's boldness that ultimately led to his undoing. You had the feeling—we all did—that sooner or later something bad was going to happen to him.'"

RFK won the Nebraska primary, and the polls predicted future victories for him in Oregon on May 28, California and South Dakota on June 4, and New York on June 18. Regardless of Bobby's growing optimism, his advisors and handlers remained critical of the candidate's failure to take proper security precautions. Pierre Salinger, sharing press agent operations during the campaign with Frank Mankiewicz, had tried putting aside the idea of assassination. But when he met up with an old friend, the French writer and statesman Romain Gary, over drinks, Gary said, "You know, Pierre, your guy will be killed."

"Why do you think so?" asked Salinger.

"He's too irresistible a temptation for the American paranoiac personality," answered the Frenchman. "He's too provocative, too rich, too young, too handsome, too photogenic, too successful, too lucky. He arouses in every 'persecuted' type a deep sense of injustice."

A few days later, Salinger arranged for RFK to have dinner with Romain Gary and his wife, actress Jean Seberg. The same subject came up. "What precautions are you taking?" the writer asked RFK.

"There's no way to protect a candidate who's stumping the country," responded Bobby. "No way at all. You've just got to give yourself to the people and trust them. From then on, it's largely a matter of luck."

They began discussing political affairs in France, and Bobby brought up Charles de Gaulle. How many attempts had been made on de Gaulle's life, he wanted to know.

"Six or seven—none of them successful," Gary responded.

"I told you—luck," Bobby said. "You can't make it without that old bitch luck."

George Plimpton joined Bobby's campaign during the third week of May. In his opinion, Bobby was a disaster waiting to happen. "The better he did in the polls, the more chances he seemed willing to take," said Plimpton. "I used to sit around with the press, the boys in the bus, and inevitably the subject of death would come up. With JFK and Martin Luther King gone, it seemed an almost forgone conclusion that someone would try to add Bobby to the list."

Plimpton recalled journalist Jimmy Breslin asking a group of reporters covering the campaign if they thought Bobby had the "stuff" to go all the way. "He has the stuff to go all the way," replied *Newsweek's* John J. Lindsay, "but he isn't going to make it. The reason is that somebody is going to shoot him. I know it and you know it . . . He's out there now waiting for him with a gun."

Feeling guilty about not being on the road show with Bobby and his entourage, Jackie Kennedy offered to join the campaign in Oregon. She likewise offered to stand in for him in South Dakota, a state in which RFK planned on spending only a few days. To avoid domestic problems with Ethel, the presidential hopeful advised his sister-in-law to stay put and do what she was doing. Her fund-raising efforts continued. Bobby would need a large infusion of money if—and when—he became his party's presidential nominee at that August's Democratic National Convention, to be held in Mayor Richard Daley's Chicago. Daley, a major backer of John F. Kennedy, had pledged to support JFK's younger brother just as ardently in the event of his nomination.

Roswell Gilpatric recalled that Jackie aided the cause as more than just a fund-raiser. She used to send Bobby copies of humorous little poems she'd written to "cheer him up." She sent Adam Wallinsky, one of his speechwriters, notes on what information to include in the candidate's presentations. She sent RFK health-food recipes for high-energy milk shakes containing fruit, nuts, grains, yogurt, and raw eggs. "Jackie still had enormous affection for Bobby," said Gilpatric. "She worried about him. She felt he was driving himself too hard. They spoke on the phone every evening, Jackie imparting all sorts of campaign advice. Not that Bobby needed her input, but he listened and as often as not followed her suggestions.

"Jackie constantly reminded RFK that in addition to his main constituency—the old, the young, the poor, and the disenfranchised—he had to draw upon a broader audience if he hoped to win a national election. She encouraged him to be pragmatic as well as idealistic. It was not enough to say that the Vietnam War had to end; he had to indicate in concrete terms *how* he intended to end it. She was currently far more interested in political affairs than she'd been when Jack was alive. We attended a party at the Park Avenue apartment of Arlene Francis and her husband, theater producer Martin Gabel, and she spent the entire evening discussing the relative merits of RFK versus Eugene McCarthy, explaining why her brother-in-law had a better chance to win the presidential election than any of his Democratic Party opponents."

Moreso than Eugene McCarthy, RFK's major potential opponent for top spot on the Democratic Party ticket was Vice President Hubert Humphrey. In a May 20, 1968, letter to RFK, Jackie wrote: "If he endorses anybody, LBJ will probably come out for Humphrey. At his best, H.H. seems disaffected, remote, not entirely plugged in—I don't consider him serious competition for you. He has beady eyes and a tinny voice. When he speaks, he sounds like he's drowning. People associate him with an unpopular administration. In the end, he won't make it any more than McCarthy."

The Oregon campaign proved more problematic than anyone in Bobby's camp expected. His lead in the statewide polls gradually dwindled. His talks on poverty, race, unemployment, and hunger were wasted on the generally well-heeled, mostly white, predominantly employed populace. After addressing a group of electronics workers outside Portland, Bobby said to Fred Dutton, "What's wrong with these people? They're unaware of what's going on—the campus riots, urban turmoil, the Vietnamese War. I don't get it." Hearing of his difficulties, Jackie sent Bobby a telegram. "Next time you give a speech up there, try wearing a knapsack. The Oregonians will love you. Camping is all they care about."

In his own campaign speeches in Oregon, Eugene McCarthy took Bobby to task, accusing him of being "a spoiled little rich kid who can't run this race without his dog, his astronaut, and his father's millions."

In his next address, RFK responded in kind. "I don't mind his taking issue with John Glenn or Dad's money," he said, "but let's leave Freckles out of this. That cocker spaniel goes everywhere with me."

"To be frank," said George Plimpton, "Freckles was sometimes a more suitable companion than Ethel, who could be very difficult, very excitable, often yelling and screaming about something or other. Fred Dutton couldn't stand her. She could be a real pain in the butt. She suffered from high blood pressure, I think, and she hated to fly. It occurred to me at one point that she might be manic-depressive and needed to be on medication. Later it turned out she was pregnant again, which may have added to her discomfort. I remember one day in particular when she carried on for hours about her hairdo. Travel brought out the worst in her. Fortunately, she was only a part-timer on the campaign trail. It was a lot easier for everyone, especially Bobby, when she wasn't around."

McCarthy won the day in Oregon with 44.7 percent to Bobby's 38.8 percent. RFK was shaken. The real winner, he told a reporter, was Hubert Humphrey, "because McCarthy won't get the Democratic nod under any circumstances." Then, in a lighter tone: "Perhaps I ought to consider sending Freckles back home to Hickory Hill."

After RFK's defeat in Oregon, winning the California primary became almost imperative. On May 29, he toured Los Angeles, dubbing it "Resurrection City" after he received the kind of ecstatic welcome he had been accorded on a regular basis prior to Oregon. California, with its large African-American and Hispanic populations, provided a natural environment for his appeal. Cesar Chavez had launched a massive voter registration drive, and Jesse Unruh, the prominent California politician, put the state party's apparatus to work on Bobby's behalf. Steve Smith took charge of the southern half of the state, establishing headquarters in Los Angeles, while RFK advisor John Seigenthaler managed

the northern half from San Francisco. With its 174 winner-take-all delegates, California was the nation's leading electoral vote state. In Jackie
Kennedy's words, it represented "the whole damn pizza."

As Bobby and his faithful troops traveled the state, the TV evening
news burst forth with stories on student takeovers at Stanford, Berkeley, the University of Chicago, and Columbia University; Abbie Hoffman, crown prince of the hippie/Yippie (Youth International Party)
subculture, calling for an end to higher education; the Black Panthers,
a paramilitary organization, threatening to crush "white supremacist
America." The Movement, as it became known, seemed to swirl around
Bobby's head. He was the Movement's object of adulation, as well as its
central target of hostility.

"You and Freckles," Jackie wired him in California, "are tomorrow's
best hope."

On Saturday, June 1, Robert Kennedy and Eugene McCarthy met
in San Francisco for an hour-long televised debate. Viewers denoted
only two major points of difference between them. McCarthy said that
if elected he would terminate J. Edgar Hoover as FBI director; RFK,
aware of the sex files on him and his family that Hoover possessed,
made no such commitment. The only other topic that provided drama
involved urban policy. And in this area, Kennedy showed himself to be
the more knowledgeable of the two. McCarthy argued that Third
World families should be dispersed from the ghetto, while Bobby called
for reconstruction of existing neighborhoods, a program similar to the
Bedford-Stuyvesant project. According to the following day's edition of
the *San Francisco Chronicle,* RFK had "mopped the floor" with
McCarthy.

On June 2, Bobby and Ethel, six of their children, Freckles, and an
assortment of aides, friends, relatives, and reporters checked into the
Ambassador Hotel in downtown Los Angeles. A bouquet of flowers and
a magnum of champagne awaited RFK in his hotel quarters (room 516,
the Royal Suite, on the fifth floor); accompanying these items was a
handwritten note, which read: "The flowers are for your room, and the
champagne is for after you win the primary. Jackie." Later that day,

Ethel described the gifts to Pierre Salinger and said, "Doesn't that woman ever stop?"

On Monday, June 3, twenty-four hours before the start of balloting, RFK rose at dawn, met with his advisors, and began an eleven-hundred-mile campaign run that took the candidate from L.A. to San Francisco, Long Beach, Watts, Venice, Santa Monica, San Diego, then back to L.A. From the airport in San Francisco, the first stop of the day, RFK's motorcade drove to Chinatown. Kristi Witker, a future television news anchor who had been on the campaign trail with Bobby from the beginning, sat in a crowded car close behind the candidate and his wife. She described the scene in Chinatown as "a mass of churning, burning humanity closing in on Bobby, their hands grabbing his hands, several of the onlookers trying to hurl themselves into his convertible. For me it was a frightening experience, but Bobby loved the feeling of that flesh-on-flesh contact he maintained with the public. I said something about all the cuff links he'd lost to crowds during the campaign. 'Nixon's worn the same pair of cuff links since 1945,' said Dick Dragne, one of Bobby's assistant press secretaries. We both laughed. Then without warning, there were repeated sharp popping sounds that made our words echo and the surrounding streets spin. Ethel had reached out and pulled Bobby down beside her. My first thought was, 'My God, it can't be—it just can't be.' And it wasn't. Someone said, 'It's firecrackers.' Ethel and Bobby sat up, and the street stopped spinning. But I remember that stark, stark feeling of terror."

Thunderous ovations greeted RFK at each of his rally stops. As he stood at a makeshift podium in Long Beach, an unshaven, disheveled-looking male bystander ran up and screamed, "Hey, Mr. Kennedy, who killed your brother?" As Rafer Johnson, the Olympic decathlon champion and the newest member of Bobby's homespun security team, stepped in front of the podium, the man shrank back into the crowd.

Sunny skies had turned to mist by the time they reached San Diego. Night had fallen as they arrived at San Diego's El Cortez Hotel, where Bobby gave another rousing speech. Afterward, while stalwarts and staff members partied late into the night in RFK's suite at the Ambassador

Hotel in Los Angeles, Bobby, Ethel, and their children went to Malibu to stay with movie director and family friend John Frankenheimer, whose most celebrated film was probably *The Manchurian Candidate*.

Physically and mentally drained, RFK nevertheless stayed up until two-thirty in the morning conversing with Frankenheimer in the director's study. "We sipped scotch and made small talk," said Frankenheimer in 2001, a year before his death. "At some point, Bobby looked at his watch and asked if he could use the telephone to call Jacqueline Kennedy. 'Won't she be asleep?' I inquired. It was three hours later in New York. 'She's expecting my call,' he said. I started to leave the room, but he beckoned me to stay. They spoke for roughly ten minutes, mostly about JFK's 1960 presidential campaign. 'Jack didn't think he'd win,' Bobby was saying. 'He didn't even expect to live very long—he had Addison's disease.' On this note, Jackie must have said something about Andy Warhol, who'd been gunned down earlier in the day by some demented feminist named Valerie Solanas; the artist was still alive. When he got off the phone, Bobby said to me, 'Did you know about Warhol?' I told him I'd heard it on the evening news. He shook his head back and forth several times. Then he said, 'This country has gone mad, absolutely mad.' "

On Tuesday, June 4, at noon, Jackie Kennedy appeared at RFK campaign headquarters in New York. Standing next to Roswell Gilpatric, who had accompanied her, she posed for press photographers. In the background loomed a poster of Robert Kennedy. Reluctantly, she agreed to an impromptu press conference.

"Do you think Bobby will win the California primary today?" asked a reporter.

"I'm keeping my fingers crossed," she said.

"If he becomes president," asked a second journalist, "will he follow up on the work John F. Kennedy started when he was president?"

"I assume he'll continue some of President Kennedy's programs," she remarked, "but I'm also certain he'll undertake a number of his own. The country faces a whole new set of problems."

The same journalist asked the former First Lady if she thought RFK would end the war in Vietnam.

"Ending the war is one of his main objectives."

"Are you planning to marry Aristotle Onassis?" shouted another correspondent.

"I'm here today in support of Senator Robert F. Kennedy," Jackie noted. "I haven't given any thought to my own future plans. I just want Bobby to win—first the California primary and then, hopefully, the presidency."

Over lunch that afternoon at the Colony, Jackie said to Gilpatric, "Bobby's different from most contemporary politicians. He's not pre-programmed or manufactured. He doesn't have some public relations firm telling him what to do or what to say. Bobby is Bobby. He's a real person, a human being. He is who he is. Even if you don't like his politics, you have to admire him for his courage and for the way he presents himself to the world."

Later that afternoon, Jackie and Gilpatric attended a rally for Bobby in front of the United Nations. Fearing further questions regarding her relationship with Aristotle Onassis, Jackie refused to speak to the press.

Bobby and Ethel slept late the morning of June 4, while their children played on the private beach adjacent to the Frankenheimer estate in Malibu. It was a windy, overcast day. The sea was rough, but the kids dashed in and out of the water. When Bobby awoke, he joined them on the beach. David Kennedy, two weeks short of his thirteenth birthday, waded into the surf with his father when suddenly a wave came and enveloped them. They disappeared beneath the churning whitecaps for a few anxious moments, and when they reemerged, Bobby had hold of his son. David was spewing up seawater, and Bobby had sustained a cut over his eye.

The candidate walked up to the swimming pool, near the house, for lunch. He was joined by Fred Dutton, novelist Budd Schulberg, and speechwriter Richard Goodwin, as well as Theodore White, who was covering the campaign for *Life*. After lunch, Bobby went to his room for a few additional hours of rest. Around three, Ethel asked Bob Galland, the children's twenty-one-year-old caretaker, and Diane Broughton to take the youngsters to the Beverly Hills Hotel, where they would be staying that night in two bungalows. After feeding the youngest of the RFK progeny and leaving them with Broughton, Galland would bring the others to the Ambassador Hotel to be with their parents.

At 6:15 p.m., John Frankenheimer drove RFK and Fred Dutton from Malibu to the Ambassador, where in RFK's suite the campaign organizers would monitor returns and, they hoped, celebrate the triumph that would catapult their man to his party's presidential nomination. As Frankenheimer gunned his car down the Santa Monica Freeway, attempting to make the forty-minute drive in half that time, Dutton turned on the radio to hear that early exit polls predicted an RFK triumph. "Hey, John, slow down," cautioned Bobby. "I want to live long enough to savor my victory."

RFK entered the fifth-floor suite at seven, an hour before the polls closed. Jean Kennedy Smith and Pat Kennedy Lawford were already there, as were Richard Goodwin, Ted Sorensen, Jesse Unruh, Dave Hackett, Jimmy Breslin, Kristi Witker, George Plimpton, Chuck Spalding, and others. All were drinking and watching last-minute updates on television. A call came from Malibu to say that Ethel had left twenty minutes earlier and would soon arrive at the hotel. Ted Kennedy, watching the election returns in San Francisco, called to wish his brother luck.

The Embassy Room, a vast ballroom on the second floor of the Ambassador, had been decorated with banners, balloons, and posters. At the front entrance, guests were handed campaign buttons that read "All the Way with RFK" and "Kennedy Power." The room had rapidly begun to fill with supporters, campaign workers, reporters, and television camera crews. Service bars on both sides of the room were dispensing free beer and wine. Champagne bottles came out when CBS-TV announced that RFK appeared to have won the South Dakota primary by a resounding two-to-one margin.

The minute the balloting in California ended, all three major television networks (CBS, NBC, and ABC) began reporting that Bobby would win the state. "A wide grin spread across his boyish face," said George Plimpton. "A loud cheer went up in the suite. Ethel reacted by bouncing up and down like a little kid on one of the beds. Bobby lit a cigar and gave several brief telephone interviews—to NBC's Sander Vanocur and CBS's Roger Mudd, among others. Somebody screeched, 'We've got it! We've got it!' Steve Smith and Fred Dutton spent the next two hours mapping out future campaign plans. 'I don't think we'll have any trouble winning the New York primary,' Smith said. At about ten, Bobby asked me to call Jackie for him. With Ethel present, he didn't want to place the call himself. So I left the suite and called her from my room down the hall. There was a good deal of static on the line, but she caught the gist of it and said, 'Tell Bobby I love him.' There was so much going on at the time that I never managed to give Bobby her message."

At 10:30 p.m., Bob Galland left the suite to bring Bobby and Ethel's children back to the Beverly Hills Hotel. At 10:45, Eugene McCarthy's face suddenly appeared on camera as he gave a brief and grudging concession speech, vowing that he had "just begun to fight." Thirty minutes later, Pierre Salinger called upstairs from the Embassy Room and assured Bobby that he could come down and deliver his victory speech with the certainty that he'd won the California primary.

Kristi Witker encountered RFK at 11:45 p.m. in the corridor outside his suite. His entourage was slowly gathering for the trek to the Embassy Room. When he saw her, he stopped and whispered, "We're having a victory party at the Factory nightclub afterward—everybody's invited. Will you come?" Elated that Bobby had won in California, Witker readily agreed to attend. "It promised to be a wonderful night," she said in later years. "Bobby was on top of the world."

By the time he appeared before the cheering throng in the ballroom of the Ambassador Hotel, the tally of the balloting gave RFK a clear-cut 5 percent victory margin over Eugene McCarthy. Standing before a bank of microphones mounted atop a three-foot-high platform, he signaled for silence and then thanked Steve Smith, Cesar Chavez, Jesse Unruh, Rafer Johnson, Rosey Grier, Ted Kennedy, Freckles, Ethel (who stood next to him), and pitcher Don Drysdale, who that very night had hurled a record-breaking sixth straight shutout for the Los Angeles Dodgers.

He ended his two-and-a-half-minute speech by promising that if he were elected president, he would unite a nation ravaged by "the divisions, the violence, the disenchantment" between blacks and whites, the poor and the more affluent, or between age groups—or over the war in Vietnam.

"We are a great country," he concluded, "an unselfish country, and a compassionate country . . . So my thanks to all of you, and it's on to Chicago, and let's win there."

As the crowd roared its approval, clapping and shouting for a good five minutes, Bobby waved and flashed the peace sign. With a parting smile, he left the platform. A press conference had been arranged by Pierre Salinger and would take place in the Colonial Room, a space usually reserved for smaller-scale affairs. To avoid the crush in the ballroom, Bobby—familiar with the Ambassador's layout from previous visits—decided to take a shortcut down a narrow corridor and through the kitchen area. While Bill Barry remained behind to help Ethel climb off the platform, RFK led the way into the hotel kitchen. Momentarily a series of gunshots could be heard, followed by a chorus of screams and the muffled sound of people scattering in all directions.

"After the rally for Bobby the afternoon of the fourth," recalled Roswell Gilpatric, "I saw Jackie back to her apartment. We had a late dinner prepared by her cook, and that's when George Plimpton called from California with news of Bobby's impending victory. Jackie seemed quite happy for him. I returned to my apartment around midnight. I went to bed but couldn't sleep. At about four in the morning, I turned on the radio. The announcer was saying something about 'the Kennedy shooting,' and my first impulse was to wonder why at this stage they would be talking about Jack Kennedy's assassination. As I continued to listen, it dawned on me that they weren't talking about Jack but about Bobby, who'd apparently been the victim of a shooting at the Ambassador Hotel. I immediately called Jackie, and she was awake. She'd already received word of the shooting, first from Chuck Spalding in Los Angeles and then from Stas Radziwill in London, who was making arrangements to fly to New York on the first available plane."

Jackie asked Gilpatric to come over as soon as possible. He dressed and caught a cab to 1040 Fifth Avenue. Caroline and John Jr. were asleep, and Jackie was on the phone with Ken O'Donnell, trying to get information.

"Jackie was determined to go to California," Gilpatric continued. "So I called up my friend Tom Watson, chairman of IBM, and asked if he could spare his private jet and crew. 'Absolutely,' he said, and he soon joined us at Jackie's apartment, where he and I sat and waited while she placed further calls. At ten-thirty in the morning, the three of us were driven out to JFK Airport in Tom's limousine. Jackie appeared to be in shock. The only comment I remember her making on the drive to the airport was, 'It can't have happened. It can't have happened. Tell me it hasn't happened.' Once we reached JFK, however, she seemed to get hold of herself. She wanted to wait for Stas Radziwill's plane to arrive from London, so he could accompany her to California. He eventually arrived, and the two of them boarded the jet and flew west."

Chuck Spalding awaited their arrival at Los Angeles International Airport. The moment she saw him, Jackie said, "What's the story, Chuck? I want it straight from the shoulder. No bullshit."

"He's dying," Spalding replied.

In the taxi to Good Samaritan Hospital, where they'd taken the mortally wounded senator, Spalding provided Jackie with a detailed chronology of events, including information he'd been given by the Los Angeles Police Department.

After completing his victory speech, Bobby had headed for the kitchen area, where he paused to shake hands with a pair of Mexican busboys. Striding past a tray rack, he walked straight into the path of the gunman, a dark, slim, twenty-four-year-old Palestinian armed with a .22-caliber revolver. An unemployed welfare recipient who had lived in Jordan for nine years before moving to California, Sirhan Sirhan faulted RFK for the senator's avowed support of Israel, particularly during the previous year's Six-Day War.

"Kennedy, you son of a bitch!" Sirhan had barked before starting to shoot. "Get the gun! Get the gun!" somebody yelled. Bullets were flying everywhere. People were running and screaming, while others froze in place, afraid to move. George Plimpton lunged at the shooter and grabbed the weapon but couldn't wrestle it out of the man's hand. Eight bullets had been fired, the first three striking Bobby at close range; five others in the room were wounded as well, though none as severely as RFK. Rosey Grier, Rafer Johnson, and three others managed to restrain Sirhan by bending him backward over a steam table, but they still couldn't get the gun away from him. It was as though the gun and his arm were fused. As they pinned him to the table, somebody shouted, "Kill him! Kill the bastard! Kill him now!" Jesse Unruh had called the police. When they arrived, they hauled Sirhan away by his arms and legs.

According to the police report, the shooting took place at 12:15 a.m., Wednesday, June 5, 1968. The first bullet struck Bobby on the right side of his head, crashing into the right hemisphere of his brain; the next two bullets hit his right armpit as he collapsed on the ground. Spalding, who had followed RFK into the kitchen with most of the rest of Kennedy's entourage, heard a mix of sounds. Someone was whining in an almost inhuman voice, "Oh no, oh no! Not again! Oh no!" Steve Smith was shouting in the distance, "Please clear the area! Please don't panic! Everything's all right!" But of course everything wasn't all right.

Bobby lay on the floor in a steadily widening pool of blood. His eyes were open. The expression in his eyes was not one of recognition, but of resignation, as if to say, "Well, they finally got me." The idea of assassination had been in the air for months. It had happened to Jack, it could as easily happen to Bobby. He had discussed this moment many times with many different people. It had been one of the most frequently talked-about subjects among his aides and advisors. But now that it had happened, it seemed to come as a total shock.

Two ambulance attendants arrived with a rolling stretcher. "Don't lift me, don't lift me," Bobby had whispered. "Oh, no, no . . . don't," he said as they gently raised him onto the gurney. He soon lost consciousness and never regained it.

Ethel Kennedy and Fred Dutton rode in the back of the ambulance with Bobby as it sped toward Central Receiving Hospital, where doctors worked frantically to stabilize the shooting victim. Realizing the futility of the situation, they recommended that he be transferred to the larger and better-equipped Good Samaritan Hospital, a half mile away. Before allowing him to be moved, Ethel insisted on ushering two priests to his bedside to administer the last rites. Only then was he transported to Good Samaritan and rushed to the ninth-floor operating room. Seeing no brain wave activity and negligible vital signs, doctors at Good Samaritan harbored little hope for Bobby's survival. At 3:15 a.m., a team of five surgeons, headed by Dr. Henry Cuneo, commenced a four-hour operation in a last-ditch effort to save the patient's life. At 7:25 a.m., Frank Mankiewicz, having set up a pressroom in the hospital, informed reporters that although surgeons had removed almost all the bullet fragments that had permeated RFK's brain, Bobby's vital signs were impaired and showed little chance for improvement. As the day proceeded, his condition worsened. Downgraded from "critical" to "extremely critical," he was being kept alive in the intensive care recovery unit by a mechanical ventilator.

Moving past police lines, television cameras, floodlights, armed security guards, news reporters, and a throng of onlookers, Jackie Kennedy, Stas Radziwill, and Chuck Spalding arrived at Good Samaritan Hospital late Wednesday afternoon. They made their way to the ninth-floor waiting room, where they found many of the same family members and friends who had sat in Bobby's suite at the Ambassador Hotel only the day before eagerly awaiting the final results of RFK's pending victory in the California primary. Jean Smith and Pat Lawford embraced Jackie, as did Steve Smith and Ted Kennedy. Teddy, who had arrived from San Francisco early that morning and had imparted the sad news by phone to Joe and Rose Kennedy at Hyannis Port, took Jackie by the hand and led her down the whitewashed hospital corridor to intensive care. Ethel sat on the inclined bed next to Bobby, holding his hand and whispering in his ear. There was no response. Tubes and lifelines connected the wounded figure to the latest in medical machinery. His head was bandaged and his eyes blackened. The respirator breathed for Bobby, forcing oxygen in and out of his inert lungs. When Ethel saw her sister-in-law standing in the room, she held out her arms. "Jackie," she said, "I'm so glad you're here."

As Jackie later reported it to Pierre Salinger, Ethel had surprised her with her warmth and cordiality, going so far as to leave the former First Lady alone in the room with her dying husband. "You've come all this way—you probably want to spend a little time alone with Bobby," she'd said.

As the hours passed, more and more friends and staff workers arrived, until they filled the waiting room and spilled into the corridors. "Steve Smith telephoned a nearby liquor store," recalled Pierre Salinger, "and had a dozen bottles of booze sent up. An intern provided us with ice and plastic cups, and we all got plastered. I mean, you needed fortification of some sort. Bobby's death marked an end to everyone's hopes and prayers for the future. And then three of his kids—Kathleen, Joe, and Bobby Jr.—showed up to see their father. The pitiful expressions on their faces said it all."

Frank Mankiewicz issued another press release at about 9:00 that evening, reporting that physicians attending the senator were discouraged by his continuing failure to show improvement following surgery.

After releasing his statement, Mankiewicz took a seat near Jackie and Jean Smith. "The Church teaches forgiveness," said Smith, "but sometimes I wonder. First Jack gets assassinated, and now Bobby. I don't think he'll make it."

At this point, Jackie remarked, "The Church is at its best only at the time of death . . . The Catholic Church understands death. I'll tell you who else understands death are the black churches. I remember at the funeral of Martin Luther King, I was looking at those faces, and I realized that they knew death. They see it all the time and they're ready for it . . . in the way in which a good Catholic is ready. We know death. As a matter of fact, if it weren't for the children, we'd welcome it."

At 12:45 a.m., Thursday, June 6, RFK's doctors met with Ethel, Jean, Pat, Teddy, and Jackie. They reminded the Kennedys that from the beginning there had been no brain activity. The senator was being kept alive by artificial means.

"Is there any hope at all of recovery?" Jackie inquired.

"None," responded Dr. Cuneo.

"What are you trying to say?" asked Ethel.

"I'm saying that by keeping Senator Kennedy tethered to a respirator, we're only prolonging the inevitable. But neither I nor any other physician can tell you what to do."

Ethel started to walk away from the group. "I won't kill Bobby," she said. "I won't do it."

According to Richard Goodwin, who had been at the hospital from the beginning, Jackie was the one who finally ordered the machines turned off. "Nobody else had the nerve to do it," said Goodwin. "The poor guy was lying there, his chest going up and down—they have those machines that keep your body going forever. And he was brain-dead, but the doctors didn't dare pull the plug. Ethel was in no shape to do anything. She was lying on the bed moaning. Teddy was kneeling in prayer at the foot of the bed."

At 1:20 a.m., Jackie asked to see Dr. Cuneo. When he appeared, she said, "We would like to disconnect the respirator."

"Are you speaking for the family?" asked the physician.

"I am," she said.

The doctor presented Jackie with a consent form, which she signed without hesitation. She returned to the intensive care unit. "It's time we let Bobby go," she said. Eventually Teddy and Ethel both thanked her for doing what they themselves couldn't do. An attendant arrived and shut down the respirator. Bobby continued to breathe on his own for a few minutes, and then gradually stopped.

Frank Mankiewicz made the announcement. The official time of death was 1:44 a.m., Thursday, June 6, 1968, twenty-five and a half hours after Sirhan Sirhan raised a pistol to Bobby's head. Robert Francis Kennedy was forty-two years old.

Chapter 12

❖

IMMEDIATELY FOLLOWING Robert Kennedy's death, an autopsy was performed in the basement of Good Samaritan Hospital by Los Angeles County chief coroner Thomas Noguchi, who six years earlier had officiated at the autopsy of Marilyn Monroe. Because RFK had been a homicide victim, representatives from the Los Angeles Police Department, the L.A. County Sheriff's Department, the Secret Service, and the FBI were present at his autopsy.

"In death, Bobby Kennedy finally received the kind of protective services he should have been given while still alive," said Mort Downey Jr., who lived in Los Angeles at the time and participated in RFK's California campaign. "Rosey Grier, Rafer Johnson, and the others meant well but weren't professionally trained and had no experience in that area. Bobby should have availed himself of either a bona fide security team or the Secret Service protection that, though not automatically bestowed, was available upon request to major presidential candidates. His failure to do so lent credence to the widely held view that Bobby had a death wish. Personally, I don't subscribe to that theory. He might have been reckless, but Bobby wasn't suicidal."

The minute Aristotle Onassis learned of RFK's death, he called Costa Gratsos. "At last Jackie's free of the Kennedys," he said. "The last link has just broke." Ari demonstrated an even more callous attitude in a follow-up conversation with Johnny Meyer. "Somebody was going to fix the little bastard sooner or later," he said.

Although Lyndon Johnson shared Ari's disdain for RFK, he dispatched Air Force One to Los Angeles to bring Kennedy's remains back to New York. Ted Kennedy helped load the casket on board and sat next to it, alone, during the entire cross-country journey. Of Joseph P. Kennedy's four sons, Teddy was now the sole survivor—he had become the titular head of one of the most celebrated (and tragic) families in America, a responsibility he wasn't wholly prepared to assume.

Jackie and Ethel sat near each other on the plane but barely spoke. "What should I have said to her?" Jackie later remarked to Roswell Gilpatric. "Hadn't I made a similar trip aboard the same plane after Jack's death less than five years earlier? I felt awful—for Ethel, and, to be honest, for myself."

Before boarding Air Force One, Jackie had spoken by telephone with Leonard Bernstein in New York. She had asked him to recommend appropriate music for Bobby's funeral. She called him again while still airborne, and they discussed Bernstein's suggestions. She then called Gilpatric. "Tell me," she said, "that this is all a bad dream, that I'm going to wake up and everything will be all right again."

At 9:00 p.m., six hours after departing Los Angeles, Air Force One landed at LaGuardia Airport and Bobby's body was transported to St. Patrick's Cathedral on Fifth Avenue. While thousands gathered outside the cathedral, Ethel, Teddy, Jackie, and other family members and friends were ushered inside. Ted spent the night with his brother's coffin; Jackie left after an hour and returned to her apartment to be with Caroline and John.

At 5:00 a.m., June 7, members of the public began filing through the cathedral to view the closed coffin of African mahogany. The procession continued until 5:00 the next morning, the line outside the church at times stretching a mile and a half up Fifth Avenue. Those at the end of the line waited for up to eight hours to pay their last respects.

At Ethel's request, Jackie telephoned Henry Lax, her personal physician, and asked him to provide her sister-in-law with a prescription for a strong sedative.

"Why does she need a sedative?" asked the doctor.

"She doesn't want to cry at Bobby's funeral," said Jackie.

"Why shouldn't she cry?" remarked Lax. "Under the circumstances, it's the most normal and natural thing to do. It's much healthier to cry than to hold everything in."

Dr. Lax finally relented and provided Jackie with the sedatives for Ethel. He suspected that she needed some for herself as well.

Beginning at 10:00 a.m., Saturday, June 8, Richard Cardinal Cushing, assisted by the newly appointed archbishop of New York, Terrence Cardinal Cooke, and a representative of Pope Paul VI, led a solemn pontifical requiem mass for Bobby. Over two thousand invited guests attended the funeral rites, including Lyndon and Lady Bird Johnson, Hubert Humphrey, Eugene McCarthy, Richard Nixon, Nelson Rockefeller, Averell Harriman, Barry Goldwater, Cary Grant, Coretta Scott King, Ralph Abernathy, and the entire Kennedy family. More than a hundred thousand mourners, stunned and saddened, many in tears, filled the immediate area surrounding St. Patrick's, shutting down midtown Manhattan traffic.

The service lasted two hours. Leonard Bernstein conducted a movement from Mahler's Fifth Symphony. Andy Williams sang "The Battle Hymn of the Republic." Senator Ted Kennedy delivered the eulogy, speaking first of his family's love for his brother, followed by his reading of passages from a 1966 anti-apartheid speech delivered by RFK during a brief visit to South Africa. Teddy concluded with words composed for the occasion by Milton Gwirtzman, a Washington lawyer and former RFK senatorial aide. "My brother need not be idealized," he said, his voice and body trembling, "or enlarged in death beyond what he was in life, to be remembered simply as a good and decent man, who saw wrong and tried to right it, saw suffering and tried to heal it, saw war and tried to stop it. Those of us who loved him and who take him to his rest today pray that what he was to us and what he wished for others will someday come to pass for all the world. As he said many times in many parts of this nation, to those he touched and who sought to touch him: 'Some men see things as they are and say why? I dream things that never were and say why not?' "

After the funeral, Jackie had an encounter with Lady Bird Johnson. Lady Bird's *A White House Diary* recorded the incident: "Then I found myself in front of Mrs. Jacqueline Kennedy. I called her name and put out my hand. She looked at me as if from a great distance, as though I were an apparition. I murmured some word of sorrow and walked on . . ."

Roswell Gilpatric, also at the funeral, attributed the incident to "Jackie's sorrow and absorption in her own thoughts." According to Gilpatric, "she had just lost the source of her safety and strength. Bobby Kennedy had been taken away from her. By the time we reached the twenty-one-car funeral train that would take Bobby's coffin from New York to Washington, D.C., she had begun to compose herself somewhat, but at the funeral itself she was extremely distraught. Within less than five years, she'd lost her husband and then the man who very possibly had been the love of her life."

Departing the funeral, Jackie spotted William Manchester in the St. Patrick's Cathedral crowd. "When Bobby first announced his candidacy for president, I'd publicly endorsed him and contributed funds to his campaign," said the author of *The Death of a President*. "When Jackie saw me at the funeral, she came up to me. 'After all the grief Bobby and I gave you over that book,' she said, 'I found it utterly gracious of you to have supported him. I want to thank you for that.' Later she sent me a letter stating more or less the same thing."

Before boarding the train, Jackie encountered Robert McNamara. Suddenly overcome by a final bout of grief, she began to cry. McNamara took her in his arms, and she sobbed on his shoulder. Aware that people were watching, she gradually pulled herself together. McNamara helped her onto the train and for a while sat next to her.

Tens of thousands of men and women, young and old, rich and poor, black and white, lined the railway tracks as the funeral train made its way to the nation's capital. Larry O'Brien remembered Ethel and Jackie walking through the train together, the former looking frazzled and dazed, the latter her usual icy, dignified self, sort of anticipating the movements of the train, holding on when it lurched or bumped, holding up Ethel as well so she wouldn't fall and get hurt.

Despite her frosty regality, Jackie was overcome by fear and anger, an anger that quickly turned to bitterness. If America had a claim on her after JFK's death, that claim was now forfeited. If she felt any doubt or obligation to consider the impact of her future actions on the political prospects of the remaining Kennedys, they were resolved by the shots that ended Bobby's life. Once again, did it matter who had pulled the trigger, or for what twisted reason?

Ethel, Jackie, and the rest of Bobby's family accompanied his body from the train station in Washington to its final resting place at Arlington National Cemetery. Some of the Kennedy children carried flowers, while others held candles. The fifteen-minute graveside ceremony was closed to the public and the only nighttime burial in the history of Arlington National Cemetery. At Jackie's suggestion, Ethel had requested there be no military presence—no gun salutes or soldiers in attendance.

The Kennedy family stood quietly, motionlessly, as Archbishop Philip M. Hannan of New Orleans gave a final, brief burial liturgy. John Glenn, serving as a pallbearer, folded the American flag that had draped Bobby's coffin during the train ride and handed it to Ted Kennedy. Teddy turned it over to Joe Kennedy, eldest son of the slain candidate, who passed it to his mother. The Harvard University band played "America." One by one, the numerous members of the family, adults and children, knelt to kiss the casket before it was lowered into the ground under a magnolia tree twenty yards from John F. Kennedy's grave and the eternal flame. Several months later, a plain white cross was placed over Robert F. Kennedy's otherwise unadorned burial plot.

"I hate this country," Jackie told Pierre Salinger a day after Bobby's funeral. "I despise America, and I don't want my children to live here anymore. If they're killing Kennedys, my kids are number one targets. I want to get out of this country."

Jackie's intention could not have been more blatant had she placed a marriage announcement on the front page of *The New York Times.* Her options had run out. In a sense, her decision to finally marry Aristotle Onassis had been made at Bobby Kennedy's grave.

With his and her children watching, and after much haggling over the terms of a prenuptial agreement, Jacqueline Kennedy and Onassis were wed on October 20, 1968. The Greek Orthodox ceremony was conducted in a small chapel on Skorpios, Ari's privately owned island off the coast of Greece. Jackie's rather inappropriate wedding present to her new husband consisted of an expensive wristwatch that had formerly belonged to JFK. As Bobby had so often predicted, the Jackie-Ari betrothal created a worldwide furor best characterized by a front-page headline in the *Los Angeles Times:* "Jackie Sells Out!" Joan Thring, an attractive Australian who worked as Rudolf Nureyev's personal assistant and became friendly with both the groom and bride, called their marriage an "out-and-out business transaction." George Smathers said that marrying Onassis was Jackie's way of "paying back" the other Kennedy women, who had constantly "flaunted their wealth and power."

Jackie may have been a living legend, but Americans now regarded Ethel Kennedy as the nation's "official" widow. In time Jackie would redeem herself in the eyes of her countrymen, but for the moment, she was perceived as something of a fallen woman, a victim of her own greed. Lady Bird Johnson revealed to White House photographer Cecil Stoughton that only after Jackie's marriage to Onassis did the current First Lady feel liberated from Mrs. Kennedy's presence and influence. "I feel suddenly free," she said. "No shadow walks beside me up and down the corridors of the White House."

Following her marriage to Onassis, Jackie wrote a letter to Rose Kennedy in which she barely mentioned her new husband, referring instead to Jack and Bobby Kennedy. "I always thought Jack was haunted by the poignancy of men dying young," she commented. She went on to say that soon after she and Jack were married, she had introduced him to "Ulysses," a poem by Alfred Lord Tennyson. "Later I showed Bobby the poem," she added, "and he fell in love with it. He often used in his speeches the lines, 'Come my friends / 'tis never [*sic*] too late to seek a newer world.' That is really what Bobby's message and dream was, wasn't it?"

Robert Kennedy's death changed the course of history. Hubert Humphrey became his party's presidential nominee at the riot-torn Democratic National Convention in Chicago in August 1968. Three months later, Richard Nixon defeated Humphrey to become president of the United States. Under Nixon's controversial leadership, the Vietnam War raged on for another four years. The Cold War intensified. Urban turmoil and student demonstrations (among them, the fatal shooting of four students at Kent State University in Ohio) escalated. Political scandal after political scandal rocked the nation, culminating in Watergate and Nixon's tearful resignation, followed by the inert administration of Gerald Ford and the haplessness of Jimmy Carter.

Rory Elizabeth Katherine Kennedy, the eleventh and last child of RFK and Ethel Skakel Kennedy, was born on December 12, 1968, six months after her father's death. Lacking Jackie's fortitude and self-confidence, Ethel never fully recovered from her husband's death. Described by family members as an "absentee" parent, Ethel experienced further loss with the subsequent deaths of two of her sons (David, in 1984, and Michael, in 1997), while a number of her other children battled drug addiction and alcoholism.

Despite Jackie's initial desire to raise Caroline and John outside the domain of the United States, she quickly changed her mind. By early 1969, she and the children had returned full-time to New York. Disillusioned with his marriage to Jackie, Aristotle Onassis soon resumed his former relationship with Maria Callas. He depicted Jackie for the benefit of Costa Gratsos as "nothing but a gold digger," and complained to Johnny Meyer that she "speaks incessantly of Bobby Kennedy." He accused Jackie of indifference following the 1973 death (while at the controls of a plane) of Alexander Onassis, his twenty-four-year-old son. In an effort to divorce his wife, Ari contacted and met more than once with attorney Roy Cohn. Onassis died on March 15, 1975, before filing separation papers. With the help of attorneys, Jackie successfully overturned her prenuptial agreement with Ari, receiving a $26 million settlement, which she gradually parlayed into a fortune worth more than $150 million.

Ten months after assassinating Robert Kennedy, following a ninety-day trial, Sirhan Sirhan was convicted of first-degree murder. The jury imposed the death sentence. For reasons he never disclosed, Ted Kennedy petitioned the Los Angeles District Attorney's office to reduce the sentence. For his part, Sirhan Sirhan filed a pro forma appeal requesting clemency. While the appeal was still in progress, the California Supreme Court abolished the state's death penalty. On June 17, 1972, Sirhan's sentence was commuted to life imprisonment.

Following Bobby's funeral, Jackie never again mentioned the names Lee Harvey Oswald or Sirhan Sirhan. "I'm not always successful at it," she told Arthur Schlesinger Jr., "but I've always done my best to think away bad thoughts." By contrast, she enjoyed reminiscing about JFK and RFK. Jokingly, she occasionally referred to Jack Kennedy's notion of the New Frontier as the "Nude Frontier." On a more serious note, she told Carl Killingsworth that of all the Kennedy brothers, "Bobby was the one who was most like his father. He was also the most like me."

As the years passed, Jackie devoted herself to raising Caroline and John. "If you don't do a good job bringing up your children," she was once quoted as saying, "then nothing else you do in life matters." In 1977, after a series of short-lived affairs, she began dating Maurice Tempelsman, a Belgian-born diamond entrepreneur with active ties to emerging African nations. Jewish, married, and the father of three grown children, Tempelsman left his wife and eventually moved into Jackie's Fifth Avenue apartment. Eager to "keep busy," Jackie became a book editor, first at The Viking Press and then at Doubleday. She and Tempelsman spent their weekends and vacations at Martha's Vineyard, where Jackie built a sprawling residence on more than 350 oceanfront acres. She continued to make public appearances on behalf of various causes but on a very selective basis. She socialized with the rest of the Kennedys but primarily on official and commemorative occasions.

In May 1993, Jackie was diagnosed as suffering from anaplastic non-Hodgkin's lymphoma, a virulent form of cancer. She died in her New York apartment on May 19, 1994, at the age of sixty-four. Her journey ended at the Kennedy grave site in Arlington National Cemetery, where she, her late husband, and his younger brother were brought together again, at last and forever.

EPILOGUE

◆

Ted Kennedy and Eunice Kennedy Shriver both passed away within weeks of the original mid-July 2009 publication of this book. In *True Compass,* Teddy's posthumously published autobiography, the longtime Massachusetts senator makes ample reference to the anguish experienced by Bobby Kennedy following the November 1963 assassination of President John F. Kennedy. Although Teddy's autobiography fails to delve into the romantic nature of Bobby's relationship with Jacqueline Kennedy, it does provide information detailing RFK's role as a surrogate father to Jack and Jackie's children, Caroline and John Kennedy Jr. *True Compass* also documents many of the ways in which Bobby helped Jackie recover from the shock and horror of her husband's murder.

Indeed, the bond that initially held the president's younger brother and widow together was forged of a mutual agony; it was so strong that the word "love" seemed almost inadequate to describe it. Yet for all the talk of how much Jackie leaned on her brother-in-law during those difficult days, there has always been too little acknowledgment of just how much he needed her, how reciprocal their relationship was.

An equally common tendency on the part of readers of *Bobby and Jackie* was simply to perceive the relationship in sexual terms. Although sexuality was undoubtedly an important aspect of their bond, it was by no means everything. The psychology behind the Bobby and Jackie liaison, the reasons for their affair—and how it changed their respective lives—are also of paramount importance and must not go unmentioned.

Bobby and Jackie were able to help each other in the wake of the president's assassination not only because of their shared grief, but because they shared, in George Plimpton's words, "a certain kind of guts." She needed him to nurse her back to normality; he needed her to remind him, as she did, that he had to go on, that he owed it to Jack. "You have to continue what you and Jack started together," she told him. She told Pierre Salinger, "Bobby's the only one I'd put my hand in the fire for." When Lyndon and Lady Bird Johnson asked her to attend a 1965 White House festival of the arts, she refused. "Bobby can't stand Johnson," she said to Larry O'Brien. "I'm not going to do anything Bobby doesn't want me to do." In a number of ways she demonstrated a greater loyalty to Bobby than she ever had to Jack, whose nonstop womanizing, particularly during his thousand days as president, had left her with a permanent scar. Forever after she remained a cynic when it came to the tradition of marriage. If nothing else, her relationship with Bobby restored her faith in love, in romance.

If RFK became Jackie's rock and refuge, she in turn meant just as much to him. "Without Jackie," he once confided to Chuck Spalding, "I don't think I'd have made it. When Jack's life ended, my hell began. I couldn't eat, sleep, or function. Jackie kept me going in a way nobody else could, not even Ethel."

The degree to which Bobby was unable to cope with the reality of his brother's death is a subject that has been downplayed in practically every book ever written about the Kennedys. "Only with Jackie could he shed that look of inconsolable grief," noted Arthur Schlesinger Jr. Although Bobby helped convince Jackie she had to go on, he had difficulty accepting his own advice. When pressed as to future plans, he at times spoke vaguely of pursuing a career as a high school history teacher. His dream for a future in public service had been shattered. His will to fight the good fight had been throttled. "How do you fight without a heart?" he wrote Jackie during one of his visits abroad. The same letter recalled a game of touch football he'd played as a teenager with both of his older brothers—Joe Jr. and Jack—in which, so eager to compete with them, he'd plowed into a wire fence, cutting his face open. "I was the seventh of nine children," he wrote. "When you come from that far down, you have to struggle to survive. Well, it seems, without Jack, I've lost the will to survive."

In another letter to Jackie he recalled the excitement of the political campaigns with Jack: Jack becoming senator; Jack becoming the president of the United States. He remembered how Jack had made him attorney general over a storm of protest. "What's so wrong with giving him a little experience before he goes out to practice law?" Jack had said at a press conference, his face breaking into a big grin, deflating criticism with his usual wry, urbane wit. "I wanted to turn down the job," the letter continues. "I wanted to take Ethel and scoot off to the South Seas. But Jack said, 'I need you.' So I stayed put and did the best I could. And now it all seems for naught."

By way of response, Jackie fired off a letter to Bobby reminding him of a conversation that had taken place between Jack and RFK in the early 1950s. The gist of it was that Jack had entered the political arena primarily because Joe Jr., the eldest brother, had been killed in World War II. If something ever happened to Jack, he expected Bobby to step into his shoes. And if anything were to happen to Bobby, Teddy would be expected to follow in Bobby's footsteps.

Showing Jackie's letter to Pierre Salinger, RFK purportedly said, "I don't know anymore. I just don't know."

It took Jackie weeks and months to get Bobby back on his feet and moving again. At first it had been Bobby who gave her the strength to move on; now she became *his* support system. She implored him to go ahead with his career, not only for his sake but for that of the Kennedy children—not only for the children, but for the country. She spent hours with him, discussing his various alternatives, including the prospect of his temporarily leaving Washington to run for the senatorial seat in New York. When he warned her that he would be regarded as a carpetbagger by the press, she gave her characteristic wave of the hand and said, "Who cares what they say? You'll win anyway." To drive home the point she placed Caroline and John Jr. at his disposal, allowing them to join their uncle on several campaign stops, a sacrifice she would never have made even for Jack. Although he wouldn't permit it, she volunteered to appear on television for the candidate. "Anything for Bobby," she told a friend.

When Bobby hesitated at one point and considered dropping out of the race, Jackie wrote out some lines from a Tennyson poem—lines that Jack had loved—and mailed them to RFK. The lines she quoted speak for themselves:

> *Though much is taken, much abides; and though*
> *We are not now that strength which in old days*
> *Moved earth and heaven, but which we are, we are.*

The verse ends with the words: *To strive, to seek, to find, and not to yield.*

With Jackie's encouragement, Bobby chose not to yield.

Although not often reported, examples abound demonstrating Jacqueline's support of her late husband's younger brother. Visitors to Bobby's Manhattan residence, for example, were quick to notice that he had transformed the apartment into a virtual shrine. Photographs of JFK were everywhere—on bookshelves, tables, and desktops. "Bobby spent hours staring at them, touching them," said Plimpton. "It was as if he couldn't let go. Finally Jackie took matters into her own hands by bringing him dozens of framed pictures of Caroline and John Jr. She placed them around the apartment, and in some cases substituted them for photos of Jack. She obviously wanted Bobby to concentrate on the here and now, not on the past."

How much Jackie helped Bobby recover from his loss—her loss as well—can be gauged by the extent to which he reengaged with the world. Despite verbal attacks from political opponents who labeled him "arrogant, overambitious, unscrupulous, a good hater like his father before him," RFK ran away with the New York senatorial race. Afterward he told the press, "Now I can go back to being ruthless again." He told journalist Oriana Fallaci that he owed his victory to Jackie. "She's the person," he said, "I feel most comfortable with. I don't have to hide my feelings with her. She understands, because she went through the same hell. And she's the one who made me understand that it's up to me to fulfill President Kennedy's reality—his dreams and visions. That's the best way, perhaps the only way, I can honor the memory of my late brother."

Fulfilling those dreams and visions were what in the end brought Bobby and Jackie so close together, and then kept them close.

An intriguing addition to the Bobby and Jackie story came to light on September 14, 2009, when CNN and The Associated Press reported the discovery of a handwritten condolence letter from Jacqueline Kennedy to Ethel penned the day after Bobby Kennedy's funeral in early June 1968. The handwritten note, which eventually turned up at the Heritage Auction Galleries in Dallas, Texas, became the focus of an FBI probe on the grounds it had purportedly been stolen from the RFK archives at Hickory Hill. The letter reads:

> *My Ethel—*
>
> *No one in the world could have ever been like you—expect maybe Bobby—We are going home now—Your phone was busy.*
>
> *You don't want any more calls, and you must be tired—I stayed up till 6:30 last night just thinking—and praying for you—and for you in the months ahead—*
>
> *I love you so much—*
>
> *You know that anything—Stas [Radziwill] will take little Bobby to Africa—I'll take them around the world + to the moon + back—anything to help you + then, now and always—*
>
> *With my deepest love*
> *Jackie*

Considering Jackie's four-year love affair with Bobby, the letter no doubt struck a false note with Ethel. In fact, according to a family insider, the letter wasn't "stolen" from the Kennedy household. Rather it was discarded by Ethel and rescued from a garbage bin by a Hickory Hill retainer; it was subsequently sold to a private collector, who later placed it on the auction block, where it was intercepted and seized by the FBI. The case is still under investigation.

ACKNOWLEDGMENTS

———◆———

I WOULD FIRST of all like to thank Mel Berger, my literary agent at William Morris Endeavor Entertainment, for his encouragement and guidance, in addition to his assistant, the always good-natured Graham C. Jaenicke. I am equally indebted to Emily Bestler, my editor at Atria Books/Simon & Schuster. Sarah Branham, also at Atria, contributed her considerable editorial skills as well. Laura Stern, Emily Bestler's assistant at Atria, deserves mention for helping to transform my manuscript into book form. My friend Gerry Visco, journalist and office manager of the Classics Department at Columbia University, was my first reader and proved invaluable as an initial line editor. The photographs that appear in this book were gathered and organized by Lewanne Jones, who provided the same service for *American Legacy,* my previous book, published in 2007. Mark Padnos, a librarian in the City University system, moonlighted as chief researcher on the project. Alma Schieren helped put together the book's bibliography. George Brown aided the cause by organizing and collating a slag heap of research material (including interview tapes and transcripts) into a cohesive mass. Victoria Carrion provided much-needed bookkeeping services. Others involved with the book, mostly in a research capacity, include Finn Dusenbery, Marilyn Farnell, Brigitte Golde, Margaret Shannon, Stefanos Tsigrimanis, and Abe Vélez.

In addition to the above, I would like to express my gratitude to

John A. Mintz Esq. for aiding in the procurement of certain previously unavailable FBI files. Archivist Michael Sampson performed the same function with respect to U.S. Secret Service materials. Martha Murphy and Martin F. McGann guided me through the myriad holdings currently housed at the National Archives. Thomas C. Taylor, associate director for policy, helped liberate never-before-seen materials at the Department of Justice. A special vote of thanks must go to Kristen Nyitray, head of special collections and university archives, State University of New York at Stony Brook, where I have placed my personal archives of Kennedy materials gathered while writing four books on the Kennedys.

The following libraries and collections were utilized in compiling information for the current volume: John F. Kennedy Presidential Library and Museum; Lyndon B. Johnson Presidential Library and Museum; Richard Nixon Library and Birthplace; Library of Congress; New York Public Library (main branch); Houghton Library (Harvard University); New York Society Library; Columbia University Library Services (manuscript division); New York University Library System; City University of New York Library System; Boston University Library (special collections); Palm Beach Historical Society; New-York Historical Society; Newport Historical Society; Boston Historical Society and Museum; Georgetown Historical Society; Washington Public Library System; White House Historical Association; Andy Warhol Museum; New York Bar Association Library; Long Island Historical Society; John F. Kennedy School of Government (Harvard University); University of Arizona Library system (manuscripts division).

I must express my gratitude to all those who agreed to be interviewed for this project. Rather than list them here, they are named (on a chapter-by-chapter basis) in the chapter notes section of this book.

Finally I want to thank Beatrice Schwartz, whose devotion and positivism, on good days and bad, made it easier and less lonely to research and write this book.

NOTES

When and where possible, the author has provided source notes within the body of the text. The following chapter notes are intended to supplement the textual references as well as to provide the reader with specific primary and secondary source information. Also included is a chapter-by-chapter listing of interviewees. For the most part, the interviews were taped and were conducted in person or by telephone; in those instances when it was either impossible or impractical to tape an interview, the author depended on handwritten notes and on the presence during the interview of a second interviewer (or researcher). In large measure, the author utilized interviews conducted specifically for this volume; to a lesser degree, the author used interviews conducted for one or more of his three earlier Kennedy biographies, the titles of which are included in the bibliography near the end of this book. Much of the interview material, including tapes and transcripts, has been placed in the author's personal archive, located in the Department of Special Collections, State University of New York at Stony Brook, Stony Brook, New York, where it is available for viewing and/or listening. It should also be pointed out that the chapter notes that follow contain occasional editorial comments that were not included in the text of the book.

CHAPTER 1

8. *"Oh, Bobby"*: William Manchester, *The Death of a President*, p. 387.
9. *"Oh my God"*: Author interview with Arthur Schlesinger Jr.
9. *"At least you have"*: ibid.
11. *"Every time I look"*: Author interview with Dave Powers.
15. *"Shall we go visit our friend?"*: Manchester, op. cit., p. 619.
15. *While Clint Hill called ahead to Arlington*: ibid., pp. 619–620.

The following oral histories, located at JFK Library, Boston, Massachusetts, were consulted for this chapter: George Burkley and John McCone.

Author interviews for this chapter were conducted with the following: Dave Powers, Ken O'Donnell, Mac Kilduff, Godfrey McHugh, William Manchester, Pierre Salinger, Arthur Schlesinger Jr., Mort Downey Jr., Larry O'Brien, Cecil Stoughton, Jack Valenti, Robert McNamara, Janet Auchincloss, Charles Spalding, Angier Biddle Duke, Peter Lawford, Marianne Strong, Peter Duchin, Courtney Evans, Burton Hersh, and Mike Mansfield.

CHAPTER 2

22. *Jayne Mansfield:* At times Jackie took a jocular view of some of JFK's lovers. Among them was the Hollywood sex siren Jayne Mansfield. In mid-1961, Mansfield told a reporter for the *Los Angeles Times* that she wanted to be remembered for her mind and not her body. The ensuing article elicited a December 1962 letter from Jackie to Bill Walton (William Walton Papers, JFK Library) in which she wrote: "Just as Jayne Mansfield wants to be remembered for her mind, so I—the recipient of many art books this Christmas—want to be remembered for her favorite gift, a plastic bathing suit cut to the navel. I will wear it to the opening of the National Cultural Center." Walton, who was gay, had given Jackie the bathing suit for Christmas '62 as a lark. Jackie closed her letter to Walton with the words: "Mad love and thanks. XO, Jackie."

23. *"Thanks, Bobby":* Author interview with George Smathers.

24. *William Holden:* Peter Evans, *Nemesis,* pp. 29–31.

25. *Judith Campbell:* Judith Campbell eventually married and became Judith Campbell Exner. According to gossip columnist Liz Smith, Exner claimed in an interview with her that JFK impregnated her while he was president; she further claimed that she underwent an abortion. Although Exner provided Smith with evidence that she underwent an abortion during Camelot, there is no proof that JFK was the father.

28. *Susan Sklover:* Author interview with Susan Sklover.

29. *Doris Lilly:* The Ted Kennedy in Belgium saga was related to the author in the course of an interview with the late Doris Lilly, whose papers can be found in Special Collections, Boston University Library System, Boston, Massachusetts.

Author interviews for this chapter were conducted with the following: Oleg Cassini, Igor Cassini, Leslie Devereux, John White, Joan Lundberg Hitchcock, Bill Walton, George Smathers, Lester Persky, Truman Capote, Susan Sklover, Morton Downey Jr., Liz Smith, Howard Oxenberg, Doris Lilly, Godfrey McHugh, Abe Hirschfeld, Diana Vreeland, Michael Diaz, Langdon Marvin, Pierre Salinger, Marty Venker, Peter Jay Sharp, Marianne Strong, Peter Lawford, and Jessie Stearns.

CHAPTER 3

36. *Theodore H. White:* White's Camelot article appeared in *Life* on December 6, 1963.

Author interviews for this chapter were conducted with the following: Theodore White, John Kenneth Galbraith, Charles Whitehouse, Pierre Salinger, and Art Buchwald.

CHAPTER 4

42. *drank herself into a stupor:* Author interview with George Smathers.

48. *Jacqueline Hirsh:* Jacqueline Hirsh oral history, JFK Library.

48. *weekly religious training class:* Joanne Frey oral history, JFK Library.

49. *"Frankly, I'm worried":* Byron Skelton letter to RFK, November 4, 1963, RFK Papers, JFK Library.

52. *adopted myth of Camelot:* Sarah Bradford, *America's Queen,* p. 242.

52. *"The sad part":* Unpublished first draft of Maud Shaw's *White House Nanny,* made available to the author by a confidential source.

52. *"his own nervous breakdown":* Ibid.

52. *imploring him not to give up:* Jacqueline Kennedy letter to RFK, January 14, 1964, RFK Papers, JFK Library.

55. *Marlon Brando:* Accounts of Jackie's encounter with Brando have appeared in previous tomes, notably Christopher Andersen's *Jackie After Jack,* pp. 105, 110–111, and Edward Klein's *Just Jackie,* pp. 68–70. According to Klein, Brando was too inebriated to perform sexually and didn't spend the night. In the first draft of a 1994 autobiography, Brando wrote not only that he spent the night and made love to Jackie but that he saw her again in New York. The first draft of Brando's autobiography, completed with the help of an unnamed ghostwriter, was followed by several other drafts prepared by Los Angeles journalist Robert Lindsey. According to a private source, the publisher of the book refused to include the Jacqueline Kennedy anecdote in the final published version; it was excised. William Trion, a close friend of Brando's, made available to the author the first draft of the actor's autobiography, and it is from this source that the author drew his information.

56. *"The two of you":* Herbert Hoover's comment reported to author by Linda Storch, a former administrative assistant to the late president.

58. *"The book changed my life":* Author interview with Larry O'Brien.

Author interviews for this chapter were conducted with the following: Pierre Salinger, George Plimpton, George Smathers, Franklin D. Roosevelt Jr., Susan Mary Alsop, Evelyn Lincoln, LeMoyne Billings, William Joyce, Philippe de Bausset, Coates Redmon, Larry O'Brien, Ken O'Donnell, Dave Powers, Peter Standford, Margot Fonteyn, Carol Granks, Pierre Dauphin, William Manchester, Truman Capote, Lester Persky, Linda Storch, Charles Spalding, Burton Hersh, and William Trion.

CHAPTER 5

60. *"I wish you were an amoeba":* Author interview with Ken O'Donnell.

60. *Gore Vidal:* Bradford, op. cit., pp. 214–215.

61. *Maureen Orth:* Maureen Orth, "When Washington Was Fun," *Vanity Fair,* December 2007.

61. *"After Jack's death":* Laurence Leamer, *The Kennedy Women,* p. 684.

62. *It reached the point:* Author interview with Pierre Salinger.

62. *with Bobby and Teddy by her side:* The July 29, 1964, television appearance of

Bobby, Teddy, and Jackie represented the second time they had thanked the American public for their condolences and good wishes. On January 14, 1964, in an abbreviated broadcast from the attorney general's office, Jackie acknowledged the receipt of some one hundred thousand letters following JFK's assassination. She promised that all the letters would be kept on file in the JFK Library, which had yet to be constructed.

63. *Joan Braden:* In addition to an interview with the author, Braden discussed her encounter with RFK in a book proposal that circulated among major publishers and was subsequently published under the title *Just Enough Rope,* her 1987 autobiography. Joan Braden and her husband, Tom, were also the models for the popular 1980s television series *Eight Is Enough.*

64. *"Jack would have wanted":* Jacqueline Kennedy letter to Ted Kennedy, no date. Confidential source.

65. *"Welcome to New York" dinner party:* Andersen, op. cit., p. 130.

65. *Chris Andersen:* Anderson, op. cit., p. 98.

66. *"the Greek's ill-gotten gains":* Author interview with Truman Capote.

67. *"I cannot tell you":* Igor Cassini provided the author with a copy of the Charlene Wrightsman letter to JFK, dated January 20, 1963.

68. *"the subject [RFK] seems to spend":* FBI restricted files, Washington D.C.

73. *Natalie Fell Cushing:* Author interview with Jan Cushing Amory.

75. *"I'm so pleased":* Author interview with Truman Capote.

76. *C. Douglas Dillon:* Jacqueline Kennedy letter to C. Douglas Dillon, October 15, 1964. Letter provided to author by C. Douglas Dillon.

76. *Secret Service files:* Although several of the Secret Service files referred to in this chapter are currently available through the National Archives, the majority are not; they were shown to the author by a confidential source.

78. *"I think it's a fabulous idea":* Author interview with Truman Capote.

79. *"I'd never seen anything":* C. David Heymann, *RFK,* p. 397. The original quotations are from the Hubert Humphrey oral history, JFK Library.

Author interviews for this chapter were conducted with the following: Ken O'Donnell, Pierre Salinger, Arthur Schlesinger Jr., Joan Braden, Evan Thomas, Samuel H. Beer, Truman Capote, Evangeline Bruce, Igor Cassini, Oleg Cassini, Jayne Wrightsman, Barbara Deutsch, Dave Powers, Courtney Evans, George Plimpton, Larry O'Brien, Andy Warhol, Jerry Bruno, John Treanor Jr., Jacob Javits, Jan Cushing Amory, Bill Walton, Coates Redmon, Susan Pollock, Diana Dubois, Peter Manso, Mary De Grace, C. Douglas Dillon, Franklin D. Roosevelt Jr., Barry Gray, Evelyn Lincoln, Kitty Carlisle Hart, and Meribelle Mode.

CHAPTER 6

81. *Mary Harrington:* Author interview with Mary Harrington.

84. *Renee Luttgen:* Author interview with Renee Luttgen.

86. *"moving in on his brother's widow":* Andersen, op. cit., p. 77.

87. *Another witness:* Maud Shaw letter to Evelyn Lincoln, February 28, 1965, confidential source. Other letters from Shaw to Lincoln are housed among the Evelyn Lincoln papers, LBJ Library, Austin, Texas.

89. *Claudine Longet:* It is worth noting that Andy Williams and Claudine Longet named their third child after Robert Kennedy. Even more noteworthy is the fact that in 1977, following her divorce from Williams, Longet was convicted of criminally negligent homicide in the shooting death of her then romantic partner, professional skier Vladimir "Spider" Sabich, at his home in Aspen, Colorado. Claiming the gun had accidentally discharged, she served a jail term of only thirty days. Longet eventually married the lawyer who defended her in the case.

93. *"wowed them": Washington Post,* March 18, 1966.

94. *"I had planned":* Maud Shaw letter to Evelyn Lincoln, March 22, 1965, LBJ Library.

Author interviews for this chapter were conducted with the following: Mary Harrington, George Plimpton, Elizabeth Dodd, Cary Reich, Renee Luttgen, Truman Capote, John Karavlas, John Meyer, Lynn Alpha Smith, Kathryn Livingston, Evelyn Lincoln, Bernard Hayworth, Mort Downey Jr., George Carpozi Jr., Mel Finkelstein, C. L. Griffen, Pierre Salinger, Hervé Alphand, Coates Redmon, Larry O'Brien, Jerry Oppenheimer, Joseph Alsop, Marie Ridder, Evangeline Bruce, William Manchester, and Edith Roades.

CHAPTER 7

97. *smeared her lips and cheeks with globs of ruby lipstick:* Another version of this anecdote can be found in Jan Pottker, *Janet & Jackie,* pp. 23–24.

97. *"federal monies which had been appropriated":* Evans, op. cit., p. 130.

101. *black-and-white film:* The alleged Monroe-RFK film emerged in the news on April 15, 2008, in a *New York Post* article by Hasani Gittens. The article stipulated that Joe DiMaggio had originally offered to purchase it for $25,000, and that it had recently been sold for $1.5 million. The article doesn't reveal the identity of the man in the film, alleging only that it could have been RFK.

105. *"a friend across Central park":* Jacqueline Kennedy letter to Robert Lowell, Houghton Library, Harvard University, Boston, Massachusetts. The phrase ("friend across the park") became the title of a Lowell poem about Jackie, which originally appeared in *Notebook 1967–68* and was later reprinted in other volumes. For further information, see C. David Heymann's *American Aristocracy.*

105. *McLean Hospital:* See C. David Heymann, *American Aristocracy,* for further details on the relationship between Jacqueline Kennedy and Robert Lowell.

107. *"Enclosed you will find":* Robert David Lion Gardiner provided the author with a copy of the letter from Aristotle Onassis.

Author interviews for this chapter were conducted with the following: John Meyer, Peter Lawford, Carl Killingsworth, George Plimpton, Taki Theodoracopulos, John Kenneth Galbraith, C. Douglas Dillon, Clark Clifford, Pierre Salinger, Paul Mathias, Katharine Graham, Blair Clark, Robert David Lion Gardiner, and Sidney Schwartz.

CHAPTER 8

109. *"What does she want"*: Author interview with George Plimpton.
113. *Nigel Hamilton:* Author interviews with Nigel Hamilton and Chuck Spalding. See also Bradford, op. cit., pp. 103–104, as well as Evans, op. cit., p. 124.
114. *series of videotaped interviews:* The videos (and video transcripts) of Truman Capote were made available to the author by Lester Persky, the late film producer, who shot the interview videos during the last two years of Capote's life.
114. *Peter Evans:* Evans, op. cit., p. 126.
123. *had "fallen in love"*: Peter Edelman oral history, JFK Library.
123. *"remote and distracted"*: Author interview with Larry O'Brien.
123. *"sooner rather than later"*: ibid.
124. *Lilly Lawrence:* Author interview with Lilly Lawrence. See also Evans, op. cit., p. 167.

Author interviews for this chapter were conducted with the following: George Plimpton, Arthur Schlesinger Jr., Larry O'Brien, Robert McNamara, Angier Biddle Duke, Jay Rutherfurd, Truman Capote, Peter Lawford, Janet Auchincloss, Carl Killingsworth, Joan Braden, Dick Banks, Pierre Salinger, Nigel Hamilton, Sarah Bradford, Franklin D. Roosevelt Jr., Lester Persky, John Meyer, Andy Warhol, George Smathers, Larry Rivers, Simon Wiesenthal, Sam Murphy, Kenneth McKnight, Diana Vreeland, Lilly Lawrence, Bill Walton, Charles Addams, and Doris Lilly.

CHAPTER 9

128. *"Why don't you turn to the Greek"*: Author interview with George Plimpton.
129. *"I obviously upset you"*: RFK letter to Katharine Graham, March 1, 1967. Letter provided courtesy of Katharine Graham.
134. *Jackie set off by herself:* Information concerning this episode based on letter from Jacqueline Kennedy to Thomas T. Hendrick, August 7, 1967, Secret Service files.
135. *Leo Lerman:* Lerman not only spoke to the London *Daily Mail* about Jackie and Lord Harlech, he included the information in his memoir, *The Grand Surprise,* p. 487.
141. *"When death ends one"*: Evans, op. cit., p. 168.

Author interviews for this chapter were conducted with the following: Sid Mandell, Dave Powers, Pierre Salinger, Anna Stigholz, Ernest Lowy, Katharine Graham, Ken O'Donnell, Larry O'Brien, George Plimpton, Mary De Grace, Truman Capote, David Susskind, David Ormsby Gore (Lord Harlech), Robert McNamara, Evangeline Bruce, Leo Lerman, Clark Clifford, John Meyer, Jack Newfield, Franklin D. Roosevelt Jr., Art Buchwald, Jan Cushing Amory, Carl Killingsworth, Ron Galella, John Kenneth Galbraith, and Bill Walton.

CHAPTER 10

147. *St. Patrick's Day parade:* James Stevenson, "Bobby on Parade," *New York Times,* March 17, 2008.

147. *Charles Masson:* There is some question as to exactly when the restaurant event transpired. David McGrath, in his article "An Immovable Feast," *Vanity Fair,* September 2008, places it in the mid-1960s. Jack Newfield, present on the occasion, consulting his diary, was certain that it took place on St. Patrick's Day 1968. Otherwise, Newfield's version of the episode, which is the version the current author reports, differs only slightly from *Vanity Fair's* presentation.

148. *Laurence Leamer:* Laurence Leamer, op. cit., p. 624.

149. *"America is going to the dogs":* Author interview with Ken O'Donnell.

149. *Bernard Fensterwald Jr.:* C. David Heymann, *A Woman Named Jackie,* pp. 482–483.

150. *"Jackie's very special":* Author interview with Pierre Salinger. See also Paul Frances, "Teddy and Jackie," *Globe,* September 8, 2008.

151. *Ron Galella:* Author interview with Ron Galella. See also Emily Nussbaum, "The Man in the Bushes," *New York* magazine, September 22, 2008.

151. *"She was the biggest hypocrite":* Nussbaum, ibid.

151. *The only scrapbook she compiled:* Author interview with Roswell Gilpatric.

154. *"I drove my car:"* Author interview with Bob Davidoff.

155. *"Mrs. Kennedy is a totally misunderstood":* Author interview with John Meyer. See also Heymann, *A Woman Named Jackie,* p. 482.

Author interviews for this chapter were conducted with the following: Ken O'Donnell, George Plimpton, Costa Gratsos, Roswell Gilpatric, John Meyer, Agnes Ash, Arthur Schlesinger Jr., Pierre Salinger, Evangeline Bruce, Ron Galella, Joan Braden, George Smathers, Eugene Girden, Jean Kennedy Smith, Bob Davidoff, and Kenneth McKnight.

CHAPTER 11

157. *Eschewing the Secret Service detail:* Secret Service protection was available to major presidential candidates who requested it. It was not until after RFK's assassination that President Johnson signed a bill making such protection mandatory.

160. *John J. Lindsay:* Author interview with George Plimpton. See also Evans, op. cit., p. 183.

161. *"If he endorses anybody":* Jacqueline Kennedy letter to RFK, May 20, 1968. Confidential source. The current author made note of the last sentence in the letter, which contains a small but apparently uncharacteristic grammatical error on Jackie's part. Presumably she meant to write, "In the end, he won't make it any more than will McCarthy." She has omitted the word *will* from the sentence.

161. *"Next time you give":* Jacqueline Kennedy telegram to RFK, May 25, 1968. Copy of the telegram provided to the author by Roswell Gilpatric.

162. *The real winner:* C. David Heymann, *RFK,* p. 483.

163. *"the whole damn pizza":* Author interview with Jean Kennedy Smith.

163. *"You and Freckles":* Jacqueline Kennedy to RFK, May 31, 1968. Copy of Jacqueline Kennedy note to RFK provided to the author by Pierre Salinger.

163. *"The flowers are for":* Author interview with Pierre Salinger.

167. *Beverly Hills Hotel:* According to a Rush & Molloy column in the *New York Post* (August 2, 2007), documentary film producer Ken Morgan claimed that he had interviewed a law enforcement officer in Los Angeles whose assignment it was to keep Ethel Kennedy out of the picture because RFK had installed a call girl in the Beverly Hills Hotel; RFK planned on spending time with the call girl following the California primary. The law enforcement officer is not identified by name in the *Post* column.

173. *"The Church is at its best":* Frank Mankiewicz oral history, JFK Library.

174. *"Is there any hope":* Author interview with George Plimpton, who spoke with Jackie shortly after the conversation between the Kennedys and RFK's physician took place.

174. *According to Richard Goodwin:* Bradford, op. cit., p. 331.

174. *"We would like to disconnect":* Author interview with George Plimpton.

Author interviews for this chapter were conducted with the following: Arthur Schlesinger Jr., Ken O'Donnell, Larry O'Brien, Pierre Salinger, George Plimpton, Roswell Gilpatric, Jean Kennedy Smith, Jeremy Larner, Kristi Witker, John Franken-heimer, William Manchester, Charles Spalding, Sarah Bradford, Costa Gratsos, John Meyer, and Margaret Shannon.

CHAPTER 12

175. *"At last Jackie's free":* Evans, op. cit., pp. 168–169.

176. *"Somebody was going to fix":* ibid., p. 188.

176. *Henry Lax:* The conversation between Jacqueline Kennedy and Dr. Lax was related to the author by Renee Luttgen, Lax's office manager and companion.

180. *With his and her children:* Also at the wedding ceremony as Jackie's guests were her mother, her stepfather, her sister, Jean Kennedy Smith, and Pat Kennedy Lawford.

180. *Joan Thring:* Evans, op. cit., p. 185.

180. *Following her marriage:* Jacqueline Kennedy letter to Rose Kennedy, December 1, 1968, JFK Library.

181. *"Come my friends":* Tennyson's lines are "Come, my friends, / 'Tis not too late to seek a newer world."

Author interviews for this chapter were conducted with the following: Mort Downey Jr., Roswell Gilpatric, Leonard Bernstein, William Manchester, Robert McNamara, Renee Luttgen, Larry O'Brien, Pierre Salinger, Costa Gratsos, John Meyer, George Smathers, Cecil Stoughton, George Plimpton, Arthur Schlesinger Jr., and Carl Killingsworth.

BIBLIOGRAPHY

✦

Aarons, Slim. *A Wonderful Time: An Intimate Portrait of the Good Life.* New York: Harper & Row, 1974.

Abbe, Kathryn McLaughlin, and Frances McLaughlin Gill. *Twins on Twins.* New York: Clarkson Potter, 1980.

Abernathy, Ralph. *And the Walls Came Tumbling Down: An Autobiography.* New York: Harper & Row, 1989.

Acheson, Dean. *Power and Diplomacy.* Cambridge, Mass.: Harvard University Press, 1958.

Adams, William Howard. *Atget's Gardens.* Garden City, N.Y.: Doubleday, 1979.

Adler, Bill. *The Kennedy Children: Triumphs & Tragedies.* New York: Franklin Watts, 1980.

Agel, Jerome, and Eugene Boe. *22 Fires.* New York: Bantam Books, 1977.

Aikman, Lonnelle. *The Living White House.* Foreword by Nancy Reagan. Washington, D.C.: White House Historical Association of the National Geographic Society, 1982.

Alderman, Eileen, and Caroline Kennedy. *In Our Defense: The Bill of Rights in Action.* New York: William Morrow & Co., 1991.

————. *The Right to Privacy.* New York: Knopf, 1995.

Alexander, Lois K. *Blacks in the History of Fashion.* New York: Harlem Institute of Fashion, 1982.

Alexander, Shana. *When She Was Bad: The Story of Bess, Hortense, Sukreet & Nancy.* New York: Random House, 1990.

Alphand, Hervé. *L'étonnement d'être: Journal, 1939–1973.* Paris: Fayard, 1977.

Alsop, Susan Mary. *To Marietta From Paris, 1945–1960.* Garden City, N.Y.: Doubleday, 1975.

Amory, Cleveland. *Who Killed Society?* New York: Harper & Brothers, 1966.

"An Honorable Profession": A Tribute to Robert F. Kennedy. Edited by Pierre Salinger. Garden City, N.Y.: Doubleday and Company, 1968.

Andersen, Christopher. *The Day John Died.* New York: William Morrow & Co., 2000.

———. *Jackie After Jack: A Portrait of the Lady.* New York: William Morrow & Co., 1998.

———. *Sweet Caroline: Last Child of Camelot.* New York: HarperCollins, 2003.

Anderson, Jack. *Washington Exposé.* Washington, D.C.: Public Affairs Press, 1967.

Angeli, Daniel, and Jean-Paul Dousset. *Private Pictures.* New York: Viking, 1980.

Anger, Kenneth. *Hollywood Babylon.* San Francisco: Straight Arrow, 1975.

———. *Hollywood Babylon II.* New York: E. P. Dutton, 1984.

Anson, Robert Sam. *"They've Killed the President!"* New York: Bantam Books, 1975.

Anthony, Carl Sferrazza. *As We Remember Her: Jacqueline Kennedy Onassis in the Words of Her Family and Friends.* New York: HarperCollins, 1997.

Ardoin, John, and Gerald Fitzgerald. *Callas.* London: Thames & Hudson, 1984.

Aronson, Steven M. L. *Hype.* New York: William Morrow & Co., 1983.

Astor, Brooke. *Footprints: An Autobiography.* New York: Doubleday, 1980.

Auchincloss, Joanna Russell, and Caroline Auchincloss Fowler. *The Auchincloss Family.* Freeport, Maine: The Dingley Press, 1957.

A Time It Was: Bobby Kennedy in the Sixties. Photographs and text by Bill Eppridge. Essay by Pete Hamill. New York: Abrams, 2008.

Bacall, Lauren. *By Myself.* New York: Knopf, 1978.

Bacon, James. *Made in Hollywood.* Chicago: Contemporary Books, 1977.

Bair, Marjorie. *Jacqueline Kennedy in the White House.* New York: Paperback Library, 1963.

Baker, Bobby. *Wheeling and Dealing: Confessions of a Capitol Hill Operator.* New York: W. W. Norton & Co., 1978.

Baker, Carlos. *Ernest Hemingway: A Life Story.* New York: Scribner, 1969.

Baldrige, Leticia. *Leticia Baldrige's Complete Guide to Executive Manners.* New York: Rawson, 1985.

———. *Of Diamonds and Diplomats.* Boston: Houghton Mifflin, 1968.

Baldwin, Billy. *Billy Baldwin Remembers.* New York: Harcourt Brace Jovanovich, 1974.

Baldwin, Billy, with Michael Gardine. *Billy Baldwin: An Autobiography.* Boston: Little, Brown and Company, 1985.

Barrow, Andrew. *Gossip: A History of High Society from 1920 to 1970.* New York: Coward, McCann & Geoghegan, 1978.

Bayh, Marvella. *Marvella, A Personal Journey.* New York: Harcourt Brace Jovanovich, 1979.

Beaton, Cecil. *Self Portrait with Friends: The Selected Diaries of Cecil Beaton 1926–1974.* Edited by Richard Buckle. New York: Times Books, 1979.

Bego, Mark. *Jackson Browne: His Life and Music.* New York: Citadel Press, 2005.

Bergin, Michael. *The Other Man: John F. Kennedy, Jr., Carolyn Bessette, and Me.* New York: ReganBooks, 2004.

Beschloss, Michael R. *Kennedy and Roosevelt: The Uneasy Alliance.* New York: W. W. Norton & Co., 1980.

Best-Loved Poems of Jacqueline Kennedy Onassis, The. Selected and introduced by Caroline Kennedy. New York: Hyperion, 2001.

Bevington, Helen. *Along Came the Witch: A Journal in the 1960's.* New York: Harcourt Brace Jovanovich, 1976.

Birmingham, Stephen. *Jacqueline Bouvier Kennedy Onassis*. New York: Grosset & Dunlap, 1978.

———. *Real Lace: America's Irish Rich*. New York: Harper & Row, 1973.

———. *"The Rest of Us": The Rise of America's Eastern European Jews*. Boston: Little, Brown and Company, 1984.

———. *The Right People: A Portrait of the American Social Establishment*. Boston: Little, Brown and Company, 1968.

Bishop, Jim. *A Day in the Life of President Kennedy*. New York: Random House, 1964.

Blackwell, Earl. *Earl Blackwell's Celebrity Register*. Towson, Md.: Times Publishing Group, 1986.

Blair, John, and Clay Blair Jr. *The Search for JFK*. New York: Berkley, 1976.

Blakey, George Robert, and Richard N. Billings. *The Plot to Kill the President*. New York: Times Books, 1981.

Blow, Richard. *American Son: A Portrait of John F. Kennedy, Jr*. New York: Henry Holt and Company, 2002.

Boller Jr., Paul F. *Presidential Anecdotes*. New York: Oxford University Press, 1988.

———. *Presidential Wives: An Anecdotal History*. New York: Oxford University Press, 1988.

Bouvier, Jacqueline, and Lee Bouvier. *One Special Summer*. Written and illustrated by Jacqueline and Lee Bouvier. New York: Delacorte Press, 1974.

Bouvier Jr., John Vernou. *Our Forebears*. Privately printed, 1931, 1942, 1944, 1947.

Bouvier, Kathleen. *To Jack with Love: Black Jack Bouvier, A Remembrance*. New York: Kensington, 1979.

Bradford, Sarah. *America's Queen: The Life of Jacqueline Kennedy Onassis*. New York: Viking, 2000.

Bradlee, Benjamin C. *Conversations with Kennedy*. New York: W. W. Norton & Company, 1975.

Brady, Frank. *Onassis: An Extravagant Life*. Englewood Cliffs, N.J.: Prentice-Hall, 1977.

Bragg, Rick. *All Over but the Shoutin'*. New York: Vintage, 1977.

Branch, Taylor. *Parting the Waters: America in the King Years, 1954–63*. New York: Simon & Schuster, 1988.

Brauer, Carl M. *John F. Kennedy and the Second Reconstruction*. New York: Columbia University Press, 1977.

Bray, Howard. *The Pillars of the Post: The Making of a News Empire in Washington*. New York: W. W. Norton & Company, 1980.

Brenner, Marie. *Great Dames: What I Learned from Older Women*. New York: Three Rivers Press, 2000.

Brokaw, Tom. *Boom! Voices of the Sixties: Personal Reflections on the '60s and Today*. New York: Random House, 2007.

Brolin, Brent C. *The Battle of St. Bart's: A Tale of Heroism, Connivance and Bumbling*. New York: William Morrow & Co., 1971.

Brown, Coco. *American Dream: The Houses at Sagaponac: Modern Living in the Hamptons*. Essays by Richard Meier and Alastair Gordon. NewYork: Rizzoli, 2003.

Bruno, Jerry, and Jeff Greenfield. *The Advance Man*. New York: William Morrow & Co., 1971.

Bryan III, J., and Charles J.V. Murphy. *The Windsor Story.* New York: William Morrow, 1979.

Bryant, Traphes, and Frances Spatz Leighton. *Dog Days at the White House: The Outrageous Memoirs of the Presidential Kennel Keeper.* New York: Macmillan Publishing Co., 1975.

Buchwald, Art. *The Establishment Is Alive and Well in Washington.* New York: Putnam, 1968.

Buck, Pearl S. *The Kennedy Women.* New York: Cowles, 1970.

Bugliosi, Vincent. *Reclaiming History: The Assassination of President John F. Kennedy.* New York: W. W. Norton & Company, 2007.

Burns, James MacGregor. *Edward Kennedy and the Camelot Legacy.* New York: W. W. Norton & Company, 1976.

———. *John Kennedy: A Political Profile.* New York: Harcourt Brace Jovanovich, 1960.

Bushnell, Candace. *Sex and the City.* New York: Warner Books, 1996.

Cafarakis, Christian, with Jack Harvey. *The Fabulous Onassis: His Life and Loves.* New York: William Morrow & Co., 1972.

Cameron, Gail. *Rose: A Biography of Rose Fitzgerald Kennedy.* New York: Putnam, 1971.

Canfield, Michael, and Alan Weberman. *Coup d'Etat in America: The CIA and the Assassination of John F. Kennedy.* New York: Third Press, 1975.

Capote, Truman. *Answered Prayers: The Unfinished Novel.* New York: Random House, 1987.

———. *A Capote Reader.* New York: Random House, 1987.

———. *Music for Chameleons.* New York: Random House, 1975.

Caroli, Betty Boyd. *First Ladies.* New York: Oxford University Press, 1987.

Carpozi Jr., George. *The Hidden Side of Jacqueline Kennedy.* New York: Pyramid Books, 1967.

Carter, Ernestine. *Magic Names of Fashion.* Englewood Cliffs, N.J.: Prentice-Hall, 1980.

Carter, Rosalynn. *First Lady from Plains.* Boston: Houghton Mifflin, 1984.

Cassini, Igor. *I'd Do It All Over Again.* New York: Putnam, 1977.

Cassini, Oleg. *In My Own Fashion: An Autobiography.* New York: Simon & Schuster, 1987.

Celebrity Homes: Architectural Digest Presents the Private Worlds of Thirty International Personalities. Edited by Paige Rense. New York: Viking Press, 1977.

Cerf, Bennett. *At Random: The Reminiscences of Bennett Cerf.* New York: Random House, 1977.

Chellis, Marcia. *Living with the Kennedys: The Joan Kennedy Story.* New York: Simon & Schuster, 1985.

Cheshire, Maxine. *Maxine Cheshire, Reporter.* Boston: Houghton Mifflin, 1978.

Childs, Marquis William. *Witness to Power.* New York: McGraw-Hill, 1975.

Churcher, Sharon. *New York Confidential.* New York: Crown Publishers, 1986.

Churchill, Sarah. *Keep on Dancing: An Autobiography.* New York: Coward, McCann & Geoghegan, 1981.

Clift, Eleanor, and Tom Brazaitis. *Madam President: Women Blazing the Leadership Trail.* New York; London: Routledge, 2003.

Clinch, Nancy Gager. *The Kennedy Neurosis.* New York: Grosset & Dunlap, 1973.

Clinton, Bill. *My Life*. New York: Knopf, 2004.

Clinton, Hillary Rodham. *Living History*. New York: Simon & Schuster, 2003.

Colby, Gerard. *DuPont Dynasty: Behind the Nylon Curtain*. Secaucus, N.J.: Lyle Stuart, 1984.

Collier, Peter, and David Horowitz. *The Kennedys: An American Drama*. New York: Summit Books, 1984.

Concise Compendium of the Warren Commission Report on the Assassination of John F. Kennedy, A. New York: Popular Library, 1964.

Condon, Dianne Russell. *Jackie's Treasures: The Fabled Objects from the Auction of the Century*. Foreword by Dominick Dunne. New York: Cader Books, 1996.

Cooney, John. *The American Pope: The Life and Times of Francis Cardinal Spellman*. New York: Times Books, 1984.

———. *The Annenbergs*. New York: Simon & Schuster, 1982.

Cooper, Lady Diana. *The Rainbow Comes and Goes*. Boston: Houghton Mifflin, 1958.

Coover, Robert. *Sesion de cine o Tocala de neuvo, Sam*. Traduccion de Mariano Antolin Rato. Barcelona: Editorial Anagrama, 1993.

Cormier, Frank. *Presidents Are People Too*. Washington, D.C.: Public Affairs Press, 1966.

Coulter, Laurie. *When John and Caroline Lived in the White House*. New York: Hyperion, 2000.

Coward, Noël. *The Noël Coward Diaries*. Edited by Graham Payn and Sheridan Morley. Boston: Little, Brown and Company, 1982.

Cowles, Virginia. *The Astors*. New York: Knopf, 1979.

Curtis, Charlotte. *First Lady*. New York: Pyramid Books, 1962.

———. *The Rich and Other Atrocities*. New York: Harper & Row, 1976.

Cutler, John Henry. *Cardinal Cushing of Boston*. New York: Hawthorne Books, 1970.

Dallas, Rita, and Jeanira Ratcliffe. *The Kennedy Case*. New York: Putnam, 1973.

Damore, Leo. *The Cape Cod Years of John Fitzgerald Kennedy*. Englewood Cliffs, N.J.: Prentice-Hall, 1967.

———. *Senatorial Privilege: The Chappaquiddick Cover-Up*. Washington, D.C.: Regnery-Gateway, 1988.

Dareff, Hal. *Jacqueline Kennedy: A Portrait in Courage*. New York: Parents' Magazine Press, 1966.

David, John H. *The Bouviers: A Portrait of an American Family*. New York: Farrar, Strauss & Giroux, 1969.

———. *The Kennedys: Dynasty and Disaster 1848–1983*. New York: McGraw-Hill, 1984.

David, Lester. *Joan—The Reluctant Kennedy: A Bibliographical Profile*. New York: Funk & Wagnalls, 1974.

David, Lester, and Irene David. *Bobby Kennedy: The Making of a Folk Hero*. New York: Dodd, Mead, 1986.

David, William, and Christina Tree. *The Kennedy Library*. Exton, Pa.: Schiffer Publishing, 1980.

Davis, Deborah. *Katharine the Great: Katharine Graham and the Washington Post*. New York: Harcourt Brace Jovanovich, 1979.

Davis, L. J. *Onassis: Aristotle and Christina*. New York: St. Martin's Press, 1986.

Davison, Jean. *Oswald's Game.* New York: W. W. Norton & Co., 1983.

Deaver, Michael K., with Mickey Hershkowitz. *Behind the Scenes.* New York: William Morrow & Co., 1988.

De Combray, Richard. *Goodbye Europe, A Novel in Six Parts.* Garden City, N.Y.: Doubleday, 1983.

de Gaulle, Charles. *Lettres, Notes et Carnets, Janvier 1964–Juin 1966.* Paris: Plon, 1987.

Delany, Kevin. *A Walk Through Georgetown: A Guided Stroll That Details the History and Charm of Old Georgetown.* Illustrated by Sally Booher. [Washington ? 1971].

Demaris, Ovid. *The Last Mafioso: The Treacherous World of Jimmy Fratianno.* New York: Times Books, 1981.

De Massy, Baron Christian. *Palace: My Life in the Royal Family of Monaco.* New York: Atheneum, 1986.

De Pauw, Linda Grant, Conover Hunt, and Miriam Schneir. *Remember the Ladies: Women in America, 1750–1815.* New York: The Viking Press, 1976.

De Toledano, Ralph. *R.F.K.: The Man Who Would Be President.* New York: Putnam, 1967.

Devi, Gayatri, and Santha Rama Rau. *A Princess Remembers: The Memoirs of the Maharani of Jaipur.* Philadelphia: J. B. Lippincott, 1976.

Dherbier, Yann-Brice, and Pierre-Henri Verlhac. *John F. Kennedy Jr.: A Life in Pictures.* New York: powerHouse Books, 2005.

Dickerson, Nancy. *Among Those Present: A Reporter's View of Twenty-five Years in Washington.* New York: Random House, 1976.

Dickinson, Janice. *Everything About Me Is Fake . . . and I'm Perfect.* New York: ReganBooks, 2004.

———. *No Lifeguard On Duty: The Accidental Life of the World's First Supermodel.* New York: ReganBooks, 2002.

Dixon Healy, Diana. *America's First Ladies: Private Lives of the Presidential Wives, 1789–1989.* New York: Atheneum, 1988.

Donovan, Robert J. *PT 109: John F. Kennedy in World War II.* New York: McGraw-Hill, 1961.

Drosnin, Michael. *Citizen Hughes.* New York: Holt, Rinehart and Winston, 1985.

Druitt, Michael. *John F. Kennedy, Jr.: A Life in the Spotlight.* Kansas City: Ariel Books, 1996.

DuBois, Diana. *In Her Sister's Shadow: An Intimate Biography of Lee Radziwill.* Boston: Little, Brown and Company, 1995.

Dumas, Timothy. *Greentown: Murder and Mystery in Greenwich, America's Wealthiest Community.* New York: Arcade Publishing, 1998.

Eban, Abba. *Abba Eban: An Autobiography.* New York: Random House, 1977.

Eisenhower, Julie Nixon. *Pat Nixon: The Untold Story.* New York: Simon & Schuster, 1986.

Englund, Steven. *Grace of Monaco.* Garden City, N.Y.: Doubleday, 1984.

Epstein, Edward Jay. *Inquest: The Warren Commission and the Establishment of the Truth.* New York: Viking, 1966.

———. *The Rise and Fall of Diamonds: The Shattering of a Brilliant Illusion.* New York: Simon & Schuster, 1982.

Evans, Peter. *Ari: The Life and Times of Aristotle Onassis.* New York: Summit Books, 1986.

————. *Nemesis: The True Story of Aristotle Onassis, Jackie O., and the Love Triangle That Brought Down the Kennedys.* New York: ReganBooks, 2004.

Evans, Rowland, and Robert Novak. *Lyndon B. Johnson: The Exercise of Power.* New York: New American Library, 1966.

Evica, George Michael. *And We Are All Mortal: New Evidence and Analysis in the John F. Kennedy Assassination.* Hartford, Conn.: University of Hartford Press, 1978.

Exner, Judith. *My Story.* New York: Grove Press, 1977.

Fairlee, Henry. *The Kennedy Promise: The Politics of Expectation.* New York: Doubleday, 1972.

Fay Jr., Paul B. *The Pleasure of His Company.* New York: Harper & Row, 1966.

Fensterwald, Bernard J. *Coincidence or Conspiracy.* New York: Zebra Books, 1977.

Fisher, Eddie. *Eddie: My Life, My Loves.* New York: Harper & Row, 1981.

Flaherty, Tina Santi. *What Jackie Taught Us: Lessons from the Remarkable Life of Jacqueline Kennedy.* New York: Perigree, 2004.

Folsom, Merrill. *More Great American Mansions and Their Stories.* New York: Hastings House Book Publishers, 1967.

Fontaine, Joan. *No Bed of Roses: An Autobiography.* New York: William Morrow & Co., 1978.

Four Days: The Historical Record of the Death of President Kennedy. Compiled by United Press International and *American Heritage* Magazine. New York: American Heritage Press, 1964.

Francisco, Ruth. *The Secret Memoirs of Jacqueline Kennedy Onassis: A Novel.* New York: St. Martin's Griffin, 2006.

Frank, Sid, and Arden Davis Melick. *Presidents: Tidbits and Trivia.* Maplewood, N.J.: Hammond World Atlas Corp., 1986.

Franklin, Marc A., David A. Anderson, and Fred H. Cate. *Mass Media Law: Cases and Materials.* 6th ed. New York: Foundation Press, 2000.

Fraser, Nicholas, Philip Jacobson, Mark Ottaway, and Lewis Chester. *Aristotle Onassis.* Philadelphia: J. B. Lippincott, 1977.

Friedman, Stanley P. *The Magnificent Kennedy Women.* Derby, Conn.: Monarch Books, 1964.

Fries, Chuck, and Irv Wilson, with Spencer Green. *"We'll Never Be Young Again": Remembering the Last Days of John. F. Kennedy.* Los Angeles: Tallfellow Press, 2003.

Frischauer, Willi. *Onassis.* New York: Meredith Press, 1968.

Fuhrman, Mark. *Murder in Greenwich: Who Killed Martha Moxley?* Foreword by Dominick Dunne. Thorndike, Maine: Thorndike, 1998.

Gabor, Zsa Zsa. *Zsa Zsa Gabor: My Story.* Written by Gerold Frank. Cleveland: World Pub. Co., 1963.

Gadney, Reg. *Kennedy.* New York: Holt, Rinehart and Winston, 1983.

Gage, Nicholas. *Greek Fire: The Story of Maria Callas and Aristotle Onassis.* New York: Knopf, 2000.

Gaines, Steven, and Sharon Churcher. *Obsession: The Lives and Times of Calvin Klein.* New York: Carol Publishing Group, 1994.

Galbraith, John Kenneth. *Ambassador's Journal: A Personal Account of the Kennedy Years.* Boston: Houghton Mifflin, 1969.

Galella, Ron. *Jacqueline.* New York: Sheed and Ward, 1974.

———. *Off-Guard: Beautiful People Unveiled Before the Camera Lens.* New York: McGraw-Hill Education, 1976.

Gallagher, Mary Barelli. *My Life with Jacqueline Kennedy.* New York: David McKay Co., 1969.

Gardiner Jr., Ralph. *Young, Gifted and Rich: The Secrets of America's Most Successful Entrepreneurs.* New York: Simon & Schuster, 1984.

Gatti, Arthur. *The Kennedy Curse.* Chicago: Regnery, 1976.

Getty, J. Paul. *As I See It: The Autobiography of J. Paul Getty.* New York: Berkley, 1976.

Giancana, Antoinette, and Thomas C. Renner. *Mafia Princess: Growing Up in Sam Giancana's Family.* New York: William Morrow & Co., 1984.

Gibson, Barbara, and Ted Schwarz. *The Kennedys: The Third Generation.* New York: Thunder's Mouth Press, 1993.

Gibson, Barbara, with Caroline Lathum. *Life with Rose Kennedy: An Intimate Account.* New York: Warner Books, 1986.

Gibson, Barbara, and Ted Schwarz. *Rose Kennedy and Her Family: The Best and Worst of Their Lives and Times.* Secaucus, N.J.: Carol Publishing Company, 1995.

Gingras, Angèle de T. *"From Bussing to Bugging": The Best in Congressional Humor.* Washington, D.C.: Acropolis Books, 1973.

Gold, Arthur, and Robert Fizdale. *Misia: The Life of Misia Sert.* New York: Knopf, 1980.

Goldman, Eric F. *The Tragedy of Lyndon Johnson.* New York: Knopf, 1979.

Goodwin, Doris Kearns. *The Fitzgeralds and the Kennedys: An American Saga.* New York: Simon & Schuster, 1987.

Goodwin, Richard N. *Remembering America: A Voice from the Sixties.* Boston: Little, Brown and Company, 1988.

Granger, Stewart. *Sparks Fly Upward.* New York: Putnam, 1981.

Gray, Earle. *Wildcatters: The Story of Pacific Petroleum and Westward Expansion.* Toronto: McClelland and Stewart, 1982.

Greenberg, Carol, and Sara Bonnett Stein. *Pretend Your Nose Is a Crayon and Other Strategies for Staying Younger Longer.* Boston: Houghton Mifflin, 1991.

Grier, Roosevelt. *Rosey, An Autobiography: The Gentle Giant.* Tulsa, Okla.: Honor Books, 1986.

Grobel, Lawrence. *Conversations with Capote.* New York: New American Library, 1985.

Guiles, Fred Lawrence. *Legend: The Life and Death of Marilyn Monroe.* New York: Stein and Day Publishing, 1984.

Gulley, Bill, and Mary Ellen Reese. *Breaking Cover.* New York: Simon & Schuster, 1980.

Guthman, Edwin. *We Band of Brothers: A Memoir of Robert F. Kennedy.* New York: Harper & Row, 1971.

Guthrie, Lee. *Jackie: The Price of the Pedestal.* New York: Drake Publishers, 1978.

Haban, Rita Miller. *Arlington National Cemetery and the Women in Military Service Memorial: A Walk in a Time Capsule.* Editor: Shirley P. Meyer. Photography: Edward Haban. 2nd pbk. ed. [Reynoldsburg, Ohio: self-published], 1998.

Halberstam, David. *The Best and the Brightest.* New York: Random House, 1972.

Hall, Gordon Langley, and Ann Pinchot. *Jacqueline Kennedy: A Biography.* New York: Frederick Fell, 1964.

Halle, Kay. *The Grand Original: Portraits of Randolph Churchill by His Friends.* Boston: Houghton Mifflin, 1971.

Hamilton, Ian. *Robert Lowell: A Biography.* New York: Random House, 1982.

Harris, Bill. *John Fitzgerald Kennedy: A Photographic Tribute.* New York: Crescent, 1983.

Harris, Fred R. *Potomac Fever.* New York: W. W. Norton and Company, 1977.

Harris, Kenneth. *Conversations.* London: Hodder & Stoughton, 1967.

Harris, Warren G. *Cary Grant: A Touch of Elegance.* Garden City, N.Y.: Doubleday, 1987.

Heller, Deanne, and David Heller. *A Complete Story of America's First Lady.* Derby, Conn.: Monarch Books, 1961.

———. *Jacqueline Kennedy: The Warmly Human Story of the Woman All Americans Have Taken to Their Heart.* New York: Monarch Books, 1961.

Hemingway, Mary Walsh. *How It Was.* New York: Knopf, 1976.

Herbert, David. *Second Son: An Autobiography.* London: Owen, 1972.

Hersh, Burton. *Bobby and J. Edgar: The Historic Face-Off Between the Kennedys and J. Edgar Hoover That Transformed America.* New York: Perseus Publishing, 2007.

———. *The Education of Edward Kennedy: A Family Biography.* New York: William Morrow & Co., 1972.

Hersh, Seymour M. *The Dark Side of Camelot.* Boston: Little, Brown and Company, 1997.

Heymann, C. David. *American Aristocracy: The Lives and Times of James Russell, Amy and Robert Lowell.* New York: Dodd, Mead, 1980.

———. *The Georgetown Ladies' Social Club: Power, Passion, and Politics in the Nation's Capital.* New York: Atria Books, 2003.

———. *Poor Little Rich Girl: The Life and Legend of Barbara Hutton.* Secaucus, N.J.: Lyle Stuart, 1984.

———. *RFK: A Candid Biography of Robert F. Kennedy.* New York: Dutton, 1998.

———. *A Woman Named Jackie: An Intimate Biography of Jacqueline Bouvier Kennedy Onassis.* New York: Carol Communications, 1989.

Hibbert, Christopher. *The Royal Victorians: King Edward VII, His Family and Friends.* Philadelphia: J. B. Lippincott, 1976.

Higham, Charles. *Marlena: The Life of Marlena Dietrich.* New York: W. W. Norton and Company, 1977.

———. *Rose: The Life and Times of Rose Fitzgerald Kennedy.* New York: Pocket Books, 1995.

———. *Sisters: The Story of Olivia de Havilland and Joan Fontaine.* New York: Putnam Publishing Group, 1984.

Hohenberg, John. *The Pulitzer Prizes: A History of the Awards in Books, Drama, Music, and Journalism, Based on the Private Files over Six Decades.* New York: Columbia University Press, 1974.

Holland, Max. *The Kennedy Assassination Tapes.* New York: Knopf, 2004.

Honan, William H. *Ted Kennedy: Profile of a Survivor.* New York: Quadrangle Books, 1972.

Hosmer Jr., Charles Bridgham. *Preservation Comes of Age: From Williamsburg to the National Trust, 1926–1949.* Vol. II. Charlottesville, Va.: University of Virginia Press, 1981.

Hurt, Henry. *Reasonable Doubt: An Investigation into the Assassination of John F. Kennedy.* New York: Holt, Rinehart and Winston, 1985.

Huste, Annemarie. *Annemarie's Personal Cook Book.* London: Bartholomew House, 1968.

Isaacson, Walter, and Evan Thomas. *The Wise Men—Six Friends and the World They Made: Acheson, Bohlen, Harriman, Kennan, Lovett, McCloy.* New York: Simon & Schuster, 1986.

Jackson, Michael. *Moonwalk.* New York: Doubleday, 1988.

Jamieson, Katherine Hall. *Packaging the Presidency: A History and Criticism of Presidential Campaign Advertising.* New York: Oxford University Press, 1984.

JFK, Jr.: The Untold Story (periodical). *Fifth Anniversary Issue.* New York: American Media Mini Mags Inc., 2004.

Joesten, Joachim. *Onassis.* New York: Tower, 1973.

John F. Kennedy Library. *Historical Materials in the John F. Kennedy Library.* Compiled and edited by Ronald E. Whealan. Boston (Columbia Point, Boston 02125): The Library, 2000.

Johnson, Lady Bird. *A White House Diary.* New York: Holt, Reinhart & Winston, 1970.

Johnson, Lyndon Baines. *The Vantage Point: Perspectives of the Presidency 1963–1969.* New York: Holt, Reinhart & Winston, 1971.

Johnson, Sam Houston. *My Brother Lyndon.* New York: Cowles, 1969.

Josephson, Matthew. *The Money Lords: The Great Finance Capitalists, 1925–1950.* New York: Weybright and Talley, 1972.

Kane, Elizabeth. *Jackie O: A Life in Pictures.* New York: Barnes & Noble Books, 2004.

Kantor, Seth. *The Ruby Cover-up.* New York: Kensington, 1978.

Kearns, Doris. *Lyndon Johnson and the American Dream.* New York: Harper & Row, 1976.

Keenan, Brigid. *The Women We Wanted to Look Like.* New York: St. Martin's Press, 1978.

Kellerman, Barbara. *All the President's Kin.* New York: The Free Press, 1981.

Kelley, Kitty. *Elizabeth Taylor: The Last Star.* New York: Simon & Schuster, 1981.

———. *His Way: The Unauthorized Biography of Frank Sinatra.* New York: Bantam Books, 1986.

———. *Jackie Oh!* Secaucus, N.J.: Lyle Stuart, 1978.

Kelly, Tom. *The Imperial Post: The Meyers, the Grahams, and the Paper That Rules Washington.* New York: William Morrow & Co., 1983.

Kennedy, Caroline. *A Family of Poems: My Favorite Poetry for Children.* New York: Hyperion Books, 2005.

Kennedy, Edward M., ed. *The Fruitful Bough: Reminiscences of Joseph P. Kennedy.* Privately printed, 1970.

Kennedy, John F. *As We Remember Joe.* Privately printed, 1945.

———. *Profiles in Courage.* New York: Harper & Row, 1964.

———. *Public Papers of the Presidents of the United States, 1961, 1962, 1963.* 3 vols. U.S. Government Printing Office, 1962, 1963, 1964.

———. *Why England Slept.* New York: Wilfred Funk, 1940.

Kennedy, Joseph P. *Hostage to Fortune: The Letters of Joseph P. Kennedy.* Edited by Amanda Smith. New York: Viking, 2001.

Kennedy, Robert F. *The Enemy Within.* New York: Harper, 1960.

————. *In His Own Words: The Unpublished Recollections of the Kennedy Years.* Edited by Edwin O. Guthman and Jeffrey Shulman. New York: Bantam Books, 1988.

————. *Thirteen Days: A Memoir of the Cuban Missile Crisis.* New York: W. W. Norton & Company, 1969.

————. *To Seek a New World.* Garden City, N.Y.: Doubleday & Company, 1967.

Kennedy Jr., Robert F. *Crimes Against Nature: How George W. Bush and His Corporate Pals Are Plundering the Country and Hijacking Our Democracy.* New York: HarperCollins Publishers, 2004.

Kennedy, Sheila Rauch. *Shattered Faith: A Woman's Struggle to Stop the Catholic Church from Annulling Her Marriage.* New York: Henry Holt and Company, 1998.

The Kennedys: A New York Times Profile. Edited by Gene Brown. New York: Arno Press, 1980.

Kern, Montague, Patricia W. Levering, and Ralph B. Levering. *The Kennedy Crisis: The Press, the Presidency, and Foreign Policy.* Chapel Hill, N.C.: University of North Carolina Press, 1983.

Kessler, Judy. *Inside People: The Stories Behind the Stories.* New York: Villard, 1994.

King, Coretta Scott. *My Life with Martin Luther King, Jr.* New York: Holt, Reinhart & Winston, 1969.

King, Larry, with Peter Occhiogrosso. *Tell It to the King.* New York: G. P. Putnam's Sons, 1988.

Klapthor, Margaret Brown. *The First Ladies.* Washington, D.C.: The White House Historical Association, 1975.

Klein, Edward. *Farewell, Jackie: A Portrait of Her Final Days.* New York: Viking, 2004.

————. *Just Jackie: Her Private Years.* New York: Ballantine Books, 1998.

————. *The Kennedy Curse: Why America's First Family Has Been Haunted by Tragedy for 150 Years.* New York: St. Martin's Press, 2003.

Knightly, Phillip, and Caroline Kennedy. *An Affair of State: The Profumo Case and the Framing of Stephen Ward.* New York: Atheneum, 1987.

Konolige, Kit. *The Richest Women in the World.* New York: Macmillan, 1986.

Koskoff, David E. *Joseph P. Kennedy: A Life and Times.* Englewood Cliffs, N.J.: Prentice-Hall, 1974.

Kramer, Freda. *Jackie: A Truly Intimate Biography.* New York: Funk & Wagnalls, 1968.

Krock, Arthur. *In the Nation: 1932–1966.* New York: McGraw-Hill, 1966.

Kwitny, Jonathan. *Endless Enemies: The Making of an Unfriendly World.* New York: Congdon & Weed, 1984.

Lamarr, Hedy. *Ecstasy and Me: My Life as a Woman.* New York: Fawcett Crest, 1967.

Lambro, Donald. *Washington—City of Scandals: Investigating Congress and Other Big Spenders.* Boston: Little, Brown and Company, 1984.

Landau, Elaine. *John F. Kennedy Jr.* Brookfield, Conn.: Twenty-First Century Books, 2000.

Lane, Mark. *Rush to Judgement: A Critique of the Warren Commission's Inquiry into the Murders of President John F. Kennedy, Officer J. D. Tippit and Lee Harvey Oswald.* New York: Holt, Reinhart & Winston, 1966.

Lanham, Robert. *The Hipster Handbook.* New York: Anchor Books, 2003.

Lash, Joseph P. *Eleanor: The Years Alone.* New York: W. W. Norton and Company, 1972.

Lasky, Victor. *J.F.K.: The Man and the Myth.* New York: Macmillan, 1963.

———*Robert F. Kennedy: The Myth and the Man.* New York: Trident Press, 1968.

Latham, Caroline, and Jeannie Sakol. *The Kennedy Encyclopedia: An Illustrated Guide to America's Royal Family.* New York: NAL Books, 1989.

Lawford, Christopher Kennedy. *Symptoms of Withdrawal: A Memoir of Snapshots and Redemption.* New York: William Morrow & Co., 2005.

Lawford, Lady May. *Bitch! The Autobiography of Lady Lawford.* Brookline Village, Mass.: Branden Books, 1986.

Lawford, Patricia Seaton, with Ted Schwarz. *The Peter Lawford Story: Life with the Kennedys, Monroe and the Rat Pack.* New York: Carroll and Graf Publishers, 1988.

Lax, Henry. *Sidelights from the Surgery.* London: Pallas, 1929.

Leamer, Laurence. *Fantastic: The Life of Arnold Schwarzenegger.* New York: St. Martin's Press, 2005.

———. *The Kennedy Women: The Saga of an American Family.* New York: Villard Books, 1994.

———. *Make-Believe: The Story of Nancy and Ronald Reagan.* New York: Harper & Row, 1983.

———. *Sons of Camelot: The Fate of an American Dynasty.* New York: William Morrow & Co., 2004.

Leaming, Barbara. *Mrs. Kennedy: The Missing History of the Kennedy Years.* New York: The Free Press, 2001.

Leary, Timothy. *Changing My Mind, Among Others: Lifetime Writings, Selected and Introduced by the Author.* Englewood Cliffs, N.J.: Prentice-Hall, 1982.

———. *Flashbacks: An Autobiography.* Los Angeles: J. P. Tarcher, 1983.

Lee, Martin A., and Bruce Shlain. *Acid Dreams: The CIA, LSD, and the Sixties Rebellion.* New York: Grove Press, 1985.

Leigh, Wendy. *Prince Charming: The John F. Kennedy, Jr. Story.* New York: Signet, 1994.

Lerman, Leo. *The Grand Surprise: The Journals of Leo Lerman.* Edited by Stephen Pascal. New York: Knopf, 2007.

Lerner, Max. *Ted and the Kennedy Legend: A Study in Character and Destiny.* New York: St. Martin's Press, 1980.

Lifton, David S. *Best Evidence: Disguise and Deception in the Assassination of John F. Kennedy.* New York: Macmillan, 1980.

Lilienthal, David E. *The Journals of David E. Lilienthal. Volume V: The Harvest Years, 1959–1963.* New York: Harper & Row, 1972.

Lilly, Doris. *Those Fabulous Greeks: Onassis, Niarchos, and Livanos.* London: W. H. Allen, 1971.

Lincoln, Anne H. *The Kennedy White House Parties.* New York: Viking Press, 1967.

Lincoln, Evelyn. *My Twelve Years with John F. Kennedy.* New York: David McKay Company, 1965.

Littell, Robert T. *The Men We Became: My Friendship with John F. Kennedy Jr.* New York: St. Martin's Press, 2004.

Logan, Joshua. *Movie Stars, Real People and Me.* New York: Delacorte Press, 1989.

Louchheim, Katie. *By the Political Sea.* Garden City, N.Y.: Doubleday, 1970.

Lowe, Jacques. *Kennedy: A Time Remembered.* London: Quartet Books, 1983.

———. *Remembering Jack: Intimate and Unseen Photographs of the Kennedys.* Boston: Bulfinch Press, 2003.

Lowell, James Russell. *Selected Literary Essays from James Russell Lowell.* Introduction by Will David Howe and Norman Zoerster. Boston: Houghton Mifflin, 1914.

Lowell, Robert. *History.* New York: Farrar, Straus & Giroux, 1973.

Macmillan, Harold. *At the End of the Day, 1961–1963.* New York: Harper & Row, 1973.

MacPherson, Myra. *The Power Lovers: An Intimate Look at Politics and Marriage.* New York: Putnam, 1975.

Maier, Thomas. *The Kennedys: America's Emerald Kings.* New York: Basic Books, 2003.

Mailer, Norman. *Marilyn.* New York: Grosset & Dunlap, 1973.

———. *Of Women and Their Elegance.* New York: Simon & Schuster, 1980.

———. *The Presidential Papers.* New York: Dell, 1963.

Makower, Joel. *Boom! Talkin' About Our Generation.* New York: Contemporary Books, 1985.

Manchester, William. *Controversy and Other Essays in Journalism, 1950–1975.* Boston: Little, Brown and Company, 1963.

———. *The Death of a President: November 1963.* New York: Harper & Row, 1967.

———. *One Brief Shining Moment: Remembering Kennedy.* Boston: Little, Brown and Company, 1983.

———. *Portrait of a President: John F. Kennedy in Profile.* Boston: Little, Brown and Company, 1962.

Manso, Peter. *Brando: The Biography.* New York: Hyperion, 1994.

———. *Mailer: His Life and Times.* New York: Simon & Schuster, 1985.

Marsh, Lisa. *The House of Klein: Fashion, Controversy, and a Business Obsession.* Hoboken, N.J.: Wiley, 2003.

Martin, John Bartlow. *Adlai Stevenson and the World: The Life of Adlai Stevenson.* Garden City, N.Y.: Doubleday and Company, 1977.

Martin, Ralph G. *Cissy: The Extraordinary Life of Eleanor Medill Patterson.* New York: Simon & Schuster, 1979.

———. *A Hero for Our Time: An Intimate Story of the Kennedy Years.* New York: Ballantine Books, 1983.

Maxwell, Elsa. *The Celebrity Circus.* New York: Appleton-Century, 1963.

———. *R.S.V.P.: Elsa Maxwell's Own Story.* Boston: Little, Brown and Company, 1954.

May, Ernest R., and Philip D. Zelikow, eds. *Kennedy Tapes, The: Inside the White House During the Cuban Missile Crisis.* Cambridge, Mass.: Belknap Press of Harvard University, 1997.

McCarthy, Dennis V. N. *Protecting the President: The Inside Story of a Secret Service Agent.* New York: William Morrow & Co., 1985.

McCarthy, Joe. *The Remarkable Kennedys.* New York: Dial Press, 1960.

McConnell, Brian. *The History of Assassination.* Nashville: Aurora Publishers, 1970.

McKnight, Frank Kenneth. *Frank-ly McKnight: A Mini-Autobiography.* Laguna Hills, Calif.: McKnight Enterprises, 1992.

McMahon MD, Edward B., and Leonard Curry. *Medical Cover-ups in the White House.* Washington, D.C.: Farragut Publishing Company, 1987.

McMillan, Priscilla Johnson. *Marina and Lee.* New York: Harper & Row, 1977.

McTaggart, Lynne. *Kathleen Kennedy, Her Life and Times.* New York: Dial Press, 1983.

Means, Marrianne. *The Woman in the White House.* New York: Random House, 1963.

Meneghini, Giovanni Battista. *My Wife Maria Callas.* New York: Farrar, Straus & Giroux, 1982.

Meyers, Joan, ed. *John Fitzgerald Kennedy . . . As We Remember Him.* New York: Atheneum, 1965.

Michaelis, David. *The Best of Friends: Profiles of Extraordinary Friendships.* New York: William Morrow & Company, 1983.

Miers, Earl Schenck. *America and Its Presidents.* New York: Grosset & Dunlap, 1959.

Miller, Alice P. *A Kennedy Chronology.* New York: Birthdate Research, 1968.

Miller, Arthur. *Timebends: A Life.* New York: Grove Press, 1987.

Miller, Hope Ridings. *Embassy Row: The Life & Times of Diplomatic Washington.* New York: Holt, Reinhart and Winston, 1969.

Miller, Merle. *Plain Speaking: An Oral Biography of Harry S. Truman.* New York: Berkley Publishing Corporation, 1973.

———. *Scandals in the Highest Office: Facts and Fictions in the Private Lives of Our Presidents.* New York: Random House, 1973.

Miller, William "Fishbait," and Frances Spatz Leighton. *Fishbait: The Memoirs of the Congressional Doorkeeper.* Englewood Cliffs, N.J.: Prentice-Hall, 1977.

Montgomery, Ruth Shick. *Flowers at the White House: An Informal Tour of the House of the Presidents of the United States.* New York: M. Barrows, 1967.

———. *Hail to the Chiefs: My Life and Times with Six Presidents.* New York: Coward-McCann, 1970.

Moon, Vicky. *The Private Passion of Jackie Kennedy Onassis: Portrait of a Rider.* New York: ReganBooks, 2005.

Mooney, Booth. *LBJ: An Irreverent Chronicle.* New York: Crowell, 1976.

Morella, Joe. *Paul and Joanne: A Biography of Paul Newman and Joanne Woodward.* New York: Dell, 1988.

Morella, Joe, and Edward Z. Epstein. *Forever Lucy: The Life of Lucille Ball.* Secaucus, N.J.: Lyle Stuart, 1986.

Morrow, Lance. *The Chief: A Memoir of Fathers and Sons.* New York: Random House, 1984.

Morrow, Robert D. *The Senator Must Die: The Murder of Robert Kennedy.* Santa Monica, Calif.: Roundtable Publishing, 1988.

Moutsatsos, Keki Feroudie. *The Onassis Women.* New York: G. P. Putnam's Sons, 1998.

Mulvaney, Jay. *Kennedy Weddings: A Family Album.* New York: St. Martin's Press, 1999.

Newfield, Jack. *Robert Kennedy: A Memoir.* New York: Berkley, 1969.

Nicholas, William. *The Bobby Kennedy Nobody Knows.* New York: Fawcett Publications, 1967.

Nin, Anais. *The Diary of Anais Nin (1947–1955), Volume 5.* New York: Harcourt Brace Jovanovich, 1974.

Niven, David. *The Moon's a Balloon.* New York: Putnam, 1972.

Nixon, Richard. *RN: The Memoirs of Richard Nixon.* New York: Grosset & Dunlap, 1978.

Nizer, Louis. *Reflections Without Mirrors: An Autobiography of the Mind.* New York: Doubleday & Company, 1978.

Noguchi, Thomas T., with Joseph Dimona. *Coroner to the Stars.* London: Corgi Books, 1983.

Noonan, William Sylvester, with Robert Huber. *Forever Young: My Friendship with John F. Kennedy, Jr.* New York: Viking, 2006.

Nowakowski, Tadeusz. *The Radziwills: The Social History of a Great European Family.* New York: Delacorte Press, 1974.

Nunnerley, David. *President Kennedy and Britain.* New York: St. Martin's Press, 1972.

Oates, Stephen B. *Let the Trumpet Sound: The Life of Martin Luther King, Jr.* New York: Harper & Row, 1982.

———. *William Faulkner: The Man & the Artist.* New York: Harper & Row, 1987.

O'Brien, Lawrence F. *No Final Victories: A Life in Politics—from John F. Kennedy to Watergate.* New York: Doubleday, 1974.

O'Donnell, Helen. *A Common Good: The Friendship of Robert F. Kennedy and Kenneth P. O'Donnell.* New York: William Morrow, 1998.

O'Donnell, Kenneth P., and David F. Powers, with Joe McCarthy. *"Johnny We Hardly Knew Ye": Memories of John Fitzgerald Kennedy.* Boston: Little, Brown and Company, 1970.

Onassis, Jacqueline Kennedy. *The Eloquent Jacqueline Kennedy Onassis: A Portrait in Her Own Words.* Edited by Bill Adler. New York: HarperCollins, 2004.

———. *In the Russian Style.* New York: The Viking Press, 1976.

———. *The Last Will and Testament of Jacqueline Kennedy Onassis.* New York: Carroll and Graf Publishers, 1997.

O'Neill, Tip, with William Novak. *Man of the House: The Life and Political Memoirs of Speaker Tip O'Neill.* New York: Random House, 1987.

Osmond, Humphry. *Predicting the Past: Memos on the Enticing Universe of Possibility.* New York: Macmillan Publishing Company, 1981.

Paper, Lewis J. *The Promise and the Performance: The Leadership of John F. Kennedy.* New York: Crown Publishers, 1975.

Parker, Robert, with Richard Rashke. *Capitol Hill in Black and White.* New York: Dodd, Mead, 1987.

Parmet, Herbert S. *Jack: The Struggles of John F. Kennedy.* New York: Dial Press, 1980.

A Patriot's Handbook: Songs, Poems, Stories, and Speeches Celebrating the Land We Love. Selected and introduced by Caroline Kennedy. New York: Hyperion, 2000.

People Weekly: Private Lives. By the editors of *People.* New York: Oxmoor House, 1991.

Persico, Joseph E. *The Imperial Rockefeller: A Biography of Nelson A. Rockefeller.* New York: Simon & Schuster, 1982.

Peters, Charles. *Tilting at Windmills: An Autobiography.* Reading, Mass.: Addison-Wesley, 1988.

Peyser, Joan. *Bernstein. A Biography.* New York: Beech Tree Books, 1987.

Phillips, John, with Jim Jerome. *Papa John: An Autobiography.* Garden City, N.Y.: Doubleday, 1986.

Phillips, Julia. *You'll Never Eat Lunch in This Town Again.* New York: Random House, 1991.

Political Profiles: The Johnson Years. New York: Facts on File, 1976.

Political Profiles: The Kennedy Years. New York: Facts on File, 1976.

Potter, Jeffrey. *Men, Money & Magic: The Story of Dorothy Schiff.* New York: Coward, McCann & Geoghegan, 1976.

Pottker, Jan. *Celebrity Washington: Who They Are, Where They Live, and Why They're Famous.* Potomac, Md.: Writer's Cramp Books, 1996.

————. *Janet and Jackie: The Story of a Mother and Her Daughter, Jacqueline Kennedy Onassis.* New York: St. Martin's Press, 2001.

Powers, Thomas. *The Men Who Kept the Secrets; Richard Helms and the CIA.* New York: Knopf, 1979.

President's Commission on the Assassination of President Kennedy, The. (The Warren Commission) *Hearings and Exhibits.* Vols. I–XXXVI. Washington, D.C.: U.S. Government Printing Office, September 1964.

Profiles in Courage for Our Time. Introduced and edited by Caroline Kennedy. New York: Hyperion, 2002.

Profiles in History: Catalogue 4. Beverly Hills, Calif.: Joseph M. Menddalena, n.d.

Rachlin, Harvey. *The Kennedys: A Chronological History 1823–Present.* New York: World Almanac Books, 1986.

Radziwill, Carole. *What Remains: A Memoir of Fate, Friendship, and Love.* New York: Scribner, 2005.

Radziwill, Lee. *Happy Times.* New York: Assouline, 2000.

Rainie, Harrison, and John Quinn. *Growing Up Kennedy: The Third Wave Comes of Age.* New York: Putnam Publishing Group, 1983.

Randall, Monica. *The Mansions of Long Island's Gold Coast.* New York: Hastings House, 1979.

Rapaport, Roger. *The Super-Doctors.* Chicago: Playboy Press, 1975.

Rather, Dan, and Gary Paul Gates. *The Palace Guard.* New York: Harper & Row, 1974.

Rather, Dan, and Mickey Herskowitz. *The Camera Never Blinks: Adventures of a TV Journalist.* New York: William Morrow & Co., 1977.

Rattray, Jeanette Edwards. *Fifty Years of the Maidstone Club, 1891–1941.* Souvenir publication privately printed for members of the club (1941).

Reeves, Richard. *President Kennedy: Profile of Power.* New York: Simon & Schuster, 1993.

Reeves, Thomas C. *A Question of Character: A Life of John F. Kennedy.* Rocklin, Calif.: Primay Publishing, 1992.

Reich, Cary. *Financier: The Biography of André Meyer: A Story of Money, Power, and the Reshaping of American Business.* New York: William Morrow & Co., 1983.

Report of the Warren Commission on the Assassination of President Kennedy. New York: Bantam Books, 1964.

Rhea, Mini. *I Was Jacqueline Kennedy's Dressmaker.* New York: Fleet, 1962.

Riese, Randall, and Neal Hitchens. *The Unabridged Marilyn: Her Life from A to Z.* New York: Congdon & Weed, 1987.

Romero, Gerry. *Sinatra's Women.* New York: Parallax, 1967.

Roosevelt, Felicia Warburg. *Doers and Dowagers.* Garden City, N.Y.: Doubleday & Co., 1975.

Rowe, Robert. *The Bobby Baker Story.* New York: Parallax Publishing Company, 1967.

Rush, George. *Confessions of an Ex-Secret Service Agent.* New York: Donald I. Fine, 1988.

Rust, Zad. *Teddy Bare: The Last of the Kennedy Clan.* Boston: Western Islands, 1971.

Salinger, Pierre. *P.S.: A Memoir.* New York: St. Martin's Press, 1995.

———. *With Kennedy.* Garden City, N.Y.: Doubleday, 1966.

Saunders, Frank, with James Southwood. *Torn Lace Curtain.* New York: Holt, Reinhart & Winston, 1982.

Schaap, Dick. *R.F.K.* New York: New American Library, 1967.

Scheim, David E. *Contract on America: The Mafia Murder of President John F. Kennedy.* New York: Shapolsky Publishers, 1988.

Schlesinger Jr., Arthur M. *The Cycles of American History.* Boston: Houghton Mifflin, 1986.

———. *The Imperial Presidency.* New York: Atlantic Monthly, 1973.

———. *Journals 1952–2000.* Edited by Andrew Schlesinger and Stephen Schlesinger. New York: Penguin 2007.

———. *Robert Kennedy and His Times.* Boston: Houghton Mifflin, 1978.

———. *A Thousand Days: John F. Kennedy in the White House.* Boston: Houghton Mifflin, 1965.

Schoenbaum, Thomas J. *Waging Peace & War: Dean Rusk in the Truman, Kennedy & Johnson Years.* New York: Simon & Schuster, 1988.

Schoor, Gene. *Young John Kennedy.* New York: Harcourt, Brace & World, 1963.

Schwartz, Charles. *Cole Porter: A Biography.* New York: Dial Press, 1977.

Sciacca, Tony. *Kennedy and His Women.* New York: Manor Books, 1976.

Sealy, Shirley. *The Celebrity Sex Register.* New York: Simon & Schuster, 1982.

Seaman, Barbara. *Lovely Me: The Life of Jacqueline Susann.* New York: William Morrow & Co., 1987.

Searls, Hank. *The Lost Prince: Young Joe, the Forgotten Kennedy.* New York: The World Pub. Co., 1969.

Sgubin, Marta, and Nancy Nicholas. *Cooking for Madam: Recipes and Reminiscences from the Home of Jacqueline Kennedy Onassis.* New York: Scribner, 1998.

Shannon, William V. *The Heir Apparent: Robert Kennedy and the Struggle for Power.* New York: Macmillan, 1967.

Shaw, Mark. *The John F. Kennedys: A Family Album.* New York: Farrar, Strauss, 1964.

Shaw, Maud. *White House Nanny: My Years with Caroline and John Kennedy, Jr.* New York: New American Library, 1965.

Shephard Jr., Tazewell. *John F. Kennedy: Man of the Sea.* New York: William Morrow & Co., 1965.

Shesol, Jeff. *Mutual Contempt: Lyndon Johnson, Robert Kennedy, and the Feud That Defined a Decade.* New York; London: W. W. Norton & Co., 1997.

Shriver, Maria. *What's Happening to Grandpa?* Illustrated by Sandra Spiedel. Boston: Little, Brown Young Readers, 2004.

Shulman, Irving. *"Jackie!": The Exploitation of a First Lady.* New York: Trident Press, 1970.

Sidey, Hugh. *John F. Kennedy, President.* New York: Atheneum, 1964.

Sills, Beverly, and Lawrence Linderman. *Beverly: An Autobiography.* New York: Bantam Books, 1987.

Silverman, Debora. *Selling Culture: Bloomingdale's, Diana Vreeland, and the New Aristocracy of Taste in America.* New York: Pantheon Books, 1986.

Slatzer, Robert F. *The Life and Curious Death of Marilyn Monroe.* New York: Pinnacle House, 1974.

Smith, Jane S. *Elsie de Wolfe: A Life in the High Style.* New York: Atheneum, 1982.

Smith, Liz. *Natural Blonde: A Memoir.* New York: Hyperion, 2000.

Smith, Malcom E. *John F. Kennedy's 13 Great Mistakes in the White House.* Smithtown, N.Y.: Suffolk House, 1980.

Smith, Marie. *Entertaining in the White House.* Washington, D.C.: Acropolis Books, 1967.

Smith, Sally Bedell. *Grace and Power: The Private World of the Kennedy White House.* New York: Random House, 2004.

Smolla, Rodney A. *Suing the Press.* New York: Oxford University Press, 1986.

Sommer, Shelley. *John F. Kennedy: His Life and Legacy.* Introduction by Caroline Kennedy. New York: HarperCollins, 2005.

Sorensen, Theodore C. *Kennedy.* New York: Harper & Row, 1965.

Sotheby's (Catalogue). *Property from Kennedy Family Homes: Hyannisport, Martha's Vineyard, New Jersey, New York, Virginia. New York Tuesday, Wednesday, & Thursday, February 15, 16, & 17th, 2005.* New York: Sotheby's, 2005.

Spada, James. *Grace: The Secret Lives of a Princess.* Garden City, N.Y.: Doubleday, 1987.

———. *John and Caroline: Their Lives in Pictures.* New York: St. Martin's Press, 2001.

———. *Peter Lawford: The Man Who Kept the Secrets.* New York: Bantam Books, 1991.

Sparks, Fred. *The $20,000,000 Honeymoon: Jackie and Ari's First Year.* New York: Bernard Geis Associates, 1980.

Spender, Stephen. *Journals 1939–1983.* New York: Random House, 1986.

Speriglio, Milo. *The Marilyn Conspiracy.* New York: Pocket Books, 1986.

Spignesi, Stephen. *J.F.K., Jr.* New York: Carol Publishing Group, 1999.

Stack, Robert, with Mark Evans. *Straight Shooting.* New York: Macmillan, 1980.

Stassinopoulos, Arianna. *Maria Callas: The Woman Behind the Legend.* New York: Simon & Schuster, 1981.

Steel, Ronald. *Walter Lippman and the American Century.* Boston: Little, Brown and Company, 1980.

Stein, Jean. *American Journey: The Times of Robert Kennedy.* New York: Harcourt Brace Jovanovich, 1970.

———. *Edie: An American Biography.* New York: Knopf, 1983.

Steinem, Gloria. *Outrageous Acts and Everyday Rebellions.* New York: Holt, Rinehart and Winston, 1983.

Storm, Tempest, with Bill Boyd. *Tempest Storm: The Lady Is a Vamp.* Atlanta: Peachtree Publishing, 1987.

Stoughton, Cecil, and Chester V. Clifton. *The Memories of Cecil Stoughton, the President's Photographer, and Major General Chester V. Clifton, the President's Military Aide.* New York: W. W. Norton & Company, 1973.

Straight, N. A. *Ariabella: The First.* New York: Random House, 1981.

Strait, Raymond. *The Tragic Secret Life of Jayne Mansfield.* Chicago: Regnery Co., 1974.

Suero, Orlando. *Camelot at Dawn: Jacqueline and John Kennedy in Georgetown, May 1954.* Photographs by Orlando Suero; text by Anne Garside. Baltimore: Johns Hopkins University Press, 2001.

Sullivan, Gerald, and Michael Kenney. *The Race for the Eighth: The Making of a Congressional Campaign: Joe Kennedy's Successful Pursuit of a Political Legacy.* New York: Harper & Row, 1987.

Sullivan, William C. *The Bureau: My Thirty Years in Hoover's FBI.* New York: W. W. Norton & Company, 1979.

Sulzberger, Iphigene Ochs. *Iphigene.* New York: Times Books, 1987.

Summers, Anthony. *Conspiracy.* New York: McGraw-Hill, 1980.

———. *Goddess: The Secret Lives of Marilyn Monroe.* New York: Macmillan, 1985.

Susann, Jacqueline. *Dolores.* New York: William Morrow & Co., 1976.

Swanberg, W. A. *Luce and His Empire.* New York: Charles Scribners Sons, 1972.

Swanson, Gloria. *Swanson on Swanson.* New York: Random House, 1980.

Sykes, Christopher. *Nancy: The Life of Lady Astor.* London: William Collins, Sons & Co., 1972.

Sykes, Plum. *Bergdorf Blondes: A Novel.* New York: Miramax, 2004.

Talbot, David. *Brothers: The Hidden History of the Kennedy Years.* New York: Free Press, 2007.

Taraborrelli, J. Randy. *Jackie, Ethel, Joan: Women of Camelot.* New York: Warner Books, 2000.

Taylor, Robert. *Marilyn Monroe in Her Own Words.* New York: Delilah-Putnam, 1983.

Teltscher, Henry O. *Handwriting, Revelation of Self: A Source Book of Psychographology.* New York: Hawthorn Books, 1971.

Ten Year Report 1966–1967 to 1976–1977. Cambridge, Mass.: The Institute of Politics, John Fitzgerald Kennedy School of Government, Harvard University, 1977.

Teodorescu, Radu. *Radu's Simply Fit.* New York: Cader Books, 1996.

terHorst, J. F., and Ralph Albertazzi. *The Flying White House: The Story of Air Force One.* New York: Coward, McCann & Geoghegan, 1979.

Teti, Frank. *Kennedy: The New Generation.* New York: Delilah, 1983.

Thayer, Mary Van Rensselaer. *Jacqueline Bouvier Kennedy.* Garden City, N.Y.: Doubleday, 1961.

———. *Jacqueline Kennedy: The White House Years.* Boston: Little, Brown and Company, 1971.

Theodoracopulos, Taki. *Princes, Playboys & High-class Tarts.* Princeton; New York: Karz-Cohl Pub., 1984.

Thomas, Evan. *Robert Kennedy: His Life.* New York: Simon & Schuster, 2000.

Thomas, Helen. *Dateline: White House.* New York: Macmillan, 1975.

Thompson, Hunter S. *Fear and Loathing in America: The Brutal Odyssey of an Outlaw Journalist, 1968–1976.* Foreword by David Halberstam; edited by Douglas Brinkley. New York: Simon & Schuster, 2000.

Thompson, Jim. *The Grifters.* Berkeley, Calif.: Creative Arts, 1975.

Thompson, Josiah. *Six Seconds in Dallas: A Micro-study of the Kennedy Assassination.* New York: Bernard Geis Associates, 1967.

Thompson, Lawrence, and R. H. Winnick. *Robert Frost: The Later Years, 1938–1963.* New York: Holt, Reinhart & Winston, 1976.

Thompson, Nelson. *The Dark Side of Camelot.* Chicago: Playboy Press, 1976.

Thorndike Jr., Joseph J. *The Very Rich: A History of Wealth.* New York: American Heritage, 1976.

Tierney, Gene, with Mickey Herskowitz. *Self-Portrait.* New York: Wyden Books, 1979.

Travell, Janet. *Office Hours: Day and Night—The Autobiography of Janet Travell, M.D.* New York: World Publishing Co., 1968.

Trewhitt, Henry L. *McNamara.* New York: Harper & Row, 1971.

Triumph and Tragedy: The Story of the Kennedys. By the writers, photographers, and editors of the Associated Press. New York: William Morrow & Co., 1968.

Troy, Ann A. *Nutley: Yesterday—Today.* Nutley, N.J.: the Nutley Historical Society, 1961.

Truman, Margaret. *First Ladies: An Intimate Group Portrait of White House Wives.* New York: Fawcett Books, 1995.

———. *Harry S. Truman.* New York: William Morrow & Co., 1972.

———. *The President's House: A First Daughter Shares the History and Secrets of the World's Most Famous Home.* New York: Ballantine Books, 2003.

Trump, Donald. *The America We Deserve.* Los Angeles: Renaissance Books, 2000.

Ungar, Sanford J. *FBI.* Boston: Little, Brown and Company, 1975.

United States Senate. *Final Report of the Select Committee to Study Governmental Operations with Respect to Intelligence Activities.* Book V. *The Investigation of the Assassination of John F. Kennedy: Performance of the Intelligence Agencies.* Washington, D.C.: U.S. Government Printing Office, April 23, 1976.

Valenti, Jack. *This Time, This Place: My Life in War, the White House, and Hollywood.* New York: Harmony Books, 2007.

Valentine, Tom, and Patrick Mahn. *Daddy's Duchess: The Unauthorized Biography of Doris Duke.* Secaucus, N.J.: Lyle Stuart, 1987.

vanden Heuvel, William, and Milton Gwirtzman. *On His Own: Robert F. Kennedy 1964–1968.* Garden City, N.Y.: Doubleday, 1970.

Van Riper, Frank. *Glenn: The Astronaut Who Would Be President.* New York: Empire Books, 1983.

Vickers, Hugo. *Cecil Beaton: A Biography.* Boston: Little, Brown and Company, 1985.

Vidal, Gore. *The Best Man.* Boston: Little, Brown and Company, 1960.

———. *Homage to Daniel Shays: Collected Essays. 1952–1972.* New York: Random House, 1972.

———. *Julian.* Boston: Little, Brown and Company, 1964.

Vreeland, Diana. *Allure.* Garden City, N.Y.: Doubleday, 1980.

Walker, John. *Self-Portrait with Donors: Confessions of an Art Collector.* Boston: Little, Brown and Company, 1974.

Wallace, Irving. *The Sunday Gentleman.* New York: Simon & Schuster, 1965.

Warhol, Andy. *Andy Warhol's Exposures.* Photographs by Andy Warhol, text by Andy Warhol with Bob Colacello. New York: Andy Warhol Books/Grosset & Dunlap, 1979.

Warren Report, The. New York: Associated Press, 1964.

Watney, Hedda Lyons. *Jackie.* North Hollywood, Calif.: Leisure Books, 1971.

Wead, Doug. *All the Presidents' Children: Triumph and Tragedy in the Lives of America's First Families.* New York: Atria Books, 2003.

Weatherby, W. J. *Conversations with Marilyn.* New York: Ballantine Books, 1977.

Weisberg, Harold. *John F. Kennedy Assassination Post Mortem.* Frederick, Md.: self-published, 1975.

———. *Whitewash.* Vols. I & II. New York: Dell, 1966; vols. III and IV, self-published, 1967.

Weiss, Murray, and Bill Hoffman. *Palm Beach Babylon: Sins, Scams, and Scandals.* New York: Carol Publishing Group, 1992.

West, Darrell M. *Patrick Kennedy: The Rise to Power.* Upper Saddle River, N.J.: Prentice-Hall, 2001.

West, J. B., with Mary Lynn Kotz. *Upstairs at the White House: My Life with the First Ladies.* New York: Coward, McCann & Geoghegan, 1973.

Whalen, Richard J. *The Founding Father: The Story of Joseph P. Kennedy and the Family He Raised to Power.* New York: New American Library, 1964.

White House Historical Association. *The White House: An Historical Guide.* Washington, D.C., 1979.

White, Ray Lewis. *Gore Vidal.* New York: Twayne Pub., 1968.

White, Theodore H. *In Search of History: A Personal Adventure.* New York: Harper & Row, 1978.

———. *The Making of the President 1960.* New York: Atheneum, 1961.

White, William S. *The Professional: Lyndon B. Johnson.* Boston: Houghton Mifflin, 1964.

Wicker, Tom. *On Press.* New York: Viking, 1975.

Wills, Garry. *The Kennedy Imprisonment: A Meditation on Power.* Boston: Little, Brown and Company, 1982.

Wilroy, Mary Edith, and Lucie Prinz. *Inside Blair House.* Garden City, N.Y.: Doubleday, 1982.

Wilson, Earl. *Show Business Laid Bare.* New York: G. P. Putnam's Sons, 1974.

———. *The Show Business Nobody Knows.* New York: Cowles Book Co., 1971.

———. *Sinatra: An Unauthorized Biography.* New York: Macmillan, 1976.

Winter-Berger, Robert N. *The Washington Pay-Off.* New York: Dell, 1972.

Wirth, Conrad L. *Parks, Politics, and People.* Norman, Okla.: University of Oklahoma Press, 1980.

Wise, David. *The American Police State: The Government Against the People.* New York: Random House, 1976.

The Witnesses. Selected and edited from the Warren Commission's Hearings by *The New York Times* with an introduction by Anthony Lewis. New York: McGraw-Hill, 1964.

Wofford, Harris. *Of Kennedys and Kings: Making Sense of the Sixties.* New York: Farrar, Straus & Giroux, 1980.

Wolff, Perry. *A Tour of the White House with Mrs. John F. Kennedy.* Garden City, N.Y.: Doubleday, 1962.

Youngblood, Rufus W. *20 Years in the Secret Service: My Life with Five Presidents.* New York: Simon & Schuster, 1973.

Ziegler, Philip. *Diana Cooper: A Biography.* New York: Knopf, 1982.

INDEX

———◆———